V&R

Antike Schriftauslegung /
Ancient Scriptural Interpretation

Band 1

Herausgegeben von Agnethe Siquans, Thomas R. Karmann,
Susanne Plietzsch und Hans-Ulrich Weidemann

Agnethe Siquans (ed.)

"Written for Our Discipline and Use"

The Construction of Christian and Jewish Identities in Late Ancient Bible Interpretation

„Zu unserer Belehrung geschrieben"

Die Konstruktion christlicher und jüdischer Identitäten in der antiken Bibelauslegung

Vandenhoeck & Ruprecht

Bibliographic information published by the Deutsche Nationalbibliothek:
The Deutsche Nationalbibliothek lists this publication in the Deutsche Nationalbibliografie;
detailed bibliographic data available online: https://dnb.de.

Typesetting: büro mn, Bielefeld
Printed and bound: ⊕ Hubert & Co. BuchPartner, Göttingen
Printed in the EU

Vandenhoeck & Ruprecht Verlage | www.vandenhoeck-ruprecht-verlage.com

ISBN 978-3-525-52219-6

Inhalt

Preface "Ancient Scriptural Interpretation" – Vorwort „Antike Schriftauslegung"

(Late) Antiquity—in its "long" definition—is the time of the emergence and formation of two religious identities: pagan Christianity facing Israel and rabbinical Judaism. The authoritative texts of both communities played a central role in this process. Both groups were heterogeneous in themselves and partly still overlapped. It is characteristic that Jews and Christians referred in part to the same Holy Scriptures, albeit partly in different versions and translations, and that these texts played a central role in the worship, piety, but also in the social and political life of the respective community. In addition, the canonical texts of the New Testament also refer in many ways to the so-called Old Testament.

Above all, the biblical texts are the subject of interpretation and part of important discourses. But they are also the focus of mutual contacts, which are manifested partly in polemical debates and in dissociation from the interpretations of the respective other, partly in positive references and reception.

The series "Ancient Scriptural Interpretation" is a forum for research into the interpretation and reception of the Holy Scriptures in Christian and Jewish texts of antiquity. The complex Jewish-Christian relations during the formative phase of post-biblical Judaism and Christianity will be examined in the context of their interpretation of Scripture.

Die (Spät-)Antike – in ihrer „langen" Definition – ist die Zeit der Entstehung und Herausbildung zweier religiöser Identitäten: die des Israel gegenüberstehenden Heidenchristentums und die des rabbinischen Judentums. Bei diesem Prozess spielten die autoritativen Texte beider Gemeinschaften eine zentrale Rolle. Beide Gruppen waren in sich heterogen und überlappten sich teilweise noch. Charakteristisch ist, dass sich Juden wie Christen teilweise auf dieselben Heiligen Schriften beriefen, wenn auch zum Teil in anderen Versionen und Übersetzungen, und dass diese Texte im Gottesdienst, in der Frömmigkeit, aber auch im sozialen und politischen Leben der jeweiligen Gemeinschaft eine zentrale Rolle spielten. Hinzu kommt, dass auch die kanonischen Texte des Neuen Testaments in vielfacher Weise auf das sogenannte Alte Testament Bezug nehmen.

Vor allem sind die biblischen Texte Gegenstand von Auslegung und Teil wichtiger Diskurse. Sie stehen aber auch im Mittelpunkt wechselseitiger Kontakte, die sich teilweise in polemischen Debatten und in Abgrenzung von den Interpretationen der jeweils anderen, teilweise in positiven Bezugnahmen und Rezeptionen manifestieren.

Die Reihe „Antike Schriftauslegung“ ist ein Forum für die Erforschung der Interpretation und Rezeption der Heiligen Schrift in christlichen und jüdischen Texten der Antike. Dabei sollen die komplexen jüdisch-christlichen Beziehungen während der formativen Phase des nachbiblischen Judentums und des Christentums im Kontext ihrer Schriftauslegung beleuchtet werden.

Vienna, January 2021

Agnethe Siquans, Thomas R. Karmann,
Susanne Plietzsch, Hans-Ulrich Weidemann

Preface – Vorwort

The present volume goes back to the symposium *"Written for Our Discipline and Use": The Construction of Christian and Jewish Identities in Late Ancient Bible Interpretation*. This symposium took place at the University of Vienna in November 2018. It was part of the project "The Saved Savior: Exodus 1–2 in Patristic and Rabbinic Interpretation" (P 28441-G24), financed by the Austrian Science Fund (FWF). I would like to thank all participants for their presentations, their contributions to the discussion and the resulting articles in this book.

I thank the co-editors of the series "Studies in Ancient Scriptural Interpretation" for their feedback.

For the editing and correction of the manuscript, I would like to express my sincere thanks to my student assistant Magdalena Pittracher and especially to Katharina Rötzer who prepared the indexes.

I would like to thank Elisabeth Hernitscheck from the publisher Vandenhoeck & Ruprecht for her active and careful support of this publication project.

Der vorliegende Band geht auf die Tagung „Zu unserer Belehrung geschrieben": Die Konstruktion christlicher und jüdischer Identitäten in der antiken Bibelauslegung zurück. Diese Tagung fand im November 2018 im Rahmen des vom „Fonds zur Förderung der wissenschaftlichen Forschung" (FWF) geförderten Forschungsprojekts „Der gerettete Retter: Ex 1–2 in patristischer und rabbinischer Interpretation" (P 28441-G24) an der Universität Wien statt. Ich danke allen Teilnehmerinnen und Teilnehmern für ihre Vorträge, ihre Diskussionsbeiträge und die daraus entstandenen Artikel in diesem Buch.

Den Mitherausgebern der neu gegründeten Reihe „Studien zur antiken Schriftauslegung" danke ich für ihre Rückmeldungen.

Für die Bearbeitung und Korrektur des Manuskripts sage ich meiner Studienassistentin Magdalena Pittracher und insbesondere Katharina Rötzer, die auch die Register erstellt hat, herzlichen Dank.

Für die umsichtige Betreuung und die engagierte Unterstützung von Seiten des Verlags danke ich Elisabeth Hernitscheck sehr herzlich.

Vienna, January 2021 Agnethe Siquans

Agnethe Siquans (Vienna)

The Construction of Christian and Jewish Identities in Late Ancient Bible Interpretation

Introduction

The quotation in the title of this volume—"written for our discipline and use," an allusion to Rom 15:4—is taken from Origen's second homily on Exodus which interprets the midwives' episode and Moses' birth and salvation as narrated in chapters one and two of the book of Exodus.[1] Origen postulates a meaning of the biblical text which he directly applies to his readers and their lives. His interpretation is part of a homily, an ethically oriented literary genre. However, other forms of Bible interpretation in Late Antiquity also imply appropriation of a later audience or readership and religious practice. Origen's use of the possessive pronoun "our" is likewise revealing; he claims the biblical text for a particular group, a community which he is part of and which he addresses in his homilies.

When we read the first chapter of his homily, we meet other groups from which Origen distances himself and his audience. These are the "friends of the letter:" *amici sunt litterae, et non putant legem spiritalem esse et spiritaliter intellegendam.* They "do not think that the Law is spiritual and is to be understood spiritually."[2] Later, he speaks about the church which is gathered from the gentiles as well as the synagogue and the Jews. Although the "friends of the letter" and the Jews are not necessarily identical, the designations are mutually exchangeable. Moreover, Christians may be "friends of the letters," but then they are often designated as "Judaizing," "Jewish" or "Jews."

Thus, Origen presents two groups of people who interpret the Bible in differing, even opposing ways: those who read it spiritually and thus appropriately (according to Origen), and those who do not read it spiritually but rather literally and whose interpretation is harshly rejected by Origen as non-Christian. This dichotomous presentation cannot veil the fact that there are also Christians who interpret the Bible literally. That Jews may read the texts spiritually does not occur to him. However, his vehement defense of the spiritual interpretation makes clear that his view is not the only one to be found among his audience or readership.

---

1 This volume arose from a symposium in Vienna in November 2018 of the same title. The symposium was part of the research project P 28441-G24 "Exodus 1–2 in Patristic and Rabbinic Interpretation," financed by the Austrian Science Fund (FWF).

2 Heine, Origen, 240.

Origen's polemic is an instrument to construct orthodox Christian identity and at the same time define the boundaries against others. His opponents are not Jews alone but also other groups of Christians who teach different doctrines and interpret biblical texts differently.

Origen's biblical interpretation as well as the exegetical writings of other patristic authors are strongly engaged with the task of constructing and defining identity. This process of self-definition includes the "establishment of community boundaries"[3] and at the same time—necessarily—the definition of others and otherness. A similar development can be shown in rabbinic texts. As Marc Hirshman states regarding the Mekhilta "[...] already in tannaitic times units of anti-Christian polemic were beginning to crystallize."[4]

Nevertheless, the scholarly views on the process of Jewish and Christian identities differ considerably. Whereas it is obvious that Christian writers deal with Jewish interpretation and Jewish tradition—both picking it up and adapting it as well as rejecting it—it is not obvious in the same way whether the Rabbis or rabbinic texts know and react to Christian doctrines, interpretations and texts. Some authors try to explain rabbinic texts independently without considering a connection to Christianity, as, for instance, Adiel Schremer did in his book *Brothers Estranged: Heresy, Christianity, and Jewish Identity in Late Antiquity* some years ago. He wants to offer a "different perspective" to allow "rabbinic Judaism to stand on its own."[5] Others try to read rabbinic and patristic texts in relation to each other, presuming mutual knowledge and contact to differing degrees.[6]

In the first centuries of the Common Era, there are no fixed entities defined as "Judaism" or "Christianity." The formation of Jewish and Christian identities is an ongoing process in Late Antiquity and thereafter. Judaism and Christianity—if we are allowed to use these terms for the first centuries—are not uniform communities during this time, but complex and internally heterogeneous.[7]

The discussion of Jewish-Christian relations has to take into consideration a number of differentiations, which several authors, including Günter Stemberger, Marc Hirshman, Edward Kessler, Burton Visotzky and others, have pinpointed. Distinctions include time, geography, language, literary genre and personal aspects of individual writers as well as political and socio-cultural circumstances. The question of sources is another important factor. Stemberger writes about rabbinic

3 Cf. Reed/Becker, Ways, 14.

4 Hirshman, Polemic Literary Units, 384.

5 Schremer, Brothers, x.

6 Cf. among others Alexander, Exegesis; Bar-Asher Siegal, The Best (and other articles by the same author); Hirshman, Rivalry; Horbury, Jews and Christians; Kamesar, Rabbinic Midrash; Kessler, Contacts; Stemberger, Contacts; Visotzky, Fathers.

7 Cf. e. g. Boyarin, Semantic Differences.

knowledge of Christian doctrine: "Information about Christian issues and beliefs was in general more indirect and casual."[8] For the Christian use of Jewish interpretations, he states (referring to Alexandria) that:

> Hellenistic-Jewish traditions, mainly Philo, still dominate, as may be seen clearly when comparing the commentary of Didymus the Blind on Zechariah with that of Jerome who used it so extensively, or even in the writings of Cyril of Alexandria.[9]

All this reminds us to take a careful and differentiated look at the sources and to be careful about general conclusions.

Jewish and Christian identities are formed in Late Antiquity and discussed in continuing delimitation from various other identities, namely Jewish, Christian, and pagan. As William Scott Green writes:

> A society does not simply discover its others, it fabricates them by selecting, isolating, and emphasizing an aspect of another people's life and making it symbolize their difference. […] In creating its others, a society confuses some part of its neighbour, and a piece of itself with itself, and construes each in terms of the other. Although designed to mark and certify divergence and discontinuity, such correspondences can forge enduring reciprocal patterns of the inside and the outside. They can reshape the naming society's picture of itself, expose its points of vulnerability, and spark in it awareness of, or reflection about, the possibility or the reality of otherness within.[10]

The construction of self-definition and the delimitation by others is thus ambiguous and proves that the others are neighbors. To define "others" and to delimitate or even divide inside and outside is even more necessary when the others are near and the differences are not obvious to all group members. As Jonathan Z. Smith notes, "The problem is not alterity, but similarity—at times, even identity."[11] He maintains that the sharpest distinctions are drawn between "near neighbors."[12] "'Otherness' is not so much a matter of separation as it is a description of interaction. […] 'Otherness' […] is a pre-eminently political category."[13] Some authors have pointed out that this persistence on drawing boundaries was indeed necessary. For instance, Wolfram Kinzig states that "on the level of popular piety there was a wider overlap between Church and Synagogue at least until the end of the

8 Stemberger, Contacts, 574.

9 Ibid., 577. It should be noted that Philo's writings were not further received in (rabbinic) Judaism.

10 Green, Otherness, 50.

11 Smith, Difference, 47.

12 Ibid., 15.

13 Ibid., 10.

fourth century, but probably far beyond."[14] And, of course, there was also an even wider overlap between opponents within the Christian and Jewish communities.

I want to add a short remark about the term "identity." Identity has been frequently problematized in recent decades. We may understand identity— specifically collective identity—courtesy of Jan Assmann who considers it to be:

> the image that a group has of itself and with which its members associate themselves. It therefore has no existence of its own, but comes into being through recognition by its participating individuals. It is as strong or as weak as its presence in the consciousness of its members and its motivating influence on their thoughts and actions.[15]

In Late Antiquity, processes of identity construction took place. The Christian claim of a new truth led to a precarious situation. All groups involved were forced to reflect upon their own position vis-à-vis opposing claims. This instigated a process of self-definition, the definition of others and delimitation by others—a process that continued during the first centuries of the Common Era. During this time, Jewish and Christian identities cannot be perceived as established facts but are in the process of formation.

This volume deals with biblical interpretation as an important aspect of the process of identity formation. From a different vantage point, it looks at biblical interpretation from the perspective of identity formation. This is, according to Smith, a political issue. Biblical interpretation is situated in a particular socio-political and cultural context and has consequences for people's religious as well as their everyday lives.

Jacob Neusner and Ernest Frerichs highlight the importance of research on Jewish-Christian relations in Late Antiquity in *To See Ourselves as Others See Us*, their volume about Christians, Jews and others in Late Antiquity. In the preface, they ask:

> Now what makes the inquiry into the reciprocal conceptions of Judaism and Christianity in these formative centuries critical? It is the simple fact that the developing theories of the other left a legacy, for both medieval and modern Western civilization, of not only intolerance but also restraint, not only a quest for universal conformity but also a capacity to sustain difference. [...] Judaism and Christianity in late antiquity present histories that mirror one another.[16]

This volume pursues the sometimes obvious, sometimes hidden traces of parallels, contacts and demarcations discernible in biblical interpretation and their relevance for the process of constructing Christian and Jewish identities.

---

14 Kinzig, "Non-Separation," 29.

15 Assmann, Memory, 113 f.

16 Neusner/Frerichs (ed.), "To See Ourselves as Others See Us," xiii.

Marc Hirshman searches for the beginnings of aggadic midrash in tannaitic literature, analyzing texts from the Tosefta, the *Sifra* and the *Mekhilta*. He asks if its development is connected in some way to the developments in Christian Bible interpretation.

Harald Buchinger presents Origen's construction of Christian identity in his Exodus interpretation, analyzing *homily 26 on Numbers*, *homily five on Exodus* and the interpretation of Exodus in *Peri Pascha*. He shows that Origen's sophisticated concept of Christian identity goes hand in hand with primitive stereotypes about Judaism and Jewish Bible interpretation.

Agnethe Siquans asks for perspectives on Christian and Jewish identities in the interpretation of Moses' birth narrative (Exod 1–2). She examines Origen's first two *homilies on Exodus*, Ephrem the Syrian's Exodus commentary, *Bavli Sota* 11a–13a, Midrash *Tanhuma* and the *Mekhilta*.

Bas ter Haar Romeny discusses the process of marking the borderlines in and of Antiochene exegesis. He first criticizes modern research trends questioning the fundamental differences between Antiochene and Alexandrian exegesis. He then shows how Diodore of Tarse and Theodore of Mopsuestia define the boundaries of acceptable exegesis.

Predrag Bukovec discusses Aphraates' anti-Jewish exegesis in his *Demonstrationes*. He asks for the literary, historical and theological context and tries to identify the Jews envisioned by Aphraates. Analysing *Dem.* 11, he shows Aphraates' procedure, his presumptions and conclusions in detail.

Günter Stemberger explores Moses' place in the story of Israel's foundation. Is the Jewish religion a "Mosaic" religion? Examination of the terms "torat Moshe," "dat Moshe," "halakhah le-Moshe mi-Sinai" and "Moshe qibbel Torah mi-Sinai" in rabbinic texts demonstrate that the answer to this question is negative.

Constanza Cordoni shows how identity and sense of place are connected in rabbinic literature. She discusses the development of the sages' perspective on the land of Israel. Different texts are concerned in various forms with the precept to dwell in the land of Israel as a religious duty.

Elisabeth Birnbaum's contribution focuses on Jerome and his stance towards himself and others in his commentary on Qohelet. His rhetoric often tends toward polemics against various groups: women, Jews, philosophers, heretics and even church leaders.

Anneliese Felber raises the question of continuity and discontinuity through the example of Mary, mother of Jesus. The church fathers clearly try to "de-judaize" Mary. Patristic perspectives on Mary put her at the center of the confrontation between Jews and Christians and the discussion of closeness and distance.

Gerhard Langer shows how Miriam is probably shaped as a counter-figure to Mary in rabbinic texts. The interpretations focus on Miriam's connection to sexuality and procreation.

The contributions in this volume present examples of group identity formation as an ongoing process—a process of inclusion and exclusion, of inside and outside, of defining oneself and constructing "others" in biblical interpretation in Late Antiquity. The question remains whether it is possible to define and construct identity without polemics, vilification and the harsh rejection of others.

Literature

Alexander, Philip S., Rabbinic and Patristic Bible Exegesis as Intertexts. Towards a Theory of Comparative Midrash, in: T. McLay (ed.), The Temple in Text and Tradition. A Festschrift in Honour of Robert Hayward, London 2015, 71–97.

Assmann, Jan, Cultural Memory and Early Civilization. Writing, Remembrance, and Political Imagination, Cambridge 2011.

Bar-Asher Siegal, Michal, "The Best of Them Is Like a Brier." On b. ʿEruvin 101a and the Jewish-Christian Dialogue in the Babylonian Talmud, in: M. Bar-Asher Siegal/W. Grünstäudl/M. Thiessen (ed.), Perceiving the Other in Ancient Judaism and Early Christianity (WUNT 394), Tübingen 2017, 131–146.

Boyarin, Daniel, Semantic Differences; or, "Judaism"/"Christianity," in: A. Y. Reed/A. Becker (ed.), The Ways that Never Parted. Jews and Christians in Late Antiquity and Early Middle Ages (TSAJ 95), Tübingen 2003, 65–85.

Green, William Scott, Otherness Within. Towards a Theory of Difference in Rabbinic Judaism, in: J. Neusner/E. S. Frerichs (ed.), To See Ourselves as Others See Us." Christians, Jews, "Others" in Late Antiquity, Chico, Calif. 1985, 49–69.

Heine, Ronald (trans.), Origen. Homilies on Genesis and Exodus (FaCh 71), Washington, D. C. 1982.

Hirshman, Marc, A Rivalry of Genius. Jewish and Christian Biblical Interpretation in Late Antiquity, Albany, N. Y. 1996.

— Polemic Literary Units in the Classical Midrashim and Justin Martyr's "Dialogue with Trypho," JQR 83, 3–4 (1993), 369–384.

Horbury, William, Jews and Christians in Contact and Controversy, Edinburgh 1998.

Kamesar, Adam, Rabbinic Midrash and Church Fathers, in: J. Neusner/A. J. Avery-Peck (ed.), Encyclopaedia of Midrash. Biblical Interpretation in Formative Judaism, Leiden 2005, 20–40.

Kessler, Edward, The Exegetical Encounter between the Greek Church Fathers and the Palestinian Rabbis, StPatr 34 (2001), 395–412.

Kinzig, Wolfram, "Non-Separation." Closeness and Co-operation between Jews and Christians in the Fourth Century, VC 45 (1991), 27–53.

Neusner, Jacob/Frerichs, Ernest S. (ed.), To See Ourselves as Others See Us." Christians, Jews, "Others" in Late Antiquity, Chico, Calif. 1985.

Reed, Annette Yoshiko/Becker, Adam H. (ed.), The Ways that Never Parted. Jews and Christians in Late Antiquity and Early Middle Ages (TSAJ 95), Tübingen 2003, 1–33.

Schremer, Adiel, Brothers Estranged. Heresy, Christianity, and Jewish Identity in Late Antiquity, Oxford 2010.

Smith, Jonathan Z., What a Difference a Difference Makes, in: J. Neusner/E. S. Frerichs (ed.), To See Ourselves as Others See Us." Christians, Jews, "Others" in Late Antiquity, Chico, Calif. 1985, 3–48.

Stemberger, Günter, Exegetical Contacts between Christians and Jews in the Roman Empire, in: M. Sæbø (ed.), Hebrew Bible/Old Testament. The History of Its Interpretation, vol. 1: From the Beginnings to the Middle Ages (until 1300), part 1: Antiquity, Göttingen 1996, 569–586.

Visotzky, Burton L., Fathers of the World. Essays in Rabbinic and Patristic Literatures (WUNT 80), Tübingen 1995.

Marc Hirshman (Hebrew University Jerusalem)

The Development of Tannaitic Aggadic Midrash and Its Relationship to Christian Readings of the Bible[1]

"But how did it all begin?" Roberto Calasso asks repeatedly in his captivating account of Greek mythology, *The Marriage of Cadmus and Harmony*. That same question has been asked no less often in attempts to understand the development of aggadic midrash. Aggadic midrash, as found already in the Tannaitic corpora—that is rabbinic works from 1–250 C. E.—is best known for its ability to elicit new meanings from Scripture by applying creative exegesis to the text. Superb research over the last century and more has tried to trace the roots of this extraordinary hermeneutic turn to antecedents such as Homeric exegesis,[2] Philonic interpretation,[3] Qumranic pesharim,[4] while others opined that the buds of this free-wheeling interpretation are present already in Scripture itself.[5] I find myself in agreement

1 This research was supported by an Israel Science Foundation grant 1991/16. I am also indebted to the fine scholars who participated in an Israel Science Foundation workshop (2199/18) on "Reading the Bible in the First and Second Centuries: Christians, Jews, Gnostics and Pagans," at the Hebrew University of Jerusalem, January 2–4, 2019.

2 The most recent contribution is the erudite work of Yakir Paz, beginning with his 2014 Hebrew University dissertation "From Scribes to Scholars: Rabbinic Biblical Exegesis in Light of the Homeric Commentaries" and a series of articles. Paz cites Saul Lieberman's 20th century definitive contributions to this field as well as the history of scholarship from the 19th century and on.

3 Maren Niehoff's intense work on Philo in her two recent books, "Jewish Exegesis and Homeric Scholarship in Alexandria" and "Philo, an Intellectual Biography" has argued forcefully for influence.

4 See Paul Mandel's balanced assessment, "Midrash Exegesis and its Precedents in the Dead Sea Scrolls," 149–168 and especially his summary on p. 167 and note 49 citing Adiel Schremer and Menahem Kister. Aharon Shemesh argued that in Qumran the word "midrash" was used to describe the genre of biblical interpretation and is more appropriate than calling the genre "pesher." See his "Biblical Exegesis and Interpretations from Qumran to the Rabbis," especially pages 467–471, with examples from aggadic exegesis.

5 Cf. the wonderful early work of Isaac L. Seeligmann, "Voraussetzungen der Midraschexegese," 150–181, followed by Michael Fishbane's excellent "Biblical Interpretation in Ancient Israel," and many others. I make special reference to Avigdor Shinan and Yair Zakovitch's essay "Midrash on Scripture and Midrash within Scripture," 257–277, who held that essentially rabbinic aggadic midrash continues exegetical moves found in the Bible itself. Zakovitch reiterates this conviction that "Biblical textual witnesses," Second Temple Literature, and "[...] above all, rabbinic literature and Jewish exegesis that fed from it all fastened themselves into the secure foundations of inner-biblical interpretation and proceeded along the paths that had already been paved within the Bible" (Zakovitch, Interpretation, 61). James Kugel downplays the range and extent of inner-biblical interpretation, certainly in comparison to the "far richer store of ancient biblical interpretation" in the Second Temple period. See Kugel, Beginning, 10–11.

with Steven Fraade's most recent assessment[6] that rabbinic aggadic midrash cannot be adequately illuminated or accounted for by these biblical and Second-Temple precedents. In our context, I am putting the question of precedents and antecedents on hold for now and will focus on the trajectory of aggadic midrash in Tannaitic literature. Can we pinpoint its inception within Tannaitic literature and chart its course over the first and second centuries?

It is striking that at the very same time that Jewish and non-Jewish Christians adopted the Hebrew Bible with a christological interpretation and so- called gnostic writers interpreted that same Bible in dualistic terms, the Jewish sages pursued a fanciful, creative and free-wheeling interpretation of the non-legal sections of the Bible that we call aggadic midrash. This aggadic midrash was appended and sometimes interwoven into the legal midrash on Exodus-Deuteronomy. Can we pinpoint when this creative non-legal exegesis began in the Tannaitic corpus?

I will treat the question from two perspectives. First, I will give a diachronic overview of the named aggada in the Tannaitic works to try to discern development. Second, I will analyze the discrete Tannaitic works to identify where and to what extent aggadic midrash is inserted and what generation of sages is represented. In this context I will be able only to begin the first analysis, and with reference only to the Tannaitic midrash on Exodus, Mekilta of Rabbi Yishmael. The reason for this choice will be explained as we proceed and I believe that the results are significant.

1. Rabban Yohanan Ben Zakkai

Let us begin with a famous description of what was taken to be Rabban Yohanan b. Zakkai's method of reading Scripture. In the Tosefta *Bava Qamma* 7:3, Rabban Yohanan is described as stating five things כמין חומר "kemin homer," a special method of reading Scripture. The great scholar of midrash, Wilhelm Bacher described Rabban Yohanan's method in the following manner:

> […] in welchen Satzungen der Thora auf ihre inneren Gründe zurückgeführt werden sollen und in denen eine maßvolle Symbolik oder Wortdeutung zu den schönsten homiletischen Anwendungen hinleitet.[7]

Bacher's characterization of Rabban Yohanan's collection of sayings that are "kemin homer" is right on the mark. This type of interpretation elicits homiletical and moral implications or lessons from Scripture. I would emphasize Bacher's description of

6 See Fraade, Early Rabbinic Midrash.

7 Bacher, Agada, 27.

them as "homiletische […] Anwendung," homiletic applications. They are, also in my view, not so much midrash, scriptural exegesis, as sermons or homilies. The Tosefta's own articulation makes this clear—"Rabban Yohanan would *say them* (אומרן) kemin homer," rather than would interpret them (דורשן). Let me analyze two examples from the list in the Tosefta *Bava Qamma* 7:6:

> ואו' מזבח אבנים לא תניף עליהן ברזל, וכי מה ראה הכתו' לפסול את הברזל יותר מכל מיני מתכות מפני שהחרב נעשית ממנו והחרב סימן פורענות והמזבח סימן כפרה, מעבירין דבר שסימן פורענות מדבר שסימן כפרה. והלא דברים קל וחומר, ומה אם אבנים שאינן לא רואות ולא שומעות ולא מדברות על שמטילות כפרה בין ישראל לאביהם שבשמי' אמ' הכת' לא תניף עליהן ברזל, בני תורה שהן כפרה לעולם על אחת כמה וכמה שלא יגע בהן אחד מן המזיקין כולן.
>
> It says, "an altar of stones. Do not wield an iron tool over them […]" (Deut. 27:5) What did Scripture see to disqualify iron above all other kinds of metals? Because the sword is made of it and the sword is a sign of retribution while the altar is a sign of atonement. We remove a thing which is a sign of retribution from a thing which is atonement. Aren't the things a *qal vahomer*? Just as stones that don't see, don't hear and don't talk, because they cast atonement between Israel and their Father in Heaven the Scripture says "Do not wield an iron tool over them," students of Torah who are atonement for the world how much more so that not one of the harmful things will touch them.

This is, as Bacher noted, wonderful homiletics, a beautiful sermon. But it is not formally exegesis. It is rather a moralizing sermon woven from the raw materials of the verse. The thrust of this remark is to arrive at the *qal vahomer*, the *a minori ad maius*-conclusion. That is why this type of sermonizing is called *kemin homer*—which I would translate: like or in the manner of a *qal vahomer*. That is also why the verb attached to this is that Rabban Yohanan would "*say them*" in the style of a *homer*—an *a minori ad maius*-locution.

This same rhetorical move is repeated in the next section of the Tosefta 7:7 which applies the same conclusion to the divine requirement that the altar be built of whole (*shelemot*, i. e. unhewn) stones (Deut 27:7). There the conclusion is

> […] אבנים מטילות שלום והלא דברים קל וחומר ומה אם אבנים שאינן לא רואות ולא שומעות ולא מדברות על שמטילות שלום בין ישראל לאביהם שבשמים אמ' המקום יהיו שלימות לפני, בני תורה שהן שלום בעולם על אחת כמה וכמה שיהיו שלימים לפני ה'.
>
> […] stones that cast peace. Aren't the things a *qal vahomer*? Just as stones that don't see, don't hear and don't talk since they cast peace between Israel and their Father in Heaven, God (*hamaqom*) says let them be whole before me, students of Torah who are peace in the world how much more so that they will be whole before God.

The parallel versions to this statement preserved in *the Mekilta d'arayot* and *Mekilta de Rabbi Yishmael* combine this homily with its predecessor:

והרי דברים ק"ו מה אם אבני מזבח שאינן לא רואות [...] אמר הכתוב לא תניף עליהן ברזל אדם שהוא עושה שלום בין איש לאשתו בין משפחה למשפחה בין עיר לעיר בין מדינה למדינה בין אומה לחברתה על אחת כמה שלא תבואנו פורענות. (מכילתא דעריות כי"ו, עמ' שפב).

Aren't these things a *qal vahomer*? Just as the stones of the altar that don't see [...] since they cast peace between Israel and their Father in heaven, Scripture said, "do not wield an iron tool over them," a person who makes peace between a man and his wife, between families, between cities, between a nation and another nation, how much more so that retribution will not come to him.

M. Kister[8] has analyzed a remarkable parallel between *Sifra Hovah* and Romans 5:12–21 wherein the same type of *a minori ad maius*-argument is employed both in the Sifra and in Paul's argumentation. Kister brings the parallels side by side. *Sifra* reads:

He (Adam) was given only one commandment, a prohibition, which he transgressed, and see how many deaths Adam was condemned (to suffer): his own and those of all his descendants [...] someone who refrains from eating *piggul* or *notar* and who fasts on the Day of Atonement—*how much more* does such a person acquire merit (מזכה) for himself and his descendants [...] (Sifra Hovah parashah 12, pereq 20)

And Paul in Romans 5:15: "For if many died through one person's trespass, how much more the grace (χάρις) and the gift (δωρεὰ) of the grace of the one man Jesus Christ abounded for the many."

Kister was surely right, as were a number of scholars whom he cites, who saw partial parallels between the texts,[9] in their agreement in general and in the use of the *qal vahomer* in specific. I do believe that this was the rhetorical device for which Rabban Yohanan was famous and shows him to be preaching in a style similar to his older contemporary Paul.

Let us take another example from the list of the Tosefta 7:5:

הרי הוא או' אשר נשיא יחטא אשרי הדור שהנשיא שלו מביא קרבן חטאת שגגה על שגגתו.

For it says, "When (*asher*) a leader sins unintentionally" (Lev 4:22 NIV), Happy (*ashrei*) is the generation that its leader brings an unintentional sin offering for his unintentional sin.

---

8 See Kister, Romans 5:12–21. The chart of comparison is on p. 413 and his incisive suggestion of the Hebrew מרובה lying behind the Greek ἐπερίσσευσεν on p. 403. One need further investigate the phrase itself (πολλῷ μᾶλλον) whether it reflects the Hebrew as hinted by Kister's placing both in bold. On the original Hebrew phrase אחת כמה על, see Haneman, Lemasoret Haketiv, 19–20. Others argue the "how much more" is a stock phrase in Greco-Roman rhetoric, see Porter, The argument, particularly 668.

9 See the list of scholars in Kister, Romans 5:12–21, 421, n. 124.

This lovely thought lacks the *qal vahomer* formulation we would expect but that formulation is preserved in the parallel text in the *Sifra Hovah*, Parasha 5:[10]

אמר רבן יוחנן בן זכאי אשרי הדור שהנשיא שלו מביא חטאת על שגגתו, אם הנשיא שלו מביא חטאת צורך לומר מה הוא הדיוט, אם על שגגתו הוא מביא צורך לו' מה הוא על זדונו
(ספרא דיבורה דחובה רפ"ה עמ' 147)

Said Rabban Yohanan ben Zakkai: Happy is the generation whose leader brings a sin offering for his unintentional sin. If the leader brings a sin offering, is there a need to say what of the common person? If for his unintentional sin he brings, is there a need to say what of his intentional sin?

I would like to suggest that this is the same rhetorical use of a passage to further the moral exhortation constructed in a similar but different *a fortiori* structure employing different terminology ("is there a need to say"?). Interestingly, Philo in his treatment of the passage in *Spec.* 1,226 (Colson, Philo, 233) points out that it there is a distinction in the sacrifices offered by the *nasi'*, *archon* in the Greek, and the commoner, *idiotes*, where the commoner offers a lesser sacrifice.

The three sermons of Rabban Yohanan we have adduced so far comply nicely with an interpretation of אומרן כמין חומר as indicating a rhetorical strategy rather than a kind of exegesis, or fanciful word play which is the hallmark of aggadic exegesis, though it is not entirely absent. We will look at the first two in the list and then return to the issue of word play.

These first two homilies in Tosefta *Bava Qamma* 7:3–4 are more elusive.

[...] מפני מה גלו ישראל לבבל יותר מכל הארצות כולם, מפני שבית אברהם אבינו משם. משלו משל למה הדבר דומה לאשה שקלקלה על בעלה להיכן משלחה? לבית אביה.

Why were Israel exiled to Babylonia over all the other lands? Because Abraham our father's home was from there. They made a parable: to what is this comparable? To a women who sinned against her husband—to where does he send her? To her father's house.

And immediately following in the Tosefta:

בלוחות הראשנים הוא אומ' והלוחות מעשה אלים[11] המה וגו' ובשניות והלוחות מעשה משה והמכתב מכתב אלים. משלו משל למה הדבר דומה למלך בשר ודם שקידש את האישה הוא מביא את הלבלר ואת הקולמוס ואת הדיו ואת השטר ואת העדים קילקלה היא מביאה את הכל דייה שיתן לה המלך כתב הכר יד שלו.

In the first tablets it says, "and the tablets are the work of God (*Elohim*)" (Ex 32:16) but in the second the tablets the work of Moses "but the writing was the writing of

10 Finkelstein, Sifra, vol. 2, 147.

11 God's name is abbreviated here.

> God (*Elohim*) (ibid.; see Ex 34:1)". They made a parable: to what is this comparable? To a king of flesh and blood who betrothed a woman. He brings the scribe and the stylist, the ink, the deed and the witnesses. She disgraced—she brings everything—it is enough that the king will give her the writing of his signature.

I believe that these two opening remarks of Rabban Yohanan in the Tosefta led Bacher to write the following:

> [...] die man mit dem Ausdrucke חומר bezeichnete, dessen Sinn schon die alten Commentatoren nicht sicher anzugeben wußten, der aber wahrscheinlich anzeigen soll, daß in der damit bezeichneten Deutung der Text mit dem ihm zugeschriebenen tiefern Sinne allegorisch oder symbolisch *verknüpft* wird. Oder aber es soll mit dem Ausdrucke כמין חומר die betreffende Schriftdeutung als etwas besonders kostbares gerühmt werden.[12]

I do not think that there is anything symbolical or allegorical in these interpretations. Rather, they are elegant rhetoric, to be prized, as Bacher suggests, for beautifully elucidating the sense of Scripture ("Schriftdeutung"). It is the comparisons, the parables, which explain God's behavior in human, albeit royal, behavior. Would it be pressing my point to say that the underlying logic of the comparisons, the parables, retain an element of the *a fortiori* argument in claiming that God's behavior accords well with that of a mortal king, though God could certainly be more exacting and extreme (דיו לבא מן הדין)?

I will grant that in two of the homilies there is a minor element of word play, *asher/ashrei* and *shelemot/shalom* but I would submit that these are more rhetorical flourishes than exegetical. The heart of the homily is not dependent on these word plays and there is no abandonment of the "logos," of the logic of the verse, as I. Heinemann characterized full bodied aggadic exegesis.

There is in the Tannaitic midrash an entire "group" named "dorshei hamurot."[13] In an article devoted to this term and others, Malchi concluded that the unique element of this approach was to make a clear correspondence of the punishment to fit the crime. This might be the case, but I think we are better served by focusing on the rhetoric and style, less so on the content and outcome. By this I mean that *kemin homer* is a kind of moralizing rhetoric which often entails an argument *a minori ad maius* or a parable to reinforce the concept. Thus, in the examples of the exile to Babylonia and the broken tablets the parables of marriage and divorce emphasize that God's behavior is in line with regular human patterns of marriage and divorce. Is putting all the expenses of the *ketuba* on the wayward bride a just punishment? Maybe or maybe not. But it certainly drives home the moralizing

12 Bacher, Agada, 29–30 (emphasis in original).

13 Once in *Semahot* 8:16 and 3x in the Bavli.

reading of Scripture. It is of course interpretation and a sensitive reading of Exodus 34:1 "*pesol lecha*—chisel for you"—on your own. But the effect and emphasis is rhetorical and does not stray very far from the "simple" meaning of Scripture. I repeat that the Tosefta speaks of *saying* these statements *kemin homer.*

Let us compare these findings with an enigmatic usage of the phrase by Rabban Gamliel in *Sifre Numbers* piska 8. Rabban Gamliel explains why the offering brought by a woman suspected of adultery, the *Sota*, brings an offering of barley rather than wheat.

שעורים, למה נאמר שהיה בדין הואיל ומנחת חוטא
באה על החטא וזו באה על החטא אם למדתי למנחת
חוטא שאינה באה אלא חטים אף זו לא תבוא אלא
חטים ת"ל שעורים אמר רבן גמליאל הניחו לי סופרים
ואומרה כמין חומר אבל נראה הוא כשם שמעשיה
מעשה בהמה כך קרבנה מאכל בהמה (ספרי במדבר פי' ח)

> "Barley," Why was this said? For it might be reasoned (in the following manner): since the meal offering of the sinner comes as a result of sin, if I learned that the meal offering of the sinner comes only from wheat this too (the sota's meal offering) will come only from wheat—therefore Scripture states "barley." Said Rabban Gamliel, "Allow me Scribes (*Soferim*) and I will say 'kemin homer.' It really is that just as her deeds are deeds of a beast, her sacrifice is the food of a beast."

Much thought has been given to Rabban Gamliel's appeal to the *Soferim*, the scribes. J. N. Epstein opined that Rabban Gamliel's reticence was because of the scribes' opposition to Philonic, allegorical exegesis. M. Kahana in his commentary on *Sifre Numbers* demurs, claiming that to the best of his memory no such opposition to Philonic exegesis appears elsewhere in rabbinic literature. Kahana sees the background here as a disagreement between the *Sifre* and the Mishnah in their respective handling of the debasement of the *Sota.*[14] In this limited and particular case, this type of *homer* reasoning lends support to the further debasement of the *Sota*, much beyond what the Torah itself prescribed. This was why Rabban Gamliel "asked permission" to use *homer* reasoning in this particular instance.

I would like to suggest another avenue of interpreting this enigmatic address by Rabban Gamliel in the *Sifre* passage. The *Sifre* makes the case that the mentioning of barley is necessary since we might have reasoned (שהיה בדין) that as in other cases of sin offerings wheat is used—therefore Scripture explicitly stipulates barley in our case. Rabban Gamliel in effect supplies a moralizing reason for the use of barley which in a certain sense supplements the previous reasoning but in another sense undercuts the reasoning. He is not deriving law or supporting it, but

14 See Kahana, Sifre, vol. 3, 112 and note 54 where he cites Epstein, Jacob N., Introduction to Tannaitic Literature. Mishnah, Tosefta and Halakhic Midrashim (Heb.), Jerusalem 1957, 398.

employing Scripture to teach a moral lesson. This is not, if you will, *beit midrashic* exegesis but rather moralizing sermons.

My hypothesis is that this technique of *kemin homer* is to be seen in the context of homiletics and not as aggadic exegesis. In all of the cases above there is no innovative reading of Scripture but rather an homiletic conclusion drawn from Scripture. In this, I find myself in full agreement with Jacob Neusner's early work on Yohanan ben Zakkai.[15] Neusner writes, very probably influenced by W. Bacher's characterization of Rabban Yohanan's scriptural work, "his known exegeses however do not reveal allegorization at all but rather homiletical moralizing."

I would like to advance the hypothesis that the more innovative free- wheeling aggadic midrash developed after Rabban Yohanan.[16]

The shift to freer exegesis is noted I believe in R. Joshua's remarks at Mishnah *Sota* 5:2–5. On two occasions R. Joshua remarks that his student R. Akiva had advanced interpretations that R. Joshua's teacher, R. Yohanan, only dared to imagine, since R. Yohanan held that there was no scriptural support for the interpretations. The two passages read:

אמר ר' יהושע
מי יגלה עפר
מעיניך רבן יוחנן בן זכאי שהיית אומר עתיד דור אחר לטהר ככר שלישי שאין לו מקרא מן
התורה שהוא טמא
והלא עקיבא תלמידך מביא לו מקרא מן התורה שהוא טמא שנאמר כל
אשר בתוכו יטמא [...]
אמר רבי יהושע
מי יגלה עפר מעיניך רבן יוחנן בן זכאי שהיית דורש כל
ימיך שלא עבד איוב את המקום אלא מיראה שנאמר איש תם וישר ירא
אלהים וסר מרע והלא יהושע תלמיד תלמידך למד שמאהבה עשה:

> Said R. Joshua, Who will lift the earth from your eyes Rabban Yohanan ben Zakkai for you used to say "a future generation will purify a third loaf that has *no verse from the Torah* and it is impure"—didn't Akiva your student *bring a verse from the Torah* that it is impure, "all in it will be impure."

> Said R Joshua, Who will lift the earth from your eyes Rabban Yohanan ben Zakkai for you used to sermonize (*doresh*) that Job served God (*hamakom*) out of fear for it says

15 See Neusner, A Life, 87–88. See also there 82: "Yohanan lived between two revolutions in Scriptural hermeneutic [...] Hillel [...] and Nahum [...] carried forward by Akiba [...]" This is challenging but I believe incorrect— especially since it would seem to me that aggadic and halakhic exegesis had different trajectories. See now Goldsmith, Midreshei Halakhah, 25–47, who argues that most of the Tannaitic midrash is comprised of brief comments rather than developed exegesis.

16 See Schwartz, Hillel, who argues vigorously that Hillel also did not engage in midrashic commentary. But David Henschke, כיצד מועיל, refutes this conclusion.

> "God fearing and avoiding evil" (Job 1:8)—didn't Joshua your student's student teach that he did it from love?

Akiva discovers a legal exegesis that Rabban Yohanan thought to be impossible in a straightforward reading of Torah. R. Joshua b. Hyrcanus advances a similarly novel and innovative reading of Job. Is this the watershed in biblical interpretation in Tannaitic circles?[17] Does the truly innovative, creative, even fanciful interpretations begin with the generation of Yohanan b. Zakkai's students at the turn of the century? More important, what brings about this seismic shift-moving from homiletic lessons based on Scripture to imaginative aggadic exegeses, which often turn Scripture on its head or at the very least divert from the logic of the verse?

2. Rabban Yohanan Ben Zakkai's Students

According to the Mishnah in *Avot* 2:8, Rabban Yohanan had five students, two of whom were noted for their piety, two for their methods of learning and one, R. Joshua, given an all embracing praise, the joy of his mother. Menahem Kahana and Daniel Boyarin, in publications stemming from their joint study of the *Mekhilta*, noted that R. Joshua had a sustained literal approach to Exodus, not veering from the *pshat*, employing terms such as *vaddai* (= "certainly"), and *kishmuo* (= "as it sounds") to indicate straightforward contextual readings. This is frequently in opposition to a rabbi named Elazar Hamodai who is, at least on one occasion, singled out for his astonishing exegesis. This sage employed the full array of inventive midrashic and allegorical exegesis. In a series of over fifty exegeses in the *Mekhilta* of Rabbi Ishmael on Exodus R. Joshua and R. Elazar Hamodai offer strikingly different, often opposing exegeses. On a number of occasions, a third opinion is also recorded, belonging to one of the leading students of Rabban Yohanan—R. Eliezer ben Hyrcanos, R. Eliezer the Great. Interestingly, R. Eliezer seems to fluctuate between a fundamentally literal approach, a fact noted fifty years ago by Yitzhak Gilat and seconded by Menahem Kahana in his study of *Mekhilta Amalek*,[18] and an extremely innovative and imaginative reading of Scripture. R. Eliezer ben Hyrcanos' predilection toward *pshat*, literal contextual interpretation, is in full agreement with R. Joshua[19] but he does also indulge in exegesis akin to R. Elazar Hamodai's pioneering exegesis.[20] R. Joshua

---

17 See Rosen-Zvi, Who Will Uncover, especially 115–116 on Job.

18 See Kahana, Mekhiltot, 70 and note 44 where he cites Gilat, R. Eliezer (heb.), 36–45.

19 Witness the "joint interpretation" attributed to R. Joshua and R. Eliezer in *Gen. Rab.* 98 (99):4 (Theodor/Albeck, Midrash Bereshit Rabbah, vol. 3, 1254–1255).

20 See my forthcoming article, "Teaching Midrash" in Hirshman/Satran (ed.), Rabbinic Study Circles.

and R. Eliezer, the two leading students of Rabban Yohanan are cited most widely in the Mishnah and are usually on opposite sides of legal opinion and disagree in the most fundamental way on legal issues! We need to explore their apparently divergent view of aggadic midrash. We will for now take a closer look at R. Eliezer and his exegesis in the Mekhilta and elsewhere and conclude with a review of R. Elazar Hamodai.

On at least three occasions R. Eliezer begins his comment with a rhetorical question: "From where do we know that [...]" So in a famous comment, repeated in the Passover Haggadah, he asserts that each plague in Egypt was fourfold (*Mekhilta of Rabbi Ishmael Beshallah* 6), relying on the recounting of the plagues in Psalms 78:49:

יְשַׁלַּח בָּם חֲרוֹן אַפּוֹ עֶבְרָה וָזַעַם וְצָרָה מִשְׁלַחַת מַלְאֲכֵי רָעִים

He inflicted his burning anger upon them,
wrath indignation trouble, a band of deadly messengers.

This is indeed intertextual, using an apposite text to interpret another text. But, I wish to claim there is no undermining of the logic of the original verses in Exodus. This is not free-wheeling, unbounded interpretation but the usual convention of "interpreting Homer through Homer" or the Bible through the Bible. So too, commenting on Exod 15:3: זֶה אֵלִי וְאַנְוֵהוּ "This is My Lord and I will extol Him", he reasons that even the maidservant at Sinai saw God more directly than the great prophets Isaiah and Ezekiel. Boyarin asserted that R. Eliezer read the *zeh*, "this," deictically rather than anaphorically. Even more likely in my view is that R. Eliezer's comment was shaped by the verses introducing the song, Ex 14:35: "The children of Israel saw the mighty hand." R. Eliezer may very well have taken the verse literally, in the same way Israel's seeing the Egyptian dead in the previous verse was to be understood quite literally. These are examples of a penchant for contextual renderings. I hope to bring examples of freer exegesis in R. Eliezer's aggadic readings.[21] We will take up one more example of R. Eliezer's exegesis soon in the context of his differing interpretation with that of his contemporary R. Elazar Hamodai. It is R. Elazar Hamodai who is the master par excellence of innovative and imaginative exegesis, and possibly, the innovator and driving force, behind this type of aggadic midrash in its early Tannaitic manifestation.

---

21 Ishay Rosen-Zvi commented on an earlier draft of this paper that indeed R. Eliezer also has more creative midrashic interpretations and he is certainly correct. I hope to deal with this in a future article (see above n. 20). Ishay and his brother Asaf Rosen-Zvi shared with me an important article they submitted comparing and contrasting exegetical techniques and formulae displayed in the legal and non-legal sections of the Mekhilta.

3. R. Elazar Hamodai

Elazar Hamodai plays a key role, arguably the most prominent role, in the Tannaitic exegesis of Exodus 15:22–18:27, which correspond to two of the nine tractates of the *Mekhilta of Rabbi Ishmael, Vayassa* and *Amalek*. He appears more than 55 times, as opposed to the precious few times, six in all, where he is quoted in Mishnah, Tosefta and *Sifre*. In the *Mekhilta*, he appears consistently as an opposing opinion to that of R. Joshua and much more rarely to that of R. Eliezer, who, only on occasion, appears as a third opinion. These differences between R. Elazar and R. Joshua were collected by W. Z. Bacher in his *Agada der Tannaiten* and were closely scrutinized by Menahem Kahana in his work on the Amalek tractate and elsewhere.

In his wonderful introduction to the Tannaitic midrash, Kahana opines that the *Sifre to Numbers* might be the oldest of the Tannaitic midrashim since the last generation of Tannaim of the early third century C. E. is absent from them.[22] By the same criterion, we might want to view these two tractates of the *Mekhilta, Vayassa* and *Amalek*, as the oldest evidence of sustained exegesis by Rabban Yohanan ben Zakkai's premier students R. Joshua and R. Eliezer, with R. Elazar Hamodai as the key dissenting voice. This precious evidence of these late first century rabbis in our midrash is complemented by another equally precious passage in the Amoraic midrash *Genesis Rabbah* (98:4).[23] In Jacob's words to Reuben we again have an extended triple debate between these three Tannaitic sages, again R. Elazar flying in the face of the simple sense of Scripture and instead reading Jacob as blessing Reuben.

Was Elazar Hamodai a contemporary of these two luminaries, students of Rabban Yohanan ben Zakkai? Whose student was he?

Tannaitic literature contains no biographical details of R. Elazar. He is portrayed in one anecdote as "sitting in front of R. Tarfon and the elders" (*Mekhilta Vayassa* 3)[24] which might suggest that he was a younger contemporary of R. Tarfon, possibly a half generation after R. Joshua and R. Eliezer. Yet the Geniza fragment of that story has R. Elazar being addressed as "our brother," which would indicate equal status.[25]

This singular figure remains elusive in our effort to fixing his dates. A legend in the Palestinian Talmud *Taanit* 4,6 depicts him as a saint fending of the Romans at Beitar by virtue of prayer and fasting, until his nephew Bar Kochva (132 C. E.!) is tricked into suspecting him as complicit with the Romans, which

22 Kahana, Halachic Midrashim, 61.

23 Theodor/Albeck, Midrash Bereshit Rabbah, vol. 3, 1253–1255.

24 Lauterbach, Mekilta, vol. 2, 113.

25 See Kahana, Fragments, 75 (Oxford MS. Heb. d. 22.6).

leads to his death. The great historian Gedaliah Alon and others accepted this as evidence for dating this sage, with his death in the 130's C. E.[26] This does not preclude his having flourished already at the beginning of the second century alongside R. Joshua and R. Eliezer. In a passage in the Babylonian Talmud *Bava Batra* 10b and a later midrash he is placed in a setting with Rabban Yohanan ben Zakkai but this is late evidence and was rejected by E. E. Urbach as a conflation of traditions.[27] More recently, S. Naeh has placed him firmly as a contemporary of the late first century author of *4 Ezra*.[28] If R. Elazar Hamodai's sobriquet, Modai, is geographical he might have lived in what was considered a town of priests—Modiin.[29]

A famous example of R. Elazar Hamodai's aggadic midrash that was viewed by R. Tarfon as "astonishing" (*matmiah*), or possibly translating more negatively, "shocking," is when R. Elazar advanced the interpretation that when the manna fell, it reached a height of sixty cubits (*Mekhilta Vayassa* 3).[30] He is rebuked by R. Tarfon: "How long will you go on making astonishing statements before us?" R. Elazar replies curtly, *"it is a verse from the Torah,"* that is to say that his interpretation is all but explicit in the Torah.[31] We should note that this is exactly the phrase used by R. Joshua above in the Mishnah introducing Akiva's startling exegesis, on the one hand. By the same token we find the same verb (*matmiah*) used by three sages, one of whom was the same R. Joshua, as a reaction to R Akiva's reaction to the grandeur of Rome as opposed to the debasement of the Temple. R. Tarfon, in another place, rebukes R. Akiva's exegesis, albeit legal, with a different verb "why do you pile on (*megabev*)."

Even more compelling is a comparison of R. Elazar's astonishing exegesis with that of R. Eliezer's interpretation of the same phenomenon—the height of the manna. I will place them alongside one another:

26 See Alon, The Jews, vol. 2, 623, 640. Alon entertains the possibility that Elazar Hamodai was a priest and does not rule out his identification with the priest Elazar who figures prominently on the Bar Kochva coins.

27 See Urbach, Tendencies, 2–3. Urbach points out that in the Pesikta d'Rav Kahana, Piska Tisa 5 (Mandelbaum, Pesikta, 21) the statement is attributed to R. Elazar ben Arak, a noted and possibly preeminent student of Rabban Yochanan, as advanced by Abba Shaul in the name of Rabban Yochanan, in Mishnah *Avot* 2:8.

28 See Naeh, The Script, especially 133 and n. 40.

29 We should note that on a few occasions the geniza reads "meyudai" which, like mudai, might be derived from the root of knowledge. This needs to be researched further.

30 Lauterbach, Mekilta, vol. 2, 113.

31 See Milikowsky's excellent essay, "Rabbinic Interpretation of the Bible. The Question of the Literal Meaning," 7–28. If my thesis here is correct, Seder Olam will be more akin to rabbinic exegesis up until R. Elazar Modai's innovations.

Mekhilta d'Rabbi Ishmael, Geniza, Ms.Heb. d.22
5VMs., according to Bar Ilan Otzar Tannarim data base (cf. Horovitz/Rabin, Mechilta, 165)

ט' וכאמתיים
על פני הארץ סביבות המחנה: ואו'
ויפל בקרב מחניהו
סביב למשכנות: י' ר' אליעזר או' הרי
הוא או' וכאמ[תים]
על פני הארץ שתי אמות היתה גבוהה
מן הארץ: אבל
המן לא נטלו אותו ישר' אלא מין
הגבוה אמרתה צא
וראה כיצד היה המן יורד ליש' יוצא
רוח צפונית והיא
מכבֶדת את המדבר והיה המטר יורד
ומכבש את
הארץ והטל עולה והרוח מנש <... ..>
ועושה אותו
כמין שלחנות ש <.. > הב והמן יורד
עליהן והיו ישר<..>
נוטלין ואוכלין: יא' הבשר עודנו: אם כך
זימן הק<..> '
למכעיסיו? על אחת כמה וכמה שישלם
שכר טוב לצדיק'
לעתיד לבא:

Lauterbach, Mekilta, vol. 2, 110:
R. Eliezer says: Behold it says: "And about two cubits above the face of the earth" (Num 11.31). The manna was two cubits high from the ground up and Israelites took it only off from the top. You must needs say: Come and see how the manna used to come down for Israel. The north wind would come and sweep the desert; then rain would come down and level the ground; then the dew would come up and the wind would blow upon it. The ground thus became a sort of golden table on which the manna would come down and from which the Israelites would take it and eat it. If God thus provided for those who provoked Him, how much the more will He in the future pay a good reward to the righteous.

Mekhilta d'Rabbi Ishmael, Oxford Ms., according to Bar Ilan Otzar Tannaim data base (cf. Horovitz/Rabin, Mechilta, 166)

כבר היה ר' טרפון והזקנים יושבים ור'
אלע' המודעי יושב לפניהם אמ' להם ר'
אלע' המודעי ששים אמה היה גובהו
של מן שהיה יורד להם לישר' אמרו לו
מודעי עד מתי את מתמיה עלינו אמ'
להם מקר' הוא מן התורה וכי איזו
מרובה מידת הטובה במידת הפורענות
מהו אומ' ביום הזה נבקעו וג' חמש
עשרה אמה מלמעלה וג' מה נפשך על
גבי ההר ט'ו אמה בבקעה ט'ו אמה
במידת הטובה מהו או' ויצו שחקים
ממעל וגו' מעוט דלתות שתים וכמה
ארובות בדלת ארבע ארבע על ארבע
שמונה שמונה על שמונה הרי שש
עשרה צא וחשב ששים אמה שהיה
גובהו של מן שהיה יורד להם לישר'

Lauterbach, Mekilta, vol. 2, 113:
Once R. Tarfon and the Elders were sitting together and R. Eleazar of Modiʿim was sitting before them. Said to them R. Eleazar of Modiʿim: Sixty cubits high was the manna that came down for Israel. Said they to him: "How long will you go on making astonishing statements before us?" Said he to them: "This can be proved from a passage of the Torah. For which measure is greater, the measure for good or the measure for evil? You must say: the measure for good. Now what does it say about the measure of evil? 'On the same day were all the fountains of the great deep broken up, and the windows of heaven were opened' (Gen. 7.11). And it says: 'Fifteen cubits upward did the waters prevail', etc. (ibid. v. 20) […] And what does it say about the measure of good? 'And he commanded the skies above and opened the doors of heaven' (Ps. 78.23). The least that 'doors' can designate is two. How many windows are there in a door? Four. Four added to four makes eight. Now, go and figure it up and you will find that the manna that came down for Israel was sixty cubits high."

Though R. Eliezer's comment is somewhat opaque it seems that he is claiming that as opposed to the quail, which Scripture states explicitly was piled two cubits high, and presumably the Israelites gathered it all, the manna was taken only from the higher level, with no stooping to gather it.[32] R. Elazar Hamodai perplexes the sages by logically inferring that if for the punishment of the Flood the waters reached fifteen cubits, the gift of the manna had to reach sixty cubits, since we've learned that God's beneficence far exceeds God's punishment. He proves this with a mathematical exercise based on Psalms.[33] His virtuoso performance is based on interweaving verses from elsewhere that treat the manna and drawing a logical, homiletical conclusion. What motivated R. Elazar's extravagant lesson? Was it the pietist in him, who was intent on glorifying God's beneficence and at the same time emphasizing its supernatural quality? These characterizations have been advanced by scholars, as we will see below.[34]

Finally, a different exegetical debate, which is most germane to our thesis, is at *Mekhilta Vayassa* 1.[35] There we find R. Elazar, the illustrious aggadist, on the attack, challenging R. Joshua over the latter's interpretation of the biblical word "nissahu." R. Joshua takes it to mean, "He raised the people of Israel." R. Elazar objects, saying that the word would have had to been written with the Hebrew letter *sin* rather than *samech* to yield that interpretation. R. Elazar understands it, in a role reversal, to be "He tested them." This direct confrontation lends additional credence to the dating of R. Elazar Hamodai above. It also shows a sensitivity to the spelling and language of Scripture. This seems to accord with the traditional stance R. Elazar Hamodai staked out in terms of the script and language of Torah.

Many scholars have identified various characteristics of R. Elazar Hamodai's approach in these *Mekhilta* passages, conveniently listed by M. Kahana in his recent contribution on the subject.[36] Bacher noted a proclivity to symbolic and allegorical interpretations, emphasizing study, prayer and fasting. Urbach noted Elazar's accentuation of the merit of the fathers, while Boyarin saw Elazar as castigating Israel for bad behavior. Kahana himself spoke of Elazar's humanism. In his most recent contribution, Kahana depicts R. Elazar as a "hasid," a pietist, who relies totally on God for his daily needs and devotes himself to study and

32 Many of the exegeses in the Mekhilta by named sages are followed by narrative expansions as here. Did R. Eliezer's comment end with the brief statement "took it only from the top up"? Or, was it he that continued with "you must needs say" and the picturesque description that follows. I, as yet, have no clear proof either way and this needs further investigation. If this is his continuation, the homily at the end is in the same style as his teacher, Rabban Yochanan ben Zakkai's *kemin homer*.

33 The eightfold argument here and the exact calculation eludes me.

34 See Kahana's depiction in the following paragraph and n. 27.

35 Horovitz/Rabin, Mechilta, 156 f.; Lauterbach, Mekilta, vol. 2, 94.

36 Kahana, Torah Study, listed on 74 and bibliographic notes 3–7.

prayer, while minimizing involvement in daily affairs.[37] Kahana also maintains the view that Elazar anchored these views with his allegorical reading of Scripture.

I think then that we will be justified to see R. Elazar as at the very least one of the Tannaitic founders, and I emphasize Tannaitic-rabbinic, of the free-wheeling, creative approach to exegesis of Scripture. Elazar's innovative approach was embraced by R. Akiva who, I would suggest, moved it into the mainstream. Early objections by the same R. Tarfon to Akiva's innovative legal exegesis,[38] as he did to R. Elazar's aggadic exegesis earlier, results in Tarfon's total capitulation[39] remarking to Akiva:

ואתה דורש ומסכים לשמועה הא כל הפורש ממך כפורש מחייו

You interpret and agree with the received tradition—
anyone who departs from you is like departing from one's own life.

Within a little less than a century in Amoraic times, midrash aggada would be as fanciful in its interpretation and as creative as some of the most imaginative literary creations of the Second Sophistic.

But why was it R. Elazar of Modiin and why at this particular point in history did this approach to biblical interpretation take hold? Why is this heated debate over exegesis preserved only in these two tractates of *Mekhilta*, spanning Exod 16–18, which contain the manna, Amalek, the beginning of the Jethro story (and briefly in fragmentary form in the Amoraic *Genesis Rabbah*)?

Urbach has suggested in his classical work *The Sages*,[40] that Elazar Hamodai's dictum in Mishnah *Avot* 3:11[41] is anti-Christian. It reads: "One who desecrates holy things, scorns the holidays, reveals faces of the Torah, and abrogates the covenant of our father Abraham and causes his friends' face to flush, even though he has good deeds, he has no place in the world to come." It would appear that this early second century sage, whom Urbach sees as battling the Christians, at the very same time, promotes an allegorical reading of Scripture and a pietistic way of life, *hasidism*. Indeed, R. Elazar Hamodai reckons the great *hasid*, Hanina ben Dosa, as one of his heroes.[42] Many scholars have noted the close correlation between this *hasidic* movement among the rabbis, including Pinhas ben Yair, Hanina ben Dosa and Honi the Circle-Drawer, and the depiction of Jesus in the gospels. Elazar then is one of this movement, and at one in the same time adopting a spiritual

37 Ibid., 93.

38 Noted already by Fraenkel, Ways, 492.

39 *Sifra Nedava* 4,4 and parallels such as Tosefta *Zevahim* 1,8.

40 Urbach, The Sages, 295–296.

41 Sharvit, Tractate Avoth, 131.

42 See Kahana, Torah Studies, 87 and n. 95, quoting S. Safrai's work on Hasidim (and I add their relation to Jesus).

non-literal reading of Scripture while demanding adherence to temple, holidays and circumcision.

Moreover, S. Naeh has shown in a wonderful article cited above[43] that Elazar stakes out the most conservative position in terms of the original language and script of the Torah. As opposed to *4 Ezra* where a new giving of the Torah is posited after Moses' Torah perished, the Tannaim debated whether the script and language had changed. Only R. Elazar Hamodai insists that the Script of the Torah never changed, a radically conservative position, held by none of the other authorities. His is a curious mix of exegetical innovation and scriptural traditionalism.

I note here that a century later Origen uses the waters of Mara, one of the key sections of R. Elazar in the Mekhilta, for a frontal and withering attack on Jewish interpretations.[44] Might these chapters Exod 16–18, with their emphasis on miracle and law (Mara), the alien enemy Amalek, and the pious convert (Jethro) have been focal points of contention between Jews and Christians in the first two centuries?

What intrigues me most is the flourishing of Tannaitic aggadic midrash in the second century. If indeed within rabbinic Judaism it begins in the time of the students of Rabban Yohanan ben Zakkai, we should ask ourselves how was this creative, midrashic enterprise construed, what "work" was it to accomplish? How cognizant was it of Christian and so called gnostic interpretations of the Jewish bible? Was this narrative playfulness mainly educational entertainment for adult audiences in synagogue on the Sabbath or a product of rabbinic study circles—*beit midrash*—of the period? Or, was it, like its Second Temple antecedents, viewed as part of the oral legends passed down along with the oral law? These and many other questions invite further study.

Literature

Sources

Colson, Francis H. (trans.), Philo. In Ten Volumes, vol. 7 (LCL 320), London, Heinemann, and Cambridge, MA., Harvard University Press, 1937; reprint 1958.

Finkelstein, Louis (ed.), Sifra on Leviticus according to Vatican Manuscript Assemani 66 with Variants from the Other Manuscripts, Genizah Fragments, Early Editions and

43 Naeh, Script, 133.

44 See Heine, Origen. On numerous occasions, Origen rhetorically ridicules the inadequacy of Jewish interpretation: "I think the Law, if it is undertaken according to the letter, is sufficiently bitter and is itself Mara" (*Hom. Exod.* VII,1; Heine, Origen, 301); "The Jews even now are at Mara" (*Hom. Exod.* VII,3; Heine, Origen, 305); "[…] let the Jews understand that already at that time our Lord's day was preferred to the Jewish Sabbath" (*Hom. Exod.* VII, 5; Heine, Origen, 308); "I wish that the Jews will tell me how the Lord is 'known in the evening' (Ex 16:6–7) and how his majesty is seen 'in the morning.'" (*Hom. Exod.* VII,7; Heine, Origen, 310) and more.

Quotations by Medieval Authorities and with References to Parallel Passages and Commentaries, vol. 2, New York 1983.
Heine, Ronald E. (ed. and transl.), Origen. Homilies on Genesis and Exodus, Washington, D.C. 1982.
Kahana, Menahem I., Sifre on Numbers, 4 vol., Jerusalem 2011–2015 (Heb.).
—, The Geniza Fragments of the Halakhic Midrashim, vol. 1, Jerusalem 2005 (Heb.).
Lauterbach, Jacob Zallel (ed.), Mekilta de Rabbi Ishmael. A critical edition on the basis of the MSS and realy editions with an English translation, introduction and notes, 3 vol., Philadelphia, Pa. 1933–1935.
Mandelbaum, Bernard (ed.), Pesikta de Rav Kahana, New York, N. Y. 1962.
Theodor, Julius/Albeck, Hanokh (ed.), Midrash Bereshit Rabbah, vol. 3, Jerusalem 1965.

Scholarly Works

Alon, Gedaliah/Levi, Gershon (ed. and transl.), The Jews in Their Land in the Talmudic Age (70–640 C.E.), 2 vol., Jerusalem 1980 and 1984.
Bacher, Wilhelm Z., Die Agada der Tannaiten. Band 1. Von Hillel bis Akiba, Strassburg 1903.
Fishbane, Michael, Biblical Interpretation in Ancient Israel, Oxford 1985.
Fraade, Steven, Early Rabbinic Midrash between Philo and Qumran, in: M. Satlow (ed.), Strength to Strength. Essays in Appreciation of Shaye J. D. Cohen, (BJS 363), Providence, R.I. 2018, 281–293.
Fraenkel, Jonah, The Ways of the Aggada and the Midrash, Givatayim 1991 (Heb.).
Goldsmith, Simcha, Were There Really *Midreshei Halakhah*?, HUCA 84–85 (2013–2014), 25–47.
Haneman, Gideon, Lemasoret Haketiv shel ktav yad hasifra hamenukad in: M. Bar-Asher (ed.), Kovetz Maamarim beleshon Hazal, part 2, Jerusalem 1980, 19–20.
Henschke, David, כיצד מועיל הפרוזבול? לתולדות ביאורה של תקנת הלל, Shenaton Ha-Mishpat Ha-Ivri/Annual of the Institute for Research in Jewish Law 22 (2001), 71–106.
Horovitz, Saul/Rabin, Yisrael Avraham (ed.), Mechilta d'Rabbi Ismael cum variis lectionibus et adnotationibus, Jerusalem 1960.
Kahana, Menahem I., Torah Study, Labor, Piety, and Realism. The Controversy between R. Joshua and R. Eleazar Ha-Modaʿi in the "Aggadah of Mekhilta," Sidra: A Journal for the Study of Rabbinic Literature 31 (2016), 73–94.
—, The Halachic Midrashim, in: S. Safrai et al (ed.), The Literature of the Sages 2. Midrash and Targum, Liturgy, Poetry, Mysticism, Contracts, Inscriptions, Ancient Science and the Languages of Rabbinic Literature, Assen/Philadelphia, Pa. 2006, 3–105.
—, The Two Mekhiltot on the Amalek Portion. The Originality of the Version of the Mekhilta d'Rabbi Ishma'el with Respect to the Mekhilta of Rabbi Shim'on ben Yohay, Jerusalem 1999 (Heb.).
Kister, Menahem, Romans 5:12–21 against the Background of Torah-Theology and Hebrew Usage, The Harvard Theological Review 100 (2007), 391–424.
Kugel, James, The Beginnings of Biblical Interpretation, in: M. Henze (ed.), A Companion to Biblical Interpretation in Early Judaism, Grand Rapids, Mich. 2012, 3–23.

Mandel, Paul, Midrashic Exegesis and its Precedents in the Dead Sea Scrolls, DSD 8 (2001), 149–168.

Milikowsky, Chaim, Rabbinic Interpretation of the Bible in the Light of Ancient Hermeneutical Practice. The Question of the Literal Meaning, in: M. Perani (ed.), "The Words of a Wise Man's Mouth are Gracious" (Qoh 10,12) (FS Günter Stemberger) (Studia Judaica 32), Berlin u. a. 2005, 7–28.

Naeh, Shlomo, The Script of the Torah in Rabbinic Thought (A). The Traditions Concerning Ezra's Changing of the Script, Leshonenu: A Journal for the Study of the Hebrew Language and Cognate Subjects 70 (2008), 125–143 (Heb.).

Neusner, Jacob, A Life of Rabban Yohanan Ben Zakkai (ca. 1–80 C. E.), Leiden 1962.

Niehoff, Maren, Jewish Exegesis and Homeric Scholarship in Alexandria, Cambridge 2011.

—, Philo. An Intellectual Biography, New Haven, Conn. 2018.

Porter, Stanley E., The Argument of Romans 5. Can a Rhetorical Question Make a Difference? JBL 110 (1991), 655–677.

Rosen-Zvi, Ishay, "Who Will Uncover the Dust from Your Eyes?" Mishnah Sotah 5 an R. Akiva's Midrash, Tarbiz 75 (2005), 95–127 (Heb.).

Schwartz, Daniel, Hillel and Scripture: From Authority to Exegesis, in: J. H. Charlesworth/L. L. Johns (ed.), Hillel and Jesus. Comparative Studies of Two Major Religious Leaders, Minneapolis, Minn. 1997, 335–362.

Seeligmann, Isaac L., Voraussetzungen der Midraschexegese, in: G. W. Anderson et al. (ed.), Congress Volume Copenhagen 1953 (VT.S 1), Leiden 1953, 150–181.

Sharvit, Shimon, Tractate Avoth through the Ages. A Critical Edition, Prolegomena and Appendices, Jerusalem 2004.

Shemesh, Aharon, Biblical Exegesis and Interpretations from Qumran to the Rabbis, in: M. Henze (ed.), A Companion to Biblical Interpretation in Early Judaism, Grand Rapids, Mich. 2012, 467–489.

Shinan, Avigdor/Zakovitch, Yair, Midrash on Scripture and Midrash within Scripture, in: S. Japhet (ed.), Studies in Bible (Scripta Hierosolymitana 31), Jerusalem 1986, 257–277.

Urbach, Ephraim E., Political and Social Tendencies in Talmudic Concepts of Charity, Zion 16 (1951), 1–27 (Heb.).

—, The Sages. Their Concepts and Beliefs, transl. I. Abrahams, Jerusalem 1975.

Zakovitch, Yair, Inner-biblical Interpretation, in: M. Henze (ed.), A Companion to Biblical Interpretation in Early Judaism, Grand Rapids, Mich. 2012, 27–63.

Harald Buchinger (Universität Regensburg)

Exegese des Exodus und Konstruktion christlicher Identität bei Origenes

Der Exodus stellt nicht nur ein Grunddatum der Geschichtskonstruktion des Volkes Israel dar; aufgrund seiner schon bei Paulus etablierten Deutung als Typos der Taufe kommt ihm auch fundamentale Bedeutung für die Konstruktion christlicher Identität zu. Aus dieser doppelten Dimension ergibt sich zwangsläufig auch die Frage nach dem Verhältnis nicht nur zwischen Israel und Kirche, sondern auch zwischen Altem und Neuem Testament, sobald ein letzteres auf den Plan tritt; auch wenn dies bekanntlich ein langer Prozess war, ist es wohl kein Zufall, dass die für christliche Bibelrezeption fundamentale hermeneutische Kategorie des Typos erstmals im Zusammenhang jener Korrelation von Exodus und den Christen belegt ist, in der Paulus in seinem Schreiben an die heidenchristliche Gemeinde von Korinth Mitte des ersten Jahrhunderts nach Christus die Exodusgeneration als „unsere Väter" bezeichnet, die „alle auf Mose getauft wurden in der Wolke und im Meer" (1 Kor 10,1 f).[1] Noch bevor ein „Neues Testament" als christliche Büchersammlung explizit dem demzufolge „Alten Testament" gegenübergestellt wird, ist ein Jahrhundert später die Auslegung der „Schrift des hebräischen Exodus" für Melito von Sardes der Anlass, als einer der ersten eine ausgefeilte hermeneutische Theorie einschließlich jener extrem antijüdischen Implikationen zu formulieren, die seither zur Last christlicher Theologie gehören.[2] Bei Origenes ist einerseits die Gegenüberstellung von Altem und Neuem Testament fait accompli, andererseits eine klare Abgrenzung seiner christlichen Gemeinde von den Juden, die er in der Regel eher schematisch darstellt, auch wenn er in Cäsarea vermutlich über differenzierte Kontakte verfügte.[3]

Trotz dieser vollendeten hermeneutischen Tatsachen und obwohl Origenes für die allegorische Deutung des Exodus auf etablierte exegetische Traditionen zurückblicken konnte,[4] ist in seiner Auslegung des Exodus eine signifikante inhaltliche und methodische Entwicklung festzustellen, die vermutlich auf die direkte

---

1 1 Kor 10,6 („das geschah als unsere τύποι"). 11 („das widerfuhr jenen τυπικῶς"); vgl. Goppelt, τύπος κτλ, 251 f.

2 Buchinger, Melito.

3 Von der umfangreichen Literatur seien hier nur die wichtigsten Monographien genannt: Bietenhard, Caesarea; de Lange, Origen; Sgherri, Chiesa.

4 Die ältere Bibliographie und die maßgeblichen Quellen erschließen Wessel, Durchzug, und Daniélou, Exodus; Langston, Exodus, und ders., Exodus IV. Christianity, sind dagegen für die Spätantike wenig ergiebig. Reiche Hinweise bietet allerdings Ledegang, Mysterium, 416–423.

oder indirekte Begegnung mit jüdischer Kritik christlicher exegetischer Konventionen zurückzuführen ist. Sie soll hier in drei Schritten anhand exemplarischer Schlüsselquellen dargestellt werden: Einem Überblick über die homiletische Auslegung des Exodus, der schon Marc Hirshman ein Kapitel gewidmet hat[5] (1), folgt eine Analyse der methodisch auf eine neue philologische Basis gestellten Überlegungen über die Bedeutung des Exodus für die christliche Identität im ersten Buch der Schrift „Über das Pascha" (2). Zuletzt werden die Transformationen des Themas im Spätwerk des Origenes dargestellt (3). Da ich in meiner Monographie über das Pascha bei Origenes[6] materiale Vollständigkeit angestrebt habe, erheben die folgenden Ausführungen keinen Anspruch auf Originalität, auch wenn sie aus der Perspektive dieses Bandes einen neuen Blick auf das Material werfen und speziell nach der Konstruktion christlicher Identität und ihrer Abgrenzung von Konstruktionen des Judentums in der Exegese des Exodus bei Origenes gefragt wird.

1. Exegese und die Konstruktion christlicher Identität in Homilien des Origenes

1.1 Überkommene Deutungen des Exodus in der 26. Numeri-Homilie

In der übertragenen Auslegung von Num 31 f in der 26. Numeri-Homilie erinnert Origenes sein Auditorium an zwei etablierte exegetische Traditionen der figurativen Exodus-Exegese:

> Dass das Bild des Auszugs aus Ägypten auf zwei Weisen aufgefaßt wird, ist sowohl von unseren Vorfahren als auch von uns selbst schon oft gesagt worden. Denn sowohl wenn einer von der Dunkelheit der Irrtümer zum Licht der Erkenntnis geführt und vom irdischen Wandel zu den geistigen Einrichtungen bekehrt wird, scheint er aus Ägypten ausgezogen und in die Wüste gekomen zu sein, das heißt jenen Zustand des Lebens, in dem er durch Schweigen und Ruhe in den göttlichen Gesetzen eingeübt und mit den himmlischen Worten vertraut gemacht werden soll; wenn er dadurch unterrichtet und angeleitet den Jordan durchschritten hat, soll er bis zum Land der Verheißung eilen, das heißt durch die Gnade der Taufe bis zu den Einrichtungen des Evangeliums gelangen. Aber auch das nannten wir ein Bild des Auszugs aus Ägypten, wenn eine Seele die Dunkelheit dieser Welt und die Blindheit des leiblichen Wesens verläßt und in jene Welt übertragen wird, die entweder als „Schoß Abrahams" wie bei

5 Hirshman, Passover; knapper vgl. Tzvetkova-Glaser, Pentateuchauslegung, 272–276. Vgl. auch Buchinger, Pascha, wo die ältere Bibliographie erschlossen ist, die darum hier nicht noch einmal detailliert referiert wird. Zur fünften Exodushomilie vgl. u. a. ebd., 790–796; zum Zusammenhang von Pascha und Exodus ebd., 407–412, zur Allegorese des „Durchgangs" ebd., 867–892.

6 Ebd.

Lazarus (Lk 16,22 f) oder als „Paradies“ wie beim Schächer, der vom Kreuz herab zum Glauben kam (Lk 23,43), bezeichnet wird.[7]

Es ist für Origenes also ein überkommener Topos, den Exodus als Typos zu verstehen (*figura* ist eine der möglichen – und auch die in der Vulgata in 1 Kor 10,6.11 verwendeten – Übersetzungen für das griechische Wort). Das übertragene Verständnis dieser typologischen Exegese konkretisiere sich einerseits in einer symbolischen Spiritualisierung, nämlich in einem Übergang von einer als Irrtum gedeuteten Dunkelheit zur in der Metapher des Lichtes angedeuteten Erkenntnis. Dieses metaphorische Verständnis realisiert sich zugleich in dem für die christliche Existenz fundamentalen Prozess der christlichen Initiation; es ist allerdings bemerkenswert, dass Origenes nicht einfach im Gefolge von 1 Kor 10 die Taufe mit dem Exodus identifiziert, sondern im Auszug aus Ägypten den Beginn des Katechumenats angedeutet sieht, während der Taufe selbst erst der Einzug ins Gelobte Land entspreche.[8] Andererseits wird der Exodus als Bild des Übergangs von der ebenfalls in platonisierender Manier metaphorisch als Dunkelheit verstandenen körperlichen Existenz dieser Welt ins Jenseits interpretiert. In systematischer Betrachtung können beide Deutungen als anthropologische Allegorien bezeichnet werden, wobei die erste neben einer moralischen Dimension außerdem eine sakramentale Typologie umfasst (wobei Typologie und Allegorie hier – wie bei Origenes selbst – als nahezu austauschbare Begriffe für eine übertragene Deutung verwendet werden).[9] In diesem homiletischen Kontext gibt Origenes nicht zu erkennen, dass die in beiden Deutungen vorausgesetzte Assoziation von Ägypten mit der „Finsternis“ nicht nur ein Stereotyp allegorischer Exodus-Interpretation darstellt, welche als Ausgangspunkt der Bewegung „vom Dunkel zum Licht“ bekanntlich zu den Grundmotiven

7 Origenes, *Hom. Num.* 26,4 (GCS 30, 249 f): *Exeundi de Aegypto figuram duobus modis accipi et a prioribus nostris et a nobis saepe iam dictum est. Nam et cum quis de errorum tenebris ad agnitionis lumen adducitur et de terrena conversatione ad spiritalia instituta convertitur, de Aegypto videtur exisse et venisse ad solitudinem, ad illum videlicet vitae statum, in quo per silentium et quietem exerceatur divinis legibus et eloquiis coelestibus imbuatur; per quae institutus et directus cum Iordanen transierit, properet usque ad terram repromissionis, id est per gratiam baptismi usque ad evangelica instituta perveniat. Sed et illam figuram esse diximus exeundi de Aegypto, cum relinquit anima mundi huius tenebras ac naturae corporeae caecitatem et transfertur ad aliud saeculum, quod vel ‚sinus Abrahae‘, ut in Lazaro, vel ‚paradisus‘, ut in latrone, qui de cruce credidit, indicatur*; zur Stelle vgl. u. a. Buchinger, Pascha, 409 f, zur Taufe bei Origenes erschöpfend Auf der Maur/Waldram, Illuminatio.

8 Zur angeblichen Überlegenheit des Jordandurchzugs gegenüber dem „Anfang des Exodus“ in Ägypten vgl. auch Origenes, *Comm. Jo.* 6, 45,233 f (GCS 10, 154); zuvor (ebd. 6, 44,227–223 [GCS 10, 153]) argumentiert Origenes die Überlegenheit der Taufe auf Josua/Jesus gegenüber jener auf Mose (vgl. 1 Kor 10,1–4).

9 Vgl. Crouzel, La distinction, in Rückgriff auch auf die umfassende terminologische Untersuchung ders., Origène.

jüdischer genauso wie christlicher Paschatheologie gehört,[10] sondern in der spätantiken Tradition eine philologische Basis in einer entsprechenden Etymologie des Namens „Ägypten" hatte.[11]

1.2 Exegese des Exodus und antijüdische Konstruktion christlicher Identität in der fünften Exodus-Homilie des Origenes

Der Exodus-Perikope selbst widmet Origenes die fünfte Homilie zum gleichnamigen Buch, die allerdings nur in der lateinischen Übersetzung durch Rufinus von Aquileia erhalten ist, dessen Text hier nicht durch Katenenfragmente überprüft werden kann. Die Predigt behandelt zumindest Ex 12,37 (Aufbruch der Israeliten) bis Ex 14,30; da die folgende Homilie mit Ex 15 einsetzt, gehörte der letzte Vers von Kapitel 14 vermutlich noch zur ausgelegten Perikope. Unter der Perspektive der Konstruktion christlicher Identität sollen hier die Einleitung der Predigt mit ihren hermeneutischen Klärungen und einem ersten summarischen Auslegungsgang über den Exodus als solchen detailliert referiert werden; es folgen knappe Bemerkungen über die anschließende geistige Auslegung der drei Stationen und die tauftheologische Zuspitzung im letzten Teil der Homilie.

Einleitung: Hermeneutische Grundlegung und summarische Auslegung

Die Einleitung zur Predigt stellt mit unmissverständlicher Deutlichkeit hermeneutische Weichen; die Exegese des Exodus ist für Origenes ein Musterbeispiel einer Konstruktion christlicher Identität einerseits in Abgrenzung vom Judentum, andererseits aber zugleich auf Basis dessen autoritativer Schriften, von denen er ausdrücklich anerkennt, dass diese zunächst nicht an die Kirche gerichtet sind – um sogleich festzuhalten, dass letztere über eine eigene traditionelle Regel des Verständnisses verfüge:

> Der „Lehrer der (Heiden-) Völker im Glauben und in der Wahrheit" (1 Tim 2,7), der Apostel Paulus, übergab der Kirche, die er aus den (Heiden-) Völkern sammelte, wie sie die Bücher des Gesetzes, die sie von anderen empfangen hatte und die ihr zuvor unbekannt und sehr fremd waren, wahrzunehmen habe, damit sie (sc. die Kirche) sich nicht, indem sie fremdartige Einrichtungen empfängt und die Regel der Einrichtungen nicht kennt, vor einer fremden Urkunde ängstige. Deshalb überliefert er an ein paar Stellen Beispiele des Verständnisses, damit auch wir im übrigen Ähnliches beobachten, damit wir nicht wegen der Gleichartigkeit der Lesung und der Urkunde glaubten, daß wir Jünger der Juden geworden seien. Er will also, dass das die Jünger Christi von den

10 Vgl. Buchinger, Pascha, 681–686.

11 Belege bei Origenes und in seinem traditionsgeschichtlichen Umfeld erschließt ders., 1015, Index s. v. Etymologien: Ägypten.

Jüngern der Synagoge unterscheide, dass wir durch geistiges Verständnis zeigen, dass das Gesetz, aufgrund dessen schlechten Verständnisses jene Christus nicht annahmen, zurecht zur Belehrung der Kirche gegeben sei.[12]

Die Benutzung derselben Schrift geht für Origenes also mit einer klaren Abgrenzung der Identität zwischen Heidenchristen und Juden einher; das formale Unterscheidungskriterium ist die geistige Auslegung (ironischerweise im Sinne jenes tieferen Schriftsinns, den die platonisierende Tradition alexandrinischer Exegese vom hellenistischen Juden Philo geerbt hatte), der inhaltliche Unterschied liegt in der Erkenntnis Christi. Während Origenes den Juden ein literalistisches Schriftverständnis zuschreibt, habe die Kirche mit 1 Kor 10,1–4 eine von Paulus überlieferte Regel des Verständnisses:

> Die Juden verstehen also nur das, dass „die Kinder Israels" aus Ägypten „aufgebrochen sind" und ihr erster Aufbruch „aus Ramses" war und sie von dort aufgebrochen „nach Sukkot" kamen und „von Sukkot aufgebrochen nach Etam" (Ex 13,20) bei Epaulis am Meer kamen (vgl. Ex 14,2), dann darauffolgend, daß ihnen dort die Wolke vorausging und jener Fels gefolgt sei, aus dem sie Wasser tranken (vgl. Ex 17,6; 1 Kor 10,4), auch daß sie durch das Rote Meer zogen und in die Wüste Sinai kamen (vgl. Ex 16,1). Wir aber wollen sehen, welche Regel des Verständnisses uns Paulus davon übergeben hat. An die Korinther schreibend, sagt er an einer bestimmten Stelle: „Wir wissen nämlich, daß unsere Väter alle unter der Wolke waren, und daß alle auf Mose getauft wurden in der Wolke und im Meer, und alle dieselbe geistige Speise aßen und alle denselben geistigen Trank tranken. Sie tranken nämlich vom geistigen Fels, der ihnen folgte; der Fels aber war Christus." (1 Kor 10,1–4)[13]

---

12 Origenes, *Hom. Exod.* 5,1 (GCS 29, 183): *‚Doctor gentium in fide et veritate' Apostolus Paulus tradidit ecclesiae, quam congregavit ex gentibus, quomodo libros legis susceptos ab aliis sibique ignotos prius et valde peregrinos deberet advertere, ne aliena instituta suscipiens et institutorum regulam nesciens in peregrino trepidaret instrumento. Propterea ergo ipse in nonnullis intelligentiae tradit exempla, ut et nos similia observemus in ceteris, ne forte pro similitudine lectionis et instrumenti Iudaeorum nos effectos esse discipulos crederemus. Hoc ergo differre vult discipulos Christi a discipulis synagogae, quod legem, quam illi male intelligendo Christum non receperunt, nos spiritaliter intelligendo ostendamus eam ad ecclesiae instructionem merito datam.*

13 Origenes, *Hom. Exod.* 5,1 (GCS 29, 183 f): *Iudaei ergo hoc solum intelligunt quia ‚profecti sint filii Istrahel' de Aegypto et prima profectio eorum fuerit ‚ex Ramesse' et inde profecti venerint ‚in Sochoth' et ‚de Sochot profecti' venerint ‚in Othon' ad Epauleum iuxta mare; tum deinde quod ibi nubes eos praecesserit et secuta sit ‚petra', de qua biberent aquam, transierint etiam per mare rubrum et venerint in desertum Sina. Nobis autem qualem tradiderit de his Paulus Apostolus intelligentiae regulam, videamus. Corinthiis scribens in quodam loco ita dicit: ‚scimus enim quia patres nostri omnes sub nube fuerunt, et omnes in Moysen baptizati sunt in nube et in mari, et omnes eandem escam spiritalem manducaverunt et omnes eundem potum spiritalem biberunt. Bibebant autem de sequenti spiritali petra; petra vero erat Christus'.* Es sei angemerkt, dass Origenes das Motiv des wandernden Felsens aus 1 Kor 10,4 in das Referat der alttestamentlichen Erzählung einträgt.

Da der Inhalt der durch Paulus autorisierten geistigen Auslegung des Exodus in der Taufe besteht, impliziert die Allegorie nicht nur eine sakramentale Konkretisierung; die Abgrenzung vom historischen Verständnis konstituiert zugleich eine Opposition zum Judentum:

> Ihr seht, wie sehr sich die Überlieferung des Paulus von der historischen Lesung unterscheidet: Was die Juden für den Durchzug des Meeres halten, nennt Paulus Taufe; was jene als Wolke ansehen, stellt Paulus als Heiligen Geist dar, und dem ähnlich will er, daß jenes verstanden werde, was der Herr in den Evangelien vorschreibt, wo er sagt: „Wenn einer nicht aus Wasser und dem Heiligen Geist wiedergeboren ist, kann er nicht in das Himmelreich eintreten." (vgl. Joh 3,5)[14]

Es folgt eine formal ähnlich durchgeführte Gegenüberstellung von Manna und Eucharistie, bevor der Prediger in einer Art Binnen-Peroratio der Einleitung als Konsequenz noch einmal eine antijüdische Abgrenzung formuliert, deren Schärfe möglicherweise nicht nur durch das tatsächliche Nebeneinander von Christen und Juden in Cäsarea motiviert ist; vielmehr lässt die Rechtfertigung der Hermeneutik des Origenes wohl auch – wenn nicht vor allem – Opposition in den eigenen Reihen gegenüber der allegorischen Auslegungspraxis des alexandrinisch geschulten Exegeten erkennen:

> Was also müssen wir tun, die wir von Paulus, dem Lehrer der Kirche, die Einrichtungen eines derartigen Verständnisses empfangen haben? Scheint es nicht recht, dass wir die uns überlieferte Regel dieser Art nach ähnlichem Beispiel auch im übrigen befolgen? Oder sollen wir, wie einige es wollen, das, was ein so großer und bedeutender Apostel überlieferte, verlassen und wieder zu „jüdischen Fabeleien" (Tit 1,14) zurückkehren? Mir jedenfalls, wenn ich das anders auslege, als es Paulus schien, glaube ich, würde es bedeuten, den Feinden Christi die Hände zu reichen und das zu sein, was der Prophet sagt: „Weh denen, die ihren Nächsten mit trübem Aufruhr tränken!" (Hab 2,15) Wir wollen also die vom seligen Apostel Paulus empfangenen Samen des geistigen Verständnisses pflegen, soweit es uns der Herr auf eure Bitten hin gnädig erhellen wird.[15]

---

14 Origenes, *Hom. Exod.* 5,1 (GCS 29, 184): *Videtis, quanto differat ab historica lectione Pauli traditio: quod Iudaei transitum maris putant, Paulus baptismum vocat; quam illi aestimant nubem, Paulus Spiritum sanctum ponit; et huic simile vult intelligi illud, quod Dominus in evangeliis praecepit dicens: ‚nisi quis renatus fuerit ex aqua et Spiritu sancto, non potest intrare in regna coelorum.'*

15 Origenes, *Hom. Exod.* 5,1 (GCS 29, 184f): *Quid igitur agendum nobis est, qui huiusmodi a Paulo ecclesiae magistro intelligentiae instituta suscepimus? Nonne iustum videtur, ut traditam nobis huiusmodi regulam simili in ceteris servemus exemplo? An, ut quidam volunt, haec, quae tantus ac talis Apostolus tradidit, reliquentes rursum ad ‚Iudaicas fabulas' convertamur? Mihi quidem si haec aliter quam Paulo videtur exponam, hoc puto esse manus dare inimicis Christi et hoc esse quod propheta dicit: ‚vae, qui potat proximum suum subversione turbulenta!' Accepta ergo a beato Paulo Apostolo semina spiritalis intelligentiae, in quantum Dominus nos precibus vestris illuminare dignabitur, excolamus.*

Auslegung der Stationen des Exodus

Nach dieser einleitenden Grundlegung und einem in den Homilien des Origenes häufig anzutreffenden Gebet um das rechte Verständnis kommentiert Origenes vor allem die Namen der in Ex 12f genannten Stationen. Ein erster Auslegungsgang geht dabei – wie meistens, wenn es um hebräische Wörter geht – von Etymologien aus, die er ausdrücklich auf jüdische Tradition zurückführt, konkret darauf, was „die Übersetzer der Eigennamen bei den Hebräern überliefern";[16] die Übersetzungen sind für ihn zugleich Anknüpfungspunkt von Allegorien (wobei Origenes auch hier den Aufbruch aus Ägypten mit dem Verlassen der dunklen Handlungen dieser Welt und der Finsternis der Irrtümer identifiziert, auch wenn er diesen Topos zum Unterschied von den anderen Ortsnamen nicht explizit etymologisch begründet).[17]

Dass die Israeliten ausgerechnet in drei Etappen zum Schilfmeer gelangen, gibt Origenes Gelegenheit zu allgemeinen Überlegungen über die Symbolik der Dreizahl, die über Vermittlung des Origenes-Kenners Ambrosius von Mailand und dessen Schüler Augustinus eine beachtliche Wirkungsgeschichte im lateinischen Westen entfalten sollten, deren eigentliche Explosion freilich erst im 20. Jahrhundert festzustellen ist:[18]

> [...] Das dritte Lager ist es, wo die göttlichen Zeichen stattfinden. Erinnere dich daran, was oben vorgelesen wurde, als Mose zum Pharao sagte: „Einen Weg von drei Tagen werden wir in der Wüste gehen und dem Herrn, unserem Gott, opfern." Das nämlich war das *Triduum*, zu dem Mose eilte und dem der Pharao widersprach; jener sagte nämlich: „Ihr sollt nicht weiter gehen." (Ex 8,28) Der Pharao erlaubte nicht, dass die Kinder Israels zum Ort der Zeichen gelangten, er erlaubte ihnen nicht, so weit fortzuschreiten, dass sie die Mysterien des dritten Tages genießen könnten. Höre nämlich den Propheten, der sagt: „Gott wird uns nach zwei Tagen auferwecken, und am dritten Tag werden wir auf(er)stehen und vor seinem Angesicht leben." (Hos 6,2) Der erste Tag ist für uns das Leiden des Erlösers, und der zweite der, an dem er in die Unterwelt abstieg;

---

16 Origenes, *Hom. Exod.* 5,2 (GCS 29, 185, hier Z. 17): [...] *apud Hebraeos tradunt interpretes nominum.*

17 Origenes, *Hom. Exod.* 5,2 (GCS 29, 185, hier Z. 4–6): *Si quis est, qui proficisci de Aegypto parat, si quis est, qui cupit obscuros mundi huius actus et errorum tenebras derelinquere, primo omnium ‚ex Ramesse' ei proficiscendum est.*

18 Das Motiv der „drei Tage" von Leiden, Tod und Auferstehung Christi scheint in der Spätantike literarisch nicht sehr breit bezeugt; liturgieformativ wurde es – anders als die Protagonisten eines der erfolgreichsten Konzepte liturgischer Erneuerung in der Mitte des 20. Jahrhunderts glaubten – allerdings erst in der jüngsten Liturgiereform des römischen Ritus wirksam, die gleichwohl einen gewaltigen Einfluss auch auf die Reform der Osterliturgie in anderen Kirchen des Westens ausübte; vgl. Buchinger, Triduum. Bei Origenes – wie vermutlich auch noch bei Ambrosius – ist eine liturgische Umsetzung des theologischen Konzeptes dieser drei Tage noch außer Reichweite, und auch Augustinus, der neben Ostern auch eine Karfreitagsfeier kannte, ging es nicht in erster Linie um die Strukturierung des Gottesdienstes; vgl. Studer, Triduum Sacrum.

> der dritte Tag aber ist der der Auferstehung. Und deshalb „ging ihnen" am dritten Tag „Gott voran, bei Tag in einer Wolkensäule, bei Nacht in einer Feuersäule" (Ex 13,21).[19]

Aus der paulinischen Allegorese des Exodus ergibt sich für Origenes auch hier eine tauftheologische Konkretion – möglicherweise ein Jahrhundert bevor Ostern in Palästina tatsächlich zum bevorzugten Tauftermin wurde.[20]

> Wenn nach dem, was wir weiter oben gesagt haben, der Apostel uns zurecht lehrt, dass in diesen Worten die Mysterien der Taufe enthalten sind, ist es nötig, dass, „die auf Christus getauft werden, auf seinen Tod getauft werden, und mit ihm begraben werden, und mit ihm" am dritten Tag „auferstehen" von den Toten (vgl. Röm 6,3 f), die er auch nach dem, was der Apostel sagt, „gemeinsam mit sich auferweckt, und gemeinsam im Himmel sitzen ließ" (vgl. Eph 2,6). Wenn du also das Mysterium des dritten Tages angenommen hast, wird Gott dich zu führen und dir selbst „den Weg" des Heils „zu zeigen" (vgl. Ex 13,21) beginnen.[21]

Am Ende der Homilie kommt Origenes noch einmal auf diese baptismale Sinnspitze zurück.[22]

Insgesamt bezeugt die Homilie nicht nur die fundamentale Bedeutung des Exodus als Typos der Taufe für die Konstruktion christlicher Identität; sie ist auch ein typisches Beispiel für die doppelte – und widersprüchliche – Konstruktion des Judentums in der Exegese des Origenes: Während er sich zur Erhellung des

---

19 Origenes, *Hom. Exod.* 5,2 (GCS 29, 186): [...] *tertia castra sunt, in quibus fiunt signa divina. Recordare, quae superius lecta sunt, cum dicebat Moyses ad Pharaonem: ‚iter trium dierum ibimus in deserto, et immolabimus Domino Deo nostro.' Hoc ergo erat triduum, ad quod festinabat Moyses et contradicebat Pharao; ille enim dicebat: ‚non eatis longius'. Non permittebat Pharao ad locum signorum pervenire filios Istrahel, non permittebat eos in tantum proficere, ut possent tertii diei mysteriis perfrui. Audi enim prophetam, qui dicit: ‚resuscitabit nos Deus post biduum, et in die tertia resurgemus et vivemus in conspectu eius'. Prima dies nobis passio Salvatoris est et secunda, qua descendit in infernum, tertia autem resurrectionis est dies. Et ideo in die tertia ‚Deus antecedebat eos, per diem in columna nubis, per noctem in columna ignis'.*

20 Buchinger, Origins. Das Schweigen des Origenes über die in Palästina sonst erst im vierten Jahrhundert bezeugte Tauffeier am Osterfest beweist natürlich nicht, dass es diese nicht schon zu seiner Zeit gegeben habe, auch wenn sie positiv vor dem vierten Jahrhundert nur für Rom und Nordafrika belegt ist; vgl. Bradshaw, Initiation.

21 Origenes, *Hom. Exod.* 5,2 (GCS 29, 186): *Quod si secundum ea, quae superius diximus, in his verbis recte nos Apostolus docet baptismi mysteria contineri, necessarium est, ut, ‚qui baptizantur in Christo, in morte ipsius baptizentur, et ipsi consepeliantur', et cum ipso die tertia resurgant a mortuis, quos et secundum hoc, quod dicit Apostolus: ‚simul secum suscitavit, simulque fecit sedere in coelestibus'. Cum ergo tibi tertii diei mysterium fuerit susceptum, incipiet te deducere Deus et ipse tibi viam salutis ostendere.*

22 Origenes, *Hom. Exod.* 5,5 (GCS 29, 190), mit ausdrücklichem Bezug auf das Hinabsteigen in das Wasser und das Heraufsteigen als ‚neuer Mensch' (vgl. Eph 2,15), um ein ‚neues Lied' zu singen."

Wortsinnes der Bibel ausdrücklich auf hebräische Traditionen beruft, um seiner Interpretation Autorität zu verleihen, unterscheidet die überkommene Regel der geistigen Auslegung die „Jünger Christi" von den „Jüngern der Synagoge";[23] bemerkenswert ist, dass beides als „Tradition" zur Sprache gebracht wird und somit Geltung beansprucht. Abgrenzung vom Judentum gehört in der Exegese des Origenes sowohl soziologisch als auch hermeneutisch zur Konstruktion christlicher Identität, auch wenn hinter der Polemik um die Berechtigung allegorischer Auslegung vielleicht vor allem hermeneutische Diskurse innerhalb der christlichen Gemeinde zu vermuten sind.

2. Eine neue philologische Basis: Pascha, Exodus und christliche Identität in der Schrift „Über das Pascha"

Die Schrift des Origenes „Über das Pascha" markiert insofern einen signifikanten Fortschritt in der Exegese des Origenes, als die Erklärung des Wortes „Pascha" der Verbindung von Taufe und Exodus eine neue philologische Basis in der Etymologie des Wortes „Pascha" selbst gibt. In der Einleitung zum ersten Buch „Über das Pascha" erklärt Origenes einerseits den Begriff „Pascha"; andererseits legt er die Hermeneutik seiner Auslegung von Ex 12 dar. Der anschließende Kommentar zum Beginn des Pesachgesetzes ist nicht nur ein Musterbeispiel für die formale exegetische Methode des Origenes, sondern auch für die Bedeutung der Exegese des Exodus für die Konstruktion christlicher Identität.

Philologische und hermeneutische Grundlegung in der Einleitung

Die Worterklärung des „Pascha" eröffnet eine qualitativ neue Dimension der Verbindung von Pascha und Exodus. Während Origenes Pascha und Exodus trotz ihres historischen und anamnetischen Zusammenhangs in seinem übrigen Schrifttum keineswegs stereotyp gemeinsam zur Sprache bringt,[24] verlegt die Erklärung des Wortes „Pascha" als „Durchgang" die Verbindung von Pascha und Exodus in die Bedeutung des Wortes selbst; philologische Worterklärung und historische Sacherklärung konvergieren nicht nur, sie koinzidieren regelrecht. Dabei scheint es, als ob Origenes die von ihm angesprochene Lernerfahrung selbst gemacht hätte:[25]

23 Die widersprüchliche Konstruktion jüdischer Exegese einerseits zur Untermauerung der wörtlichen Auslegung, andererseits als Gegenbild zur geistigen Interpretation des Origenes ist auch eine wesentliche Erkenntnis der leider unpublizierten Dissertation von Clements, „Peri Pascha", hier u. a. 34 f.

24 Zur narrativen und anamnetischen Zusammengehörigkeit von Pascha und Exodus vgl. Buchinger, Pascha, 407–412.

25 De Lange, Origen, 96: „It very much sounds as if Origen himself has been made to learn this lesson the hard way, and to put right his ideas about the etymology of *pascha*." Auch Clements,

> Die meisten der Brüder, vielleicht sogar alle, nehmen an, dass die Benennung des Pascha nach dem Leiden (πάθος) des Erlösers benannt sei, während das Fest, wenn es übersetzt wird, Durchgang (διάβασις) ist. Weil nun an diesem Fest das Volk aus Ägypten auszieht, wird es folgerichtig „Phash" genannt, das heißt Durchgang. […] Und wenn einer von den Unsrigen voreilig im Zusammentreffen mit Hebräern sagte, dass das Pascha wegen des Leidens so benannt werde, wird er von ihnen verlacht werden als einer, der überhaupt nicht versteht, was die Bedeutung aufgrund der Benennung ist.[26]

Nach der Wort- und Sacherklärung folgt im zweiten Schritt der Einleitung die Darlegung der Hermeneutik. Origenes unterscheidet dabei zwei Ebenen: einmalige Geschichte und bleibende Bedeutung; dem Pesachgesetz und dem historischen Exodus „damals (τότε)" stellt er gegenüber, dass nach 1 Kor 5,7 „(als) unser Pascha Christus geopfert wurde", woraus sich ergebe, dass die Christen „bis heute (μέχρι σήμερον)" zum Subjekt sowohl des Pesachgesetzes als auch des durch den Namen des Pascha bezeichneten Exodus würden:

> Weil das Volk damals (τότε) aus Ägypten auszieht, wird ihnen auf passende Weise das Gesetz dieses Festes gegeben wie folgt: <Es folgt ein Exzerpt aus Ex 12>. Und wenn das geschehen ist, zieht das Volk aus Ägypten aus, und die Erstgeburt der Ägypter wird vernichtet und der Pharao ändert nach dem Exodus der Hebräer seinen Sinn (vgl. Ex 14,5), und gemeinsam mit dem Heer und den Wagen zieht er aus, sie zu verfolgen (vgl. Ex 14,9), und so wird er im Roten Meer versenkt (vgl. Ex 15,4), und Mose zieht mit dem Volk durch das Meer hindurch.
>
> Dass aber auch bis heute (μέχρι σήμερον) sowohl das Pascha geschieht und das Schaf geschlachtet wird und das Volk aus Ägypten auszieht, lehrt auch uns der Apostel, wenn er sagt: „Auch unser Pascha nämlich wurde geopfert, Christus, damit wir nicht im alten Sauerteig und nicht im Sauerteig der Schlechtigkeit und Bosheit, sondern in den Mazzot der Lauterkeit und Wahrheit feiern." (1 Kor 5,7 f) Wenn aber „(als) unser Pascha" Jesus „Christus geopfert wurde", dann ziehen diejenigen, die Christus opfern, aus Ägypten aus und ziehen durch das Meer durch […][27]

Pascha, 170 u. ö., betont die Bedeutung der philologischen Erkenntnis für die Verdichtung des Zusammenhangs von Pascha und Exodus in der Theologie des Origenes.

26 Origenes, *De pascha* 1,1–3 (Papyrus p. 1 f): Οἱ μὲν γὰρ πλεῖστοι τῶν ἀδ[ελ]φῶν, τάχα δὲ καὶ οἱ πάντ[ες], τὴν ὀνομασίαν λαμβάνο[υσι]ν τοῦ πάσχα παρὰ τὸ πάθο[ς το]ῦ σ(ωτῆ)ρ(ο)ς κεκλῆσθαι τῷ ὀνόματι τοῦ πάσχα […] [ὅ]περ εἰ ἑρμηνευ[θ]είη, ἐστὶν [δι]άβασις. Ἐπεὶ [γ]ὰρ ἐν ταύτῃ τῇ [ἑο]ρτῇ ὁ λαὸς ἐξ Α[ἰγύπτου] ἐξ[έρχε]ται, ἀκολούθως φ[ας'] κα[λ]εῖ[ται, τοῦτ' ἔσ]τιν διάβασ[ις]. […] Καὶ εἴ τις προπετέστερον τῶν ἡμετέρων Ἑβραίοις συμβαλὼν λέγοι τὸ πάσχα διὰ τὸ πάθος τοῦ σ(ωτῆ)ρ(ο)ς οὕτως ὠνομάσθαι, καταγέλαστος ὑπ' αὐτῶν ἔσται ὡς ὅλως οὐκ ἐπιστάμενος τί τὸ σημαινό‹μενο›ν ἐκ τῆς ὀνομασίας. Der Papyrus wird nach der Editio princeps zitiert: Guéraud/Nautin, Origène. Da dadurch trotzdem das Prinzip der Ergänzung von interner und externer Zitation gewahrt bleibt und um unnötige Komplikationen zu vermeiden, wird die Seitenangabe der Edition nicht auch noch wiedergegeben.

27 Origenes, *De pascha* 1,5–8 (Papyrus p. 2 f): Ἐπεὶ ὁ λαὸ[ς ὁ Ἑ]βραίων τότ[ε] ἐξ[έρ]χετ[α]ι τ[ὴν Αἴγυπτον, ὁ] νόμο[ς] ε[ἰκότως αὐ]τοῖς τα[ύτ]ης τῆς ἑορτῆς δίδοται οὕ[τ]ως κα[τ]' ο[ἴ]κους, ὅπως ἕκαστοι πρόβατο[ν] ἄρσεν τέλει[ον ἄ]μωμον λαβό[ντ]ες θύσω[σιν καὶ π]ρὸς ἑ[σ]π[έ]ραν φάγω[σιν

Im hermeneutischen Rahmen einer platonisierenden Exegese besteht die abschließend zusammengefasste Aufgabe des Exegeten darin, „dass der Vernunft auf vollkommenere Weise der dem Geschehen in der Geschichte (ἱστορία) innewohnende Sinn (νοῦς) gezeigt werde".[28]

Die Konstruktion christlicher Identität in der Exegese von Ex 12,1f

Der anschließende Kommentar zu Ex 12,1f wendet nicht nur dieses hermeneutische Programm einer Auslegung auf den zwei Ebenen des platonisierenden Weltbildes an, sondern durchläuft in geradezu exemplarischer Weise jene vier Methodenschritte, in denen seine Exegese von den philologischen Klärungen (1) und der historischen Auslegung (2) zur „Wahrheit" oder „Wirklichkeit" (3) fortschreitet, die auch die Basis für die abschließende, meist moralische Anwendung für die Gegenwart (4) bietet.[29]

Das einleitende Zitat des Lemmas dient im ersten Schritt der Vergewisserung über den auszulegenden Text; als zweiter Methodenschritt folgt die historisch-sachliche Auslegung: Es sei eben „‚der erste unter den Monaten des Jahres' (Ex 12,2), als sie aus Ägypten auszogen". Zu dieser Erklärung des Sachverhalts gehört auch die Berufung auf – angebliche – jüdische Praxis: „Und soweit es der Geschichte entspricht, so ist dieser der erste Monat, und die Juden begehen jedes Jahr dieses Fest ‚am Vierzehnten des ersten Monats', indem sie nach dem ihnen durch Mose gegebenen Gesetz ‚entsprechend den Häusern ein Schaf opfern' (vgl. Ex 12,3.6; Num 9,3)."[30] Die hermeneutische Funktion Christi markiert den Überstieg auf die

---

ὀπτὸ]ν πυ[ρὶ] οὔτε ὠμὸν οὔ[τε ἡ]ψήμενον ἐν ὕδατι ἵν' οὕ[τως] ὁ ὀλεθρεύων τὰ πρωτότ[οκα τ]ῶν Αἰγυπτίων μὴ θίγῃ αὐτῶν τὰς φλιὰς τῶν θυρῶν αὐτῶν ὁρῶν τῷ αἵματι κεχρισμένας. Καὶ τούτων γενομένων ὁ λαὸς τὴν Αἴγυπτον ἐξέρχεται καὶ τὰ πρωτότοκα τῶν Αἰγυπτίων ἀπόλυται, καὶ ὁ Φαραὼ μετὰ τὴν τῶν Ἑβραίων ἔξοδον μεταμέλεται, καὶ ἅμα τῇ στρατιᾷ καὶ τοῖς ἅρμασιν καταδιώκων αὐτοὺς ἐξέρχεται, καὶ οὕτως ἐν τῇ Ἐρυθ[ρ]ᾷ θαλάσσῃ καταποντίζε[τα]ι, καὶ Μωϋσῆς σὺν τῷ λ[αῷ] διὰ τῆς θαλάσσης διέρχετ[αι. Ὅ]τι δὲ καὶ μέχρι σήμερον [κ]αὶ τὸ πάσχα γίνεται καὶ τ[ὸ] πρόβατον θύεται καὶ ὁ λαὸς [ἐξ] Αἰγύπτου ἐξέρχεται, κα[ὶ ὁ ἀ]πόστολος ἡμᾶς διδάσκε[ι λέ]γων· „Καὶ γὰρ τὸ πάσχα ἡμ[ῶν] ἐτύθη χ(ριστό)ς, ὥστε ἑορτάζω[με]ν μ[ὴ ζύ]μῃ παλαιᾷ μηδὲ ζ[ύμῃ] κα[κί]ας καὶ πονηρία[ς ἀλλὰ ἀζύ]μοις εἰλικριν[είας καὶ ἀληθε]ίας". Εἰ δὲ τὸ π[άσχα ἡμῶν ἐτ]ύθη Ἰ(ησοῦ)ς Χ(ριστό)ς, ‹οἱ› Χ(ριστὸ)ν θ[ύοντες Αἴγυ]πτον ἐξέρ[χο]ντ[αι καὶ τὴν θάλασσα]ν δι[έρ]χον[ται] καὶ τ[ὸν] Φαρ[αὼ κ]α[τα]πον[τι]ζόμενον ὄψο[ν]ται […].

28 Origenes, *De pascha* 1,9 (Papyrus p. 3): [Ἵ]να δὲ λό[γῳ ἐν]τε[λ]έστερον ὁ [ν]οῦς ὁ ἐγ[κε]ίμενο[ς] περὶ τὰ γενόμε[να] περὶ τῆς ἱστορίας δειχθῇ […].

29 Vgl. Torjesen, Hermeneutical Procedure, 138–147; es versteht sich von selbst, dass Origenes nicht immer wie hier alle vier Methodenschritte durchläuft, wie auch der Streit um einen zwei-, drei- oder mehrfachen Schriftsinn der Komplexität seines Denkens nicht gerecht wird.

30 Origenes, *De pascha* 1,10f (Papyrus p. 3f): Εἶπεν δὲ Κ(ύριο)ς πρὸς Μωϋσῆν καὶ Ἀαρὼν ἐν γῇ Αἰγύπτῳ λέγων· ὁ μὴν οὗτος ὑμῖν ἀρχὴ μηνῶν, πρῶτός ἐστιν ὑμῖν ἐν τοῖς μησὶν τοῦ ἐνιαυτοῦ. Τοῦτον τὸν μῆνα ἀρχὴν μηνῶν λέγει εἶναι ὁ θ(εὸ)ς πρὸς Μωϋσῆν καὶ Ἀαρών, καὶ πρῶτον αὐτὸν ἐν τοῖς μησὶν τοῦ ἐνιαυτοῦ αὐτοῖς εἶνα[ι], ἡνίκα τὴν Αἴγυπτον ἐξέ[ρχο]νται· καὶ ὅσον μὲν κατὰ [τὴ]ν

Ebene der übertragenen Auslegung, die im dritten Schritt entfaltet wird; dabei ist bemerkenswert, dass die Erfüllung von Gesetz und Propheten nicht historisch in der Passion gesehen wird,[31] sondern im Aufweis des wahren Sinnes von Pascha und Exodus für die Christen:

> Da aber Christus „kam, nicht um das Gesetz oder die Propheten aufzulösen, sondern zu erfüllen“ (Mt 5,17), zeigte er uns, was das wahre Pascha sei, der wahre Durchgang aus Ägypten; und es ist für den, der durchgeht, dann ein „Anfang der Monate“, wenn es der Monat des Durchzugs aus Ägypten wird, wie für ihn ein Anfang einer anderen Geburt wird, eines neuen Wandels, der für den geschieht, der die Finsternis verlässt und „zum Licht kommt“ (vgl. Joh 3,20 f); ich rede gleichsam passend zum Symbol, das durch Wasser denen gegeben wird, die „zum Glauben an Christus gekommen sind“ (1 Kor 15,19) und das „Bad der Wiedergeburt“ (Tit 3,5) genannt wird. Was bedeutet eine Wiedergeburt anderes als den Anfang einer neuen Geburt?[32]

Die personale Zuspitzung der moralischen Allegorese auf die zweite Person kann als vierter und letzter Schritt eines typischen Auslegungsganges verstanden werden, der in der Aneignung des biblischen Wortes in seiner allegorischen Deutung an sein Ziel kommt:

> In einen vollkommenen Wandel und eine vollkommene Liebe hineingelangen muß einer, damit er noch in der gegenwärtigen Welt hören kann: „Dieser Monat ist ein Anfang der Monate“ (Ex 12,2) für dich.[33]

Schulbuchmäßige Exegese des Exodus und Konstruktion christlicher Identität fallen hier zusammen; zur übertragenen Auslegung gehören existentielle und intellektuelle Aspekte genauso wie die inhaltliche Dimension des Glaubens an Christus und die Konkretion in der sakramentlichen Feier der Initiation. Indem

---

ἱστορίαν, οὗτος αὐτὸς πρ[ῶτο]ς μήν ἐστιν καὶ ταύτην ἄγ[ουσι]ν οἱ Ἰουδαῖοι κατ᾽ ἔτος τὴν ἑο[ρτ]ὴν τῇ τεσσαρεσκαιδεκάτῃ [το]ῦ πρώτου μηνὸς κατ᾽ οἴκου[ς] πρόβατον κατὰ τὸν διὰ Μω[ϋσ]έως αὐτοῖς δοθέντα νόμο[ν] ‹θύοντες›, […].

31 Dass das Pascha keinen Typos der Passion darstellt, ist schon vor der Schrift „Über das Pascha“ ein Grundgedanke der Paschatheologie des Origenes; vgl. Buchinger, 1Kor 5,7 als Schlüssel, 238–264, und ders., Pascha passim, insbesondere 708–783.

32 Origenes, *De pascha* 1,12 f (Papyrus p. 4): ἐπειδὴ δὲ ὁ Χ(ριστὸ)ς ἦλθεν [οὐ κ]αταλῦσαι τὸν νό[μον] ἢ τ[οὺς] προφήτας ἀλλὰ [πλ]ηρ[ῶσαι, ἔ]δειξεν ἡμῖν τί [τὸ ἀληθινὸν] πάσ[χα, ἡ διάβασις] ἡ ἀληθινὴ ἡ [ἐξ Αἰγύπτου,] καὶ ἔστι τ[ῷ διαβαίνοντι] τότε ἀρ[χὴ μηνῶν, ὅτε γίνεται] ὁ μὴν ὁ τ[ῆς] δια[βάσε]ως τ[ῆς] Α[ἰγ]ύπτου, ὥσπε[ρ α]ὐτῷ γ[εν]νήσεως γίν[εται ἀρ]χή [τις ἑ]τέρας, κ[αινῆς π]ολιτ[είας γι]νομένη[ς καταλί]πον[τι] τὸ σκότος κ[αὶ ἐρχ]ομένῳ πρὸς τὸ φῶς, λ[έγω] οἰκείω[ς] ὡς πρὸς τὸ σύμ[βολ]ον τὸ δι᾽ ὕδατος διδόμ[ενον] τοῖς εἰς Χ(ριστὸ)ν ἠλπικόσ[ι]ν, ὃ [λο]υτρὸν παλιγγενεσίας ὠνόμασται. Ἡ γὰρ παλιγγενεσία τί ἕτερον ἢ ἑτέρας γενέσεως ἀρχὴν σημαίνει;

33 Origenes, *De pascha* 1,14 (Papyrus p. 4 f): Τελείας δὲ πολιτείας καὶ τελείας ἀγάπης ἐντὸς γενέσθαι δεῖ, ἵνα τις ἔτι ἐν κόσμῳ τῷ ἐνεστῶτι ὢν ἀκοῦσαι δυνηθῇ· Ὁ μὴν οὗτος ἀρχὴ μη[ν]ῶν ἐστιν σοί.

die Christen in der moralischen Allegorese in die Rolle Israels einrücken und sich den Bedeutungsgehalt des Exodus aneignen, wird der österliche Hinübergang auch unabhängig von 1 Kor 10 zu einem Typos der Taufe, wobei Origenes die Hermeneutik hier in der Kategorie der „Wahrheit/Wirklichkeit (ἀλήθεια)" formuliert. Origenes konstruiert christliche Identität also durch das formal-methodische Vorgehen und die charakteristische platonisierende Hermeneutik seiner Exegese.

Die eschatologische Deutung des Exodus in der Einzelauslegung von Ex 12,11

In der weiteren Einzelauslegung von Ex 12,11 findet sich auch die zweite Origenes zufolge schon von seinen Vorgängern übernommene Deutung des Exodus: die auf den Tod des Christen. Mit dem Hinweis auf die Schuhe mache der Text „auch etwas überaus Deutliches über die Auferstehung des Fleisches klar, das ebenfalls mit uns ausziehen wird, wenn wir aus Ägypten ausziehen: wir müssen nämlich ‚die Glieder auf der Erde abtöten: Unzucht, Unreinheit, Zügellosigkeit, Götzendienst' (Kol 3,15; Gal 5,19 f) und so weiter, und so aus Ägypten ausziehen."[34] Moralische Allegorese gehört ebenso wie die eschatologische Symbolik zur Konstruktion christlicher Identität in der Exegese von Details des Exodus.

Traditionelle Typologie im Finale des zweiten Buches „Über das Pascha"

Im zweiten Buch „Über das Pascha" wendet Origenes die Etymologie des Pascha als „Hinübergang (ὑπέρβασις)" nicht anthropologisch, sondern christologisch: Nicht die Glaubenden, sondern Christus selbst ist hier das Subjekt des Hinübergangs;[35] damit gibt Origenes der zu seiner Zeit längst traditionellen Auffassung vom österlichen Descensus und Ascensus Christi und der von ihm Erlösten ebenfalls eine philologische Basis in der Bedeutung des Wortes „Pascha" selbst. Auch wenn er sich weiterhin der von ihm abgelehnten Passionstypologie des Pascha enthält, formuliert er das Osterkerygma nicht nur in der Kategorie des Typos,[36] sondern auch im Rückgriff auf die traditionelle Deutung des Exodus, deren Dunkel- und Licht-Metaphorik er an dieser Stelle ausdrücklich in der Etymologie unter anderem des Wortes „Ägypten" verwurzelt:

---

34 Origenes, *De pascha* 1,111 (Papyrus p. 37 f): ἐν τούτῳ δὲ καὶ ἐμφανέστερόν τι δηλοῖ τὰ περὶ τῆς ἀναστάσεως σαρκός, συνεξερχομένης καὶ αὐτῆς ἡμῖν τὴν Αἴγυπτον ἐξιοῦσιν· νεκρῶσαι γὰρ ἡμᾶς τὰ μέλη δεῖ τὰ ἐπὶ τῆς γῆς πορνείαν ἀκαθάρσίαν ἀσέλγειαν εἰδωλολατρίαν καὶ τὰ ἑξῆ[ς] καὶ οὕτω τὴν Αἴγυπτον ἐξε[λθ]εῖν.

35 Origenes, *De pascha* 2,28 f (Papyrus p. 47 f): Φάγεσθε αὐτὸ μετὰ σπουδῆς, πάσχα ἐστὶν κ(υρί)ῳ, ὅ ἐστιν ὑπέρβασις κ(υρί)ου. Ὁ γὰρ ὑπερβὰς τοὺς ὅρους τοὺς θείους διὰ τὴν ἐν Ἀδὰμ παρακοὴν οὗτός ἐστιν κ(ύριο)ς ὁ τοῦ θανάτου τὸ κέντρον ἀμβλύνας […].

36 Das Wort kommt in Origenes, *De pascha* 2, nur an dieser Stelle vor.

> Aus der Knechtschaft des „Weltenherrschers der Finsternis dieses Äons" (Eph 6,12) befreite uns das wahre Schaf, das ist Christus Jesus, dessen Typos das in Ägypten geschlachtete Schaf wurde, das die Hebräer damals aus der Macht des Herrschers über Ägypten damals entriss, das Finsternis heißt, der Pharao aber Zerstreuer, der die im Licht der Tugend durch seine Herrschermacht zerstreut, das heißt durch die Gedanken derer, die in Finsternis leben.[37]

Auch hier dienen die Hebräer und ihr Exodus, deren Bedeutung für den Ausleger nur in der Geschichte „damals (τότε)" besteht, in erster Linie der Konstruktion christlicher Identität, die einerseits auf moralischer Praxis, andererseits auf der Erlösung durch Christus beruht, als dessen Typos das Pascha mit dem Gros altkirchlicher Autoren angesprochen wird.

3. Die Überwindung des eschatologischen und hermeneutischen Vorbehalts im österlichen Transitus

Im Spätwerk des Origenes ist eine weitere Entwicklung im Verständnis des Exodus zu beobachten: In der Apologie „Gegen Kelsos" benützt Origenes die philonische Variante der Worterklärung als διαβατήρια, um eine eschatologische Deutung des als „Hinübergang" verstandenen Pascha zu entfalten; in der von 1 Kor 5,7 geleiteten Erkenntnis überwindet der „Vollkommene" gewissermaßen den eschatologischen Vorbehalt. Um seine festkritischen Ausführungen gegenüber dem Einwand zu bekräftigen, dass auch die Christen eine Osterfeier kennen, relativiert er die Bedeutung zeitgebundener Feste zugunsten einer zeitlichen Entschränkung der Bedeutung äußerer religiöser Praxis in der Erkenntnis:

> Wer erkannt hat, dass „(als) unser Pascha Christus geopfert wurde" (1 Kor 5,7), und dass man feiern muß (vgl. 1 Kor 5,8), indem man vom Fleisch des Wortes ißt, dann gibt es keinen Zeitpunkt, zu dem er nicht das Pascha begeht, das „Hinübergang" übersetzt wird; er geht immer im Gedanken und im Wort und in jeder Tat von den Dingen dieser Welt zu Gott hinüber und eilt (vgl. Ex 12,11?) zu seiner Stadt.[38]

---

37 Origenes, *De pascha* 2,34 (Papyrus p. 49): Τῆς γὰρ δουλείας τοῦ κοσμοκράτορος τοῦ σκότους τούτου τοῦ αἰῶνος ἀπήλλαξεν τὸ ἀληθινὸν πρόβατον, ὅ ἐστιν Χ(ριστὸ)ς Ἰ(ησοῦ)ς, οὗ τύπος ἐγένετο ‹τὸ› ἐν Αἰγύπτῳ σφαγὲν πρόβατον, ῥυσάμενος τοὺς τότε Ἑβραίους ἐκ τῆς ἐξουσίας τοῦ τότε ἄρχοντος Αἰγύπτου, ὃ καλεῖται σκότος, Φαραὼ δ‹ὲ δ›ιασκεδαστής ὃς διασκεδαννύει τὰ ἐν φωτὶ τῆς ἀρετῆς ἔργα διὰ τῆς αὐτοῦ ἀρχοντικῆς ἐξουσίας, τοῦτ' ἔστιν διανοίας ἐν σκότει ζώντων.

38 Origenes, *Cels.* 8,22 (SC 150, 224): ὁ νοήσας ὅτι τὸ πάσχα ἡμῶν ἐτύθη Χριστὸς, καὶ χρὴ ἑορτάζειν ἐσθίοντα τῆς σαρκὸς τοῦ λόγου, οὐκ ἔστιν ὅτε οὐ ποιεῖ τὸ πάσχα, ὅπερ ἑρμηνεύεται διαβατήρια, διαβαίνων ἀεὶ τῷ λογισμῷ καὶ λόγῳ καὶ πάσῃ πράξει ἀπὸ τῶν τοῦ βίου πραγμάτων ἐπὶ τὸν θεόν, καὶ ἐπὶ τὴν πόλιν αὐτοῦ σπεύδων.

Die Möglichkeit und das Ziel der Überwindung des eschatologischen Vorbehalts durch die Erkenntnis machen deutlich, dass sich der eschatologische Vorbehalt für Origenes vor allem als hermeneutische Differenz darstellt; beide können in strikter Identität durch Erkenntnis überwunden werden. Ganz im Sinne des alexandrinischen Konzepts des „Christentums als Intellektuellen-Religion"[39] konstruiert Origenes christliche Identität in erster Linie mit Hilfe einer vom Neuen Testament im allgemeinen und dem Christus-Kerygma im besonderen informierten Erkenntnis, ohne freilich die moralischen Dimensionen zu vernachlässigen.

Es lässt sich zusammenfassen: Mit verschiedenen Methoden konstruiert Origenes durch die Exegese des Exodus christliche Identität; er bedient sich dabei überkommener Typologien genauso wie der Etymologien, die er ironischerweise aus dem hellenistischen Judentum übernommen hat. Unterscheidend ist für ihn eine charakteristische Exegese, deren Form durch platonisierende Transzendierung des historischen und wörtlichen Sinnes zugunsten einer übertragenen Deutung charakterisiert ist und deren Inhalt spezifisch christlich – und häufig christologisch – kodiert ist. Die für Origenes in den meisten Kontexten konstitutive Opposition zur Konstruktion eines angeblich literalistischen Judentums zeigt freilich, mit wie simplifizierenden Klischees, um nicht zu sagen: primitiven – und in der historischen Wirkung äußerst fatalen – Stereotypien ein derart anspruchsvolles Programm der Konstruktion christlicher Identität durch Exegese des Exodus einhergehen konnte.

Literatur

Quellen

Baehrens, Wilhelm A., Origenes Werke. Band 6. Homilien zum Hexateuch in Rufins Übersetzung, Bd. 1: Die Homilien zu Genesis, Exodus und Leviticus (GCS 29), Leipzig 1920.

Baehrens, Wilhelm A., Origenes Werke. Band 7. Homilien zum Hexateuch in Rufins Übersetzung, Bd. 2: Die Homilien zu Numeri, Josua und Judices (GCS 30), Leipzig 1921.

Borret, Marcel, Origène. Contre Celse. Vol. 4. Livres VII et VIII (SC 150), Paris 1969.

Guéraud, Octave/Nautin, Pierre, Origène, Sur la Pâque. Traité inédit publié d'après un papyrus de Toura (CAnt 2), Paris 1979.

Preuschen, Erwin, Origenes Werke. Band 4. Der Johanneskommentar (GCS 10), Leipzig 1903.

39 Die Formulierung stammt von Fürst, Christentum.

Forschungsliteratur

Auf der Maur, Hans Jörg/Waldram, Joop, Illuminatio verbi divini – confessio fidei – gratia baptismi. Wort, Glaube und Sakrament in Katechumenat und Taufliturgie bei Origenes, in: H. J. Auf der Maur/L. Bakker/A. van de Bunt/J. Waldram (Hg.), Fides Sacramenti. Sacramentum Fidei. Studies in honour of Pieter Smulders, Assen 1981, 41–95.

Bietenhard, Hans, Caesarea, Origenes und die Juden (FDV 1972), Stuttgart 1974.

Bradshaw, Paul F., „Diem baptismo sollemniorem": Initiation and Easter in Christian Antiquity, in: E. Carr/S. Parenti/A.-A. Thiermeyer/E. Velkovska (Hg.), ΕΥΛΟΓΗΜΑ. Studies in Honor of Robert Taft, S. J. (StAns 110 = ALit 17), Roma 1993, 41–51 [Ndr. in: M. E. Johnson (Hg.), Living Water, Sealing Spirit. Readings on Christian Initiation (A Pueblo Book), Collegeville, Minn. 1995, 137–147].

Buchinger, Harald, Melito, „Israel" und die Bibel beider Testamente, in: R. Roukema/H. Amirav (Hg.), The ‚New Testament' as a Polemical Tool. Studies in Ancient Christian Anti-Jewish Rhetoric and Beliefs (NTOA 118), Göttingen 2018, 73–90.

—, Was There Ever a Liturgical Triduum in Antiquity? Theological Idea and Liturgical Reality, EO 27 (2010), 257–270.

—, Pascha bei Origenes (IThS 64), Innsbruck 2005.

—, Towards the Origins of Paschal Baptism: The Contribution of Origen, StLi 35 (2005), 12–31.

—, 1Kor 5,7 als Schlüssel der Paschatheologie des Origenes. Das Pascha der Juden, das Opfer Christi und das Pascha der Christen – eine Aporie?, ZNW 91 (2000), 238–264.

Clements, Ruth Anne, „Peri Pascha": Passover and the Displacement of Jewish Interpretation Within Origen's Exegesis (Ph. D. Diss.), Cambridge, Mass. 1997.

Crouzel, Henri, La distinction de la „typologie" et de l'„allegorie", BLE 65 (1964), 161–174.

—, Origène et la „connaissance mystique" (ML.T 56), Paris 1961.

Daniélou, Jean, Exodus, RAC VII (1969), 22–44.

de Lange, Nicholas Robert Michael, Origen and the Jews. Studies in Jewish-Christian Relations in Third-Century Palestine (UCOP 25), Cambridge, Mass. 1976.

Fürst, Alfons, Christentum als Intellektuellen-Religion. Die Anfänge des Christentums in Alexandria (SBS 213), Stuttgart 2007.

Goppelt, Leonhard, τύπος κτλ, ThWNT VIII (1969), 246–260.

Hirshman, Marc, Passover and the Exodus in Origen's Writings and Rabbinic Midrashim, in: ders., A Rivalry of Genius. Jewish and Christian Biblical Interpretation in Late Antiquity (SUNYJ), Albany, N. Y. 1996, 67–81, Endnoten 142–146.

Langston, Scott M., Exodus Through the Centuries (Blackwell Bible Commentaries), Malden, Mass. 2006.

—, Exodus, The. IV. Christianity. A. Greek and Latin Patristics through Medieval Times, EBR VIII (2014), 484–486.

Ledegang, Freddy, Mysterium Ecclesiae. Images of the Church and its Members in Origen (BEThL 156), Leuven 2001.

Sgherri, Giuseppe, Chiesa e Sinagoga nelle opere di Origene (SPMed 13), Milano 1982.

Studer, Basil, Zum Triduum Sacrum bei Augustinus von Hippo, in: I. Scicolone (Hg.), La celebrazione del Triduo Pasquale. Anamnesis e mimesis. Atti del III Congresso

Internazionale di Liturgia. Roma, Pontificio Istituto Liturgico, 9–13 Maggio 1988 (StAns 102 = ALit 14), Roma 1990, 273–286.
Torjesen, Karen Jo, Hermeneutical Procedure and Theological Method in Origen's Exegesis (PTS 28), Berlin 1986.
Tzvetkova-Glaser, Anna, Pentateuchauslegung bei Origenes und den frühen Rabbinen (Early Christianity in the Context of Antiquity 7), Frankfurt a. M. 2010.
Wessel, Klaus, Durchzug durch das Rote Meer, RAC IV (1959), 370–389.

Agnethe Siquans (University of Vienna)

The Construction of Christian and Jewish Identities in Interpretations of Exodus 1–2

Biblical interpretation was crucial to the formation of Christian and Jewish identities in Late Antiquity.[1] It established a common basis for Judaism and Christianity while at the same time separating them from one another.

One of the most significant characters in the Hebrew Bible as well as the New Testament is Moses.[2] Although he plays different roles in Jewish and Christian traditions, and although Jewish and Christian interpretations do not always focus on the same episodes or aspects of Moses's life, he is a major figure in both religions. One important narrative for both Judaism and Christianity, is the story of Moses's birth, rescue and youth in Exodus 1–2. Chapter one connects the story of the children of Israel in Egypt with the preceding book of Genesis and the Joseph story. Jacob's family multiplies and becomes a people. In response, the Egyptians oppress the Hebrews and take measures to prevent them from growing even more numerous. Next, Pharaoh commands two midwives to kill the male Hebrew newborns, but they do not obey him. His subsequent order to throw all male babies into the Nile provides the background for Moses's birth and rescue by Pharaoh's daughter, which occurs in chapter 2. Later, the grown-up Moses kills an Egyptian overseer, flees to Midian, takes refuge with Jethro the priest, and marries one of his daughters. Exodus 1–2 are the opening chapters of the whole Exodus story and therefore significant for the characterization of Moses, who is the book's central human character and the savior of God's people.

The present article focuses on patristic and rabbinic interpretations of these two chapters of the Bible. The primary sources analyzed are two patristic texts—Origen's first two homilies on the Book of Exodus and Ephrem the Syrian's Exodus commentary—as well as three rabbinic writings: Bavli *Sota* 11a-13a, Midrash *Tanhuma* and the *Mekhilta*. Other Jewish and Christian texts are also examined to complement the overall picture.[3]

---

1 This article and the symposium at which its theses were presented and discussed is part of the research project, financed by the Austrian Science Fund (FWF): "The Saved Saviour: Exodus 1–2 in Patristic and Rabbinic Interpretation" (P-28441-G24).

2 Cf. for an introduction and overview: Heither, Schriftauslegung; Krochmalnik, Schriftauslegung; Langston, Exodus; Stemberger, Mose.

3 Of these, Philo's *Life of Moses* and Josephus' *Antiquities* turned out to be especially interesting as sources for later Christian interpretations. For example, Gregory's *Life of Moses* takes up Philo's *Vita* from a Christian perspective.

These texts are products of their social, cultural, and religious contexts and in turn contribute to the construction of identity of the interpretive communities and to the demarcation of those communities from others. Admittedly, it is easier task to reconstruct this process in many Christian texts, which explicitly deal with questions of identity and self-definition. However, midrash also has to be read within its socio-cultural context even if the connection is not as manifest as in contemporaneous Christian texts.[4] As Gerhard Langer writes: "Gottesbild, Weltbild, Offenbarungsvorstellung, Lehre und zentrale Stellung der Tora zählen zu den entscheidenden 'Subtexten' einer rabbinischen Auslegung von Midrasch, die im Rahmen des exegetischen Vorgehens 'eingespielt' werden und die im Zuge einer Analyse konkreter rabbinischer Texte jeweils zu erheben sind."[5] There is, thus, a connection between the biblical past and the rabbinic present.

Part 1 of this article presents examples of discourse on identity in Origen's Exodus homilies, Ephrem's commentary, the Bavli passage on Exodus 1:8–2:9, Midrash *Tanhuma* in the Standard and Buber versions, and some passages from the *Mekhilta* dealing with Exodus 1–2. Part 2 discusses possible traces of reactions to Christian interpretation in rabbinic texts.

1. Identity Construction in Interpretations of Exodus 1–2

1.1 Origen's Homilies on Exodus 1 and 2

Origen's homilies on the Old Testament books were delivered in Caesarea between 245 and 250.[6] They were written in Greek, but are preserved only in Rufinus's Latin translation. Homily is an ethically-oriented literary genre that applies biblical interpretation directly to the lives of listeners of readers. Origen's use of the possessive pronoun "our" is revealing: He claims the biblical text for a particular group, a community to which he belongs and which he addresses. Origen's biblical

4 Cf. Langer, Midrasch, 68: "Grundsätzlich werden die Ideale der Rabbinen auch in den Bibeltext hineinprojiziert. Dazu gehören der Vorrang des Studiums und der Lehre, die mit der höchsten Wertschätzung der Tora verbunden wird, und die vielen Beispiele für richtiges und toragemäßes Verhalten, für Bescheidenheit und Tugendhaftigkeit." For a contrasting position cf. Kugel, Two Introductions. That references are more implicit in midrash may also be due to the literary genre. The context of Christian texts that are written by individual authors can be more easily detected than the contexts of midrash as collections of tradition(s). Nevertheless, rabbinic literature does not convey a uniform picture either, as Lavee, Rabbinic Literature, 330 f, states: "Rabbinic literature gives us access to a variety of views and perceptions. [...] The sources do not provide a coherent and consistent theology." He even asks "whether such coherence existed at the time." (331)

5 Langer, Midrasch, 93.

6 For the dating of the homilies cf. Grappone, Annotazioni, 52; for an introduction to the homilies on Exodus see Heine, Origen, 1–43.

interpretation—like of other patristic authors—is strongly engaged with the task of constructing and defining identity. This process of self-definition includes the "establishment of community boundaries,"[7] which inevitably entails the definition of others and otherness. A passage from Origen's second homily, interpreting Moses's rescue from the river by Pharaoh's daughter, shows this clearly.

At the outset, Origen states that the biblical text is "filled with great mysteries" (*repleta immensis mysteriis*)[8] and that it would thus take too much time to explain it in detail. He then focuses on the aspects of the text, that are important *pro ecclesiae aedificatione*, "for the edification of the Church."[9] Origen identifies Pharaoh's daughter with "the Church which is gathered from the Gentiles"[10] and supports this with a quotation from Psalm 45.

This typological interpretation further proceeds as follows: Pharaoh's daughter finds Moses, who has been abandoned by his people. For Origen, as for the New Testament, Moses represents the law. This law, he says, was locked up until the church gathered from the gentiles found it and opened it. Only then was Moses able to grow up, because the church accepted the law and understood it correctly, that is, spiritually.

Origen then interprets the wages, that Pharaoh's daughter gives Moses's mother in terms of the church and the synagogue: The synagogue receives freedom from idolatry—from the church as payment for nurturing the law in its childhood.

Origen maintains that the gentile Christians' father was Pharaoh, who is identified with the devil. In accepting Christ, gentile Christians turned away from Pharaoh. Like Pharaoh's daughter, they came to the river, which symbolizes baptism. Pharaoh's daughter is thus the ancestor, the *typos*, of all gentiles who are baptized into Christianity. Thus, this character, who is a bit suspect in rabbinic literature because she is or was an idolater,[11] becomes Christian. Origen even maintains that she is the one who redeemed the Jews from idolatry—the complete reverse of the rabbinic perspective discussed. The concluding doxology beseeches Christ to give Christians the knowledge of the great, strong, and spiritual Moses.

In this interpretation, Pharaoh's daughter represents Origen's audience, which consisted of gentile Christians. They could identify with her, as a convert.

Interestingly, Moses is also "on the Christian side," but only when he (i.e., the law) is understood correctly, as the "spiritual law" (referring to Rom 7:14). This implies, of course, that Jews do not understand the law correctly. Thus, Moses has been adopted by the church and no longer belongs to the synagogue.

---

7 Cf. Reed/Becker, Ways, 14.

8 Latin text: Baehrens, Origenes Werke; English translation: Heine, Origen, here 245.

9 Heine, Origen, 245.

10 Heine, Origen, 246.

11 Cf. e.g. Miralles Maciá, Judaizing.

The synagogue, then, is represented by Moses's mother, though Origen does not say this explicitly. She is the one who abandons him and later nurtures him for Pharaoh's daughter, that is, the church. Due to his typological construction, Origen takes a critical stance toward Moses's mother that is not found anywhere else in patristic literature.

Origen interprets the book of Exodus from a distinctly Christian perspective. Therefore, the positive characters are pre-figurations of Christians and the negative ones are identified as the pagans. The Jews are situated in between: Moses was one of them and they took care of him, but they did not accept him spiritually. Thus, they can no longer lay claim to him. The biblical book of Exodus which is part of the law—that is part of "Moses"— is adopted by the Christians.

However, Origen rejects not only Jews, but all who do not understand Scripture and the law of Moses spiritually, including Christians. Origen constructs a "we"-group, an in-group, which he aims to persuade of his particular view of Christianity and Christian biblical interpretation. In his theoretical treatise *De principiis* IV,2,4, Origen maintains the relevance of the literal sense of Scripture (though not for every biblical passage). But in his second homily on Exodus, he ignores it and exclusively promotes the spiritual sense, which—unlike in his first homily—he does not distinguish from Scripture's moral meaning. Crouzel has shown that for Origen the moral sense is a subspecies of the spiritual sense of Scripture.[12] This means that a proper understanding of Scripture corresponds (ideally, at least) to the right Christian lifestyle. Origen's spiritual interpretation has two reference points: the church—that is, the community—and the individual, especially his or her interior life. Origen's biblical interpretation in the homilies is not primarily about doctrine or faith, but spiritual practice.

Origen's opponents belong to two groups: pagans and Jews. While they are differentiated from each other, in Origen's fundamentally dichotomous worldview, both are on the "other" side. He identifies Christians as spiritual, heavenly, good, and chaste and all others as carnal, earthly, bad, and licentious. Although he concedes that the Jews had the law and took care of it in the past, in the present they are situated on the same side as the pagans who were evil from the beginning. The decisive distinction between (real) Christians and Jews is spiritual biblical interpretation.

1.2 Ephrem the Syrian

Ephrem wrote his biblical commentaries in Edessa after 363.[13] His commentaries on Genesis and Exodus are preserved in Syriac and use a methodology different from Origen's. Ephrem prefers a literal exegesis and takes up numerous traditions

12 Cf. Crouzel, Origène, 114; Lies, Schriftauslegung.

13 Syriac text: Tonneau, Sancti Ephraem; English translation: McVey/Mathews Jr./Amar, St. Ephrem; for an introduction to Ephrem's interpretation cf. Griffith, Ephraem.

otherwise known from Jewish writings. Especially in the first chapters of his commentary, the influence of Philo's *Vita Mosis* is manifest. In his commentary on Exodus 1 and 2, Ephrem hews close to the biblical text. References to his contemporary situation are rarely visible, as they are in his poetic compositions. However, at some points, his particular theological convictions are perceptible, such as when he stresses the free will of Pharaoh's daughter.

Ephrem does not explicitly discuss hermeneutics or methods of biblical interpretation, nor does he speak about church and synagogue or Christians and Jews. He simply retells the Exodus story, but with a specific focus: His interpretation concentrates on the character of Moses. The structural center of his narrative is—as in the biblical book—the conflict between God and Pharaoh, which he presents as a conflict between life and death. Contrasting metaphors, such as life-death and light-darkness, are a characteristic feature of his language in general. Moses represents and performs God's justice and mercy. He is the authorized savior of the Hebrews from the beginning of the narrative. Ephrem's Moses is characterized by beauty, integrity, legitimacy, and authority. He is unambiguously Hebrew. Unlike in the biblical text, Jethro's daughters do not describe Moses as an Egyptian (cf. Exod 2:19). Moreover, Ephrem mentions that Moses learned from his mother and sister about his Hebrew origin.

The women in the biblical narrative—the midwives, Moses's mother and sister, Pharaoh's daughter and Jethro's daughters—play an important role for Ephrem: All of them are positive characters, regardless of their religion. Ephrem has no problem with Pharaoh's daughter or Zipporah being idolaters. He mentions this explicitly but suggests that it cannot impede God's plan.

Ephrem addresses a readership that needs comfort in the face of life mortal danger. In his commentary, he is not concerned with polemics against opponents within or adjacent to his Nicean Christian community, as he is elsewhere in his writings. Rather, he assures his readers that everything that happens corresponds to God's plan and that life will prevail over death, God over Satan.

Implicitly, Ephrem positions his readers on God's side. Exodus is read as a Christian book, without reflection or discussion. Ephrem never mentions Jews or Judaism or the synagogue or even the church and the Christians. There are only a few hints, like the mention of martyrdom and the discussion on free will, that identify Ephrem's interpretation as Christian. Modern scholars have often been puzzled by the midrashic character of Ephrem's exegesis and its coexistence with the harsh polemics against Jews in his hymns.[14] Elena Narinskaya states that "there may have been a tradition of biblical exegesis common to both Jews and Christians, of Semitic origin."[15] If this is the case, it is likely that Ephrem did not perceive

14 Cf. e.g. Drijvers, Jews; Friedl, Ephräm; Griffith, Ephraem; McVey, Polemic; Narinskaya, Ephrem; Shepardson, Rhetoric; idem, Anti-Judaism.

15 Narinskaya, Ephrem, 178.

his biblical interpretation as specifically "Jewish" but rather as the common way of interpreting Scripture. Discussions and polemics can be found in his liturgical compositions rather than in his interpretations.

1.3 Bavli *Sota* 11a–13a

The Babylonian Talmud contains a passage with a continuous interpretation of Exodus 1:8–2:9. Such longer interpretive passages are, as Stemberger has remarked, quite rare in the Babylonian Talmud.[16] "Anders als so viele andere babylonische Aussagen zu biblischen Texten verwendet unser Abschnitt diese nicht als Belegtext in einer Diskussion, sondern arbeitet den Bibeltext abschnittsweise der Reihenfolge nach ab, jeweils ohne irgendwelche Einleitung mit dem jeweiligen Lemma des Bibeltextes beginnend."[17] Stemberger dates this midrashic section to the sixth century.

In this text, the authors' and presumed readers' identity is defined by knowledge of God's will, his people's history and the correct interpretation of Scripture. The Hebrews play an important part in this text. They act in full accord with God's will. The rabbinic interpreters demonstrate this by quoting numerous biblical verses. The "others" are defined by ignorance: The Egyptian soothsayers, Pharaoh's counsellors, and Pharaoh's daughter do not know how to interpret Scripture correctly—but interestingly, they do know Scripture and quote from it. The soothsayers and counsellors draw incorrect conclusions from the texts, while Pharaoh's daughter expresses a correct idea without understanding it: "*And Pharaoh's daughter said unto her, Take this child away* (Exod 2:9). R. Ḥama b. Ḥanina said: She prophesied without knowing what she prophesied—*Heliki* ['take away']—behold what is thine [*ha sheliki*]." (*bSota* 12b)[18] Pharaoh's daughter is made a proselyte in the Bavli, as she goes to the river to cleanse herself of the idolatry of her father's house. The rabbis' attitude toward proselytes is ambivalent—they are simultaneously welcomed and rejected—and becomes more negative over time.[19] Thus, Pharaoh's daughter clearly does not belong to the Egyptians, but she also does not belong to the Hebrews. In any case, idolatry is a prominent attribute of the "others," which *bSota* 11a–13a ascribes to the Egyptians but never to the Hebrews during their stay in Egypt.

Thus, one important marker of identity is the proper understanding of Scripture. On the meta-level this marks the rabbis as the only legitimate authorities for Jewish interpretation. Anything outside the boundaries they draw, outside their "fence," is illegitimate.

16 Cf. Stemberger, Midrasch.

17 Stemberger, Mose, 17.

18 English translation: Epstein (ed.), Talmud, 65.

19 Cf. Lavee, Boundaries; idem, Proselytes.

Circumcision is twice mentioned as a positive marker defining Hebrew identity. The text also emphasizes Moses's special status by stating that he was born circumcised.

Another element of identity construction is genealogy. Commenting on Exod 1:21 ("and because the midwives feared God, he gave them houses"), the Bavli offers an elaborate interpretation of the term "houses." The two midwives, Shiphrah and Puah—the latter of whom is identified with Miriam—are given a prominent position in their people's history. The midrash makes Miriam David's ancestor by presenting her as Kaleb's wife and identifying her with a number of less-known and otherwise unimportant biblical characters. The text links different biblical books in an effort to define Israel's identity.

1.4 Midrash *Tanhuma* (printed and Buber version)

Midrash *Tanhuma* belongs to the category of so-called homiletic midrashim. Marc Bregman assigns the major part of Midrash *Tanhuma* on Genesis and Exodus to sixth- or seventh-century Palestine.[20]

Whereas the biblical text of Exodus 1 and 2 hardly mentions God, the midrash establishes a close connection between Israel and God. Exod 1:1 ("and these are the names of the sons of Israel") provides the redactors with an opportunity to praise God's name. Several verses from Psalms, Job, and Nehemiah expressing the strength of God's name are quoted. The interpretation of the names of the individual tribes underlines the solidarity and equality within Israel. This is not only a statement about the biblical text but also an exhortation to readers to maintain this solidarity and equality.

Midrash *Tanhuma* emphasizes the massive proliferation of the Israelites in Egypt.

> *And Joseph died, and all his brethren* (Exod. 1:6). Nevertheless, *the children of Israel were fruitful and increased abundantly* (ibid., v.7). R Yannai declared: Each woman bore six children at one time, while (because each word in the biblical verse is in the plural from, thus implying a minimum of two) other say that each one bore twelve, for the word *paru* ("were fruitful") indicates two; *veyishresu* ("and increased abundantly"), two; *vayirbu* ("and multiplied"), two, *vaya'asmu* ("and waxed"), two; *bime'od me'od* ("exceedingly mighty"), two; and *the land was filled with them* (ibid.), two, totaling twelve in all (*Tanhuma Shemot* 5).[21]

The midrash ascribes this proliferation to God and stresses the role of the women, thereby admonishing the contemporary female recipients of the text to follow their example. Reproduction is presented as another way to strengthen Israel's community.

---

20 Bregman, Tanhuma-Yelammedenu, 5*.

21 English translation: Berman, Midrash, 321 f.

Israel's identity and even its existence is endangered not primarily by Pharaoh, but by the Israelites themselves (*Tan Shemot* 5, *TanB Shemot* 7):

> The prophet said: They have dealt treacherously against the Lord, for they have begotten strange children; now shall the new moon devour them with their portions (Hos. 5:7). That is to say, they gave birth to children, but neglected to circumcise them. This teaches us that after Joseph's death the people disregarded the covenant of circumcision, saying: Let us be like the Egyptians. When the Holy One, blessed be He, observed this, He suppressed the love He bore them, as it is said: He turned their heart to hate His people (Ps. 105:25).[22]

According to this text, problems arise when Israel abandons God and his Torah. This is proved by a quotation of Hos 5:7. Only when Israel rejects YHWH can the new Pharaoh take action against Israel. The next paragraph points to the imminent salvation that comes from God and no one else. Israel asks God for mercy. This makes clear that Israel's existence is dependent on God's election and its continued devotion to him. The explicit mention of circumcision emphasizes the importance of Torah observance. Inner unity and a focus on the community and its wellbeing are decisive factors, ideals that this midrash wants to teach its readership.

The printed version of the midrash includes a passage on Moses's relation to idolaters. He is defended against the implicit accusation of contact with idolaters and perhaps complicity in Israel's idolatry. Any connection to idolatry or idolaters would be problematic. Thus, *Tanhuma* emphasizes that Pharaoh's daughter and Jethro had rejected idolatry before they met Moses. In Exod 2:19, Jethro's daughters describe Moses, the man they met at the well, as an Egyptian. The rabbis found this objectionable and interpreted the passage in a clever way: It did not mean that Moses was an Egyptian, but that the Egyptian whom Moses killed was the cause of his flight to Midian. Any doubt concerning Moses's Hebrew identity is dispelled.

1.5 The *Mekhilta de-Rabbi Ishmael*

The *Mekhilta* is the oldest of the rabbinic texts examined here, originating in the second half of the third century.[23] It begins with Exodus 12, but traditions concerning Exodus 1–2 are scattered throughout the text.[24]

The question of Hebrew identity appears in three passages: one on the cities Pithom and Ramses, one on the use of Hebrew language, and one on the relationship between Moses and Jethro.

---

22 Berman, Midrash, 322.

23 Cf. Stemberger, Einleitung, 253; more detailed in Stemberger, Datierung.

24 Critical edition: Horovitz/Rabin, Mechilta.

The opposition between Egyptians and Hebrews is visible throughout the text and clearly corresponds to the biblical presentation. Contrasting forms of religious practice are associated with the two groups. The dichotomy between proper and improper worship plays an important role in the demarcation of the Hebrews from the Egyptians and the Midianites. Pithom is indirectly characterized as a place of idolatry (*Beshallah* 2).

Moses's close relation to the Midianites is problematized in the text as well (*Amalek* 3). Moses wants to marry Jethro's daughter and accepts Jethro's condition not to circumcise his firstborn. Thus, Moses accepts that his first son Gershom will be an idolater. The midrash criticizes Moses by means of a reference to Exod 4:24–26. In verse 24, God tries to kill Moses, whereas in verse 25 Zipporah circumcises her son. The midrash considers whether God in fact wanted to kill the son rather than Moses, which is grammatically possible. Several rabbis criticize Moses for postponing Gershom's circumcision. Only Rabbi Jose defends Moses. The text thus makes clear that Moses's behavior was at least questionable. Neither Jethro nor Zipporah is made responsible for the failure to circumcise Gershom.

The rabbinic interpreters consider circumcision central to Jewish identity. The citation of multiple rabbis in this passage underlines the importance of the topic. With Gershom's circumcision by Zipporah, the case is settled for Moses. However, the midrash uses this narrative as a warning not to neglect circumcision and accentuates its significance as an identity marker.

Another passage important for the definition of Israelite or Jewish identity is *Mekhilta Pisha* 5. According to this passage, four merits justify Israel's redemption from Egypt: They did not fornicate, they did not slander, and they did not change their names or their language. In the discussion of language, there is an explicit reference to Moses's dialogue with his Hebrew brothers who are oppressed by forced labor, in Exodus 2. Again, doubt about Moses's identity is apparent. By explicitly describing the Hebrews as his brothers, the midrash makes clear what group Moses belongs to. Language defines belonging. The same is true for Joseph, who is also discussed in this passage. Like Moses, Joseph lived among Egyptians but spoke Hebrew. The other examples (Exod 5:3 and Gen 14:13) refer to language as well but also focus on worship.

Overall, the midrash communicates that the Hebrews' identity is defined by worship of the one God and rejection of idolatry. This becomes manifest in the use of the Hebrew language and, of course, circumcision. Susanne Plietzsch understands the halakha in the *Mekhilta* as "Teil eines weiter ausgreifenden Vorhabens […] die Demonstration eines Rückgriffs auf den biblischen Narrativ im Zuge einer autoritativen Neuformulierung jüdischen Selbstverständnisses."[25] This statement is also valid for the aggadic passages just examined.

25 Plietzsch, Sache, 248.

2. Traces of Reactions to Christianity in Rabbinic Texts

According to Philip Alexander, "Christianity figures little in traditional Jewish sources. Yet appearances can be deceptive. The very lack of explicit reference can be exploited as an apologetic device to support the view that Judaism is the older faith and so possesses at least prima facie a superior claim to legitimacy."[26] Moshe D. Herr is convinced that certain aggadic statements can only be understood as anti-Christian polemic,

> which contributed significantly to the flowering of the aggadah in Ereẓ Israel. This, as opposed to the situation in Babylonia, is indicated by Abbahu's statement in a conversation with sectarians (minim): "We [of Ereẓ Israel] who frequently meet with you, set ourselves the task of thoroughly studying it [i. e., the Bible], but they [i. e., those of Babylonia] do not study it so carefully" (Av. Zar. 4a).[27]

Where can traces of such an apologetic discourse be found?[28] First, topics of conflict between Jews and Christians are an interesting field of research. These include circumcision, sexuality, and asceticism (especially Mary's virginity) and questions of monotheism and Trinitarian dogma. Particularly interesting are cases where Jewish and Christian interpretations are strikingly different or even conflict and do not show any common ground. Yet, Philip Alexander urges caution: "In general the Rabbis' direct contacts with Christianity were slight, and their knowledge of the finer points of Christian doctrine slighter still."[29] The following discussion thus concentrates on topics of conflict, the affirmation or rejection of which is central to the self-definition of rabbinic Judaism. These are circumcision, the question of a woman giving birth free of pain, and the Holy Spirit.

2.1 Circumcision

Circumcision is a matter of ritual practice, not of doctrine, and it is a central issue in patristic and rabbinic texts. This was not previously the case to such an extent. As Judith Frishman states,

> The concern about the isolation and even survival of Judaism and the Jewish people is obviously fueled by a new reality: Christianity was steadily gaining ground, conversion to Judaism was becoming more difficult but also less attractive and circumcision (and other Jewish practice) was often subject to Roman repression.[30]

---

26 Alexander, Parting, 1.

27 Herr, Church Fathers, 554.

28 For criteria to identify points of contact between Jewish and Christian texts or teachings, cf. Kessler, Encounter, 401; Visotzky, Fathers, 19; Stemberger, Contacts.

29 Alexander, Parting, 19.

30 Frishman, Abraham, 177.

Tan Shemot 5/*TanB Shemot* 7 informs the readers that the disregard of circumcision by Israel was a more serious problem than the external threat from Pharaoh. Pharaoh only had power over Israel when they abandoned God and his laws. Here the rabbis emphasize the importance of circumcision in response to those who reject and denigrate it.[31]

Origen's polemic against Judaism in his second homily on Exodus (2,4) addresses this topic more generally. He asserts that Jews are not capable of understanding the law spiritually and thus correctly. The Jewish understanding of the law is denigrated as literal and obsolete. In other texts, such as *Hom. Num.* 6,4,1, Origen contrasts the "circumcision of the flesh" and the "circumcision of the heart." He also mentions observance of the Sabbath and New Moon and the offering of sacrifices. Circumcision is one of the most mentioned and criticized aspects of Torah observance in patristic texts.

That circumcision was perceived as characteristic of Judaism is apparent in the seemingly natural assumption that Pharaoh's daughter recognizes Moses as a Hebrew child by his circumcision. This assumption is also found in Christian texts, such as Theodoret of Cyrus.[32] Following Paul (Rom 2; 3:1), the Jews are frequently designated "those of the circumcision" in patristic writings.[33] Circumcision appears as a feature of Judaism and a marker of difference between Jews and Christians. It is thus plausible that rabbinic texts—perhaps as a reaction to the Christian rejection of circumcision—preach circumcision as an important marker of belonging to the Jewish community.

2.2 Pregnancy and Birth Free of Pain

In *Sota* 12a, the Bavli asserts that Jochebed's pregnancy and Moses's birth proceeded without pain. This is based on the idea that the righteous women are exempted from the decree against Eve. Günter Stemberger argues that this is a reaction to the Christian tradition that Mary's childbirth was free of pain, which may have been known to the rabbis.[34] It was not an elite doctrine but a popular idea.

31 For ancient texts about circumcision cf. Blaschke, Beschneidung. Maier, Jüdische Auseinandersetzung, 189 f, denies the Christian background of the rabbinic discussion on circumcision: "Die Angriffe gegen die Beschneidung gehörten für jüdisches Bewußtsein schon längst zu den Hauptmerkmalen der Infragestellung durch die feindliche Umwelt." According to Maier, the texts give no specific Christian reasons for the rejection of circumcision.

32 Cf. Theodoret, *quaest. III in Exod.*

33 Cf. e. g. Eusebius, *Ecl. proph.* IV (PG 22, 1208A–B); Basilius, *Comm. Isa.* 208 (PG 30, 476D–480A); Cyrillus Alexandrinus, *Comm. Joel.* (PG 71, 376D–381C). Circumcision is also mentioned as a characteristic of Jews in pagan texts: cf. Horaz, *Sermones* 1,9,70 (*curtis Iudaeis*).

34 Stemberger, Mose, 29–30.

A comparison with Josephus complements and corroborates Stemberger's argument. The statement in the Bavli is indeed noteworthy and cannot be entirely explained on the basis of the biblical text. In Exod 1:19, the midwives inform Pharaoh that the Hebrew women—in contrast to the Egyptians—bear their children before the midwives arrive. This suggest that Hebrew women, including Jochebed, had easy childbirths. According to Exod 2:2–3, Jochebed hid the infant Moses for three months. Then, the biblical narrative tells us, she could not hide him any longer. This raises the question of why. A widespread interpretation asserts that soldiers were looking for Hebrew children to kill them.[35]

Josephus, in *A. J.* 2,218, combines the two ideas: of easy delivery and scouts searching for children.

> However, their belief in the promises of God was confirmed by the manner of the woman's delivery, since she escaped the vigilance of the watch, thanks to the gentleness of her travail, which spared her any violent throes.[36]

This interpretation emerges from the biblical text: Josephus obviously knows the tradition about the soldiers or spies and asks why Jochebed was initially able to hide the baby. The answer is an explanation for the textual gaps in Exodus 2.

Whereas Josephus says that the pain was not overwhelming, the Talmud speaks of a birth without any pain, which is a further development or even a new idea. As Christian tradition interpreted Mary as the "new Eve," the allusion to Eve further supports the view that Christian discussions were the backdrop for this tradition in the Bavli.

2.3 The Holy Spirit

Mekhilta Shira 10 mentions the Holy Spirit, רוח הקדש, as the source of Miriam's prophecy about Moses's birth.[37] Bavli *Sota* 11a presents the same tradition but replaces the Holy Spirit with the Shekhina. It is possible that this exchange was a reaction to Christian ideas.

In Luke 1:26–28, the archangel Gabriel announces Jesus's birth to Mary. Her pregnancy is caused by the Holy Spirit (Luke 1:35). According to the *Mekhilta* (second half of the third century), Moses's birth is also prophetically announced, and the Holy Spirit effects Miriam's prophecy.

35 Cf. e. g. *bSota* 12a: The Egyptians brought children to places where they thought a Hebrew child was born. When the children cried, they provoked the newborns to cry as well. So the babies were discovered. Cf. Ephrem, *Comm. Exod.* 2,1 who speaks of a search for children. Cf. further *Exod. Rab.* 1:20; Targum Pseudo-Jonatan; Philo, *Mos.* 1,10.

36 Thackeray (transl.), Josephus, 259.

37 That Miriam predicted Moses's birth is a widespread Jewish tradition: cf. Tervanotko, Denying.

However, the tradition about Miriam's prophecy reaches back even further. Pseudo-Philo's *Liber Antiquitatum Biblicarum* in the first century C. E. mentions it and ascribes the prophecy to the Holy Spirit (*L. A. B.* 9:10).[38]

The fact that Miriam has the same name as Mary, the mother of Jesus, was used for typological interpretations by the church fathers.[39] They saw a strong parallel between the two Miriams or Marias. Did Jewish authors also perceive this parallel? Did the *Liber Antiquitatum Biblicarum* add the Holy Spirit to the narrative to create a parallel to the tradition about Jesus's birth? This question remains open.

In the tradition about Miriam's prophecy in *Sota* 11a, the Holy Spirit is not mentioned. But it does appear it in *Sota* 11b: Miriam "cried out" (פועה) through the Holy Spirit. Here the Spirit is mentioned again without further discussion. However, there is a difference between the two passages in Bavli *Sota* 11a and 11b that is—in my opinion—essential: In the second passage about Miriam's speaking (*Sota* 11b), the Spirit is not presented as a person, whereas in the first passage (*Sota* 11a) it is. The Holy Spirit seems to stand on the riverbank and be personally present. Perhaps this prevented the editors of the Talmud from letting the Spirit appear in this episode.[40]

It is possible that the disappearance of the Holy Spirit from this tradition is a reaction to Christian claims. Especially in connection with the announcement of the savior's birth it can be tricky to speak about the Holy Spirit in the face of Christian Trinitarian theology. Moreover, it should be considered that at the time when the Talmud was redacted, the doctrine of Trinity was further developed, especially at the First Council of Constantinople in 381. At the time of the *Liber Antiquitatum Biblicarum* and the *Mekhilta*, this was not yet the case, and it was easier to speak about the Holy Spirit.

However one evaluates these observations, the development of differences between rabbinic and patristic interpretations is obvious. Whether these rabbinic interpretations are reactions to Christian doctrine or an independent development, they show the common ground as well as the boundaries between the two traditions. There certainly was some interaction, but it was probably indirect. The rabbis knew Christian doctrines and traditions, often superficially but sometimes more profoundly, and rejected them by turning in another direction in their own interpretations or by creating parallel countertraditions including the claim of greater antiquity. Marc Hirshman speaks of "hidden controversy."[41] Reactions to the challenge of different interpretations and teachings can be varied:

---

38 In Josephus, *A. J.* 2, 212–216, it is Amram, the father, who foresees Moses's birth. Josephus does not mention the Spirit at all.

39 Cf. Siquans, Prophetinnen, 82–102.

40 Similarly, in Tan *Shemot* 9 the Holy Spirit is mentioned only as the source of Moses's knowledge and not as a personally present entity.

41 Hirshman, Rivalry, 129.

> One can simply disregard it and fail to address it altogether, either explicitly or implicitly. One can insist on adhering to known ways, dismissing any attempt to change them because of external causes, and remain oblivious to all other views, whether similar or different. An alternative approach may choose to conceal any material that might be helpful to the opponent, at least for the time being. A third approach might be to adopt the rival's claims and imprint them with our own seal of "authenticity," in other words, "judaize" the appealing exegeses or ideologies or our opponent's doctrine.[42]

The examples discussed above exemplify several possible reactions: insisting on adhering to known ways in the case of circumcision, adopting the rival's claim in the case of Jochebed's childbirth, and disregarding the Holy Spirit in certain contexts.

3. Conclusion

Günter Stemberger observes that midrash "kommt aus dem Bewußtsein einer untrennbaren Zusammengehörigkeit Israels und seiner Bibel, weshalb Midrasch immer auch *Aktualisierung* ist, die Gegenwartsbedeutung des Textes bzw. der biblischen Geschichte stets von neuem zu erheben hat."[43] This statement can be extended to all scriptural interpretation. Interpreters answer to the needs of their time and their audience. They presume that Scripture is meaningful for their contemporaries and try to build a bridge between the old text and the new questions that arise from their own particular situation. In times of insecurity concerning the authority and legitimacy of competing interpretations, scriptural exegesis becomes an important factor in constructing, ascertaining, and renewing one's own identity and delimitating it from others who share the same scriptures. This sometimes produces, but also preserves, common ground on which dialogue can later be built.

Literature

Sources

Baehrens, Wilhelm A., Origenes Werke. Band 6. Homilien zum Hexateuch in Rufins Übersetzung, Bd. 1: Die Homilien zu Genesis, Exodus und Leviticus (GCS 29), Leipzig 1920.

Berman, Samuel E., Midrash Tanhuma-Yelammedenu. An English Translation of Genesis and Exodus from the printed version of Tanhuma-Yelammedenu with an introduction, notes, and indexes, Hoboken, N. J. 1996.

42 Ibid., 129–130.

43 Stemberger, Einleitung, 235.

Buber, Salomon (ed.), Midrash Tanḥuma al ḥamishah ḥumshe torah, Wilna 1885, repr. Jerusalem 1964.
Cohn, Leopold/Wendland, Paulus (ed.), Philonis Alexandrini opera quae supersunt, Bd. 1, Berlin 1896, Bd. 3, Berlin 1898, Bd. 4, Berlin 1902, repr. Berlin 1962.
Díez Macho, Alejandro (ed.), Targum palaestinense in Pentateuchum. Additur Targum Pseudojonatan ejusque hispanica versio, vol. 2 Exodus (BPM ser. 4), Madrid 1980.
Epstein, Isidor (ed.), The Babylonian Talmud, Seder Nashim 3, London 1936.
Fernández Marcos, Natalio/Sáenz-Badillos, Angel (ed.), Theodoreti Cyrensis Quaestiones in Octateuchum: Editio critica (Textos y estudios "Cardenal Cisneros"), Madrid 1979.
Heine, Ronald (transl.), Origen. Homilies on Genesis and Exodus (FaCh 71), Washington, D.C. 1982.
Horovitz, Saul/Rabin, Yisrael Avraham (ed.), Mechilta d'Rabbi Ismael cum variis lectionibus et adnotationibus, Jerusalem 1960.
McVey, Kathleen (Ed.)/Edward G. Mathews Jr./Joseph P. Amar (transl.), St. Ephrem the Syrian. Selected Prose Works (The Fathers of the Church 91), Washington, D.C. 1994.
Migne, Jacques Paul (ed.), Basilius, Opera omnia quae existant (PG 30), Paris 1888.
—, Eusebius Pamphili Caesariensis Episcopus, Eclogae propheticae (PG 22, 1017–1262), Paris 1857.
—, S. Cyrillus Alexandrinus Episcopos, Commentarius in Ioelem prophetam (PG 71, 376D–381C), Paris 1864.
Thackeray, Henry St. J. (transl.), Josephus. Jewish Antiquities, Books 1–3 (LCL 242), London 1991.
Tonneau, Raymond-Marie (ed.), Sancti Ephraem Syri in Genesim et in Exodum Commentarii (CSCO 152/153), Louvain 1955.
Zundel, Henokh (ed.), Midrash Tanhuma ʿal Ḥamishah ḥumshe Torah: ʿim ha-perushim ha-mefursamim ʿEts Yosef, ʿAnaf Yosef, Jerusalem 1960.

Scholarly Works

Alexander, Philip S., "The Parting of the Ways" from the Perspective of Rabbinic Judaism, in: J.D.G. Dunn (ed.), Jews and Christians. The Parting of the Ways A.D. 70 to 135, Tübingen 1992, 1–26.
Blaschke, Andreas, Beschneidung. Zeugnisse der Bibel und verwandter Texte (TANZ 28), Tübingen 1998.
Bregman, Marc, The Tanhuma-Yelammedenu Literature. Studies in the Evolution of the Versions, Piscataway, N.J. 2003 (English and Hebrew).
Crouzel, Henri, Origène, Paris 1985.
Drijvers, Han J.W., Jews and Christians at Edessa, JJS 36 (1986), 88–102.
Friedl, Alfred, Ephräm der Syrer, in: W. Klein (ed.), Syrische Kirchenväter, Stuttgart 2004, 36–56.
Frishman, Judith, "And Abraham Had Faith". But in What? Ephrem and the Rabbis on Abraham and God's Blessing, in: E. Grypeou/H. Spurling (ed.), The Exegetical Encounter between Jews and Christians in Late Antiquity (JCPS 18), Leiden/Boston, Mass. 2009, 163–179.

Grappone, Antonio, Annotazioni sulla cronologia delle omelie di Origene, Augustinianum 41 (2001), 27–58.

Griffith, Sidney H., Ephraem the Exegete (306–373). Biblical Commentary in the Works of Ephraem the Syrian, in: C. Kannengiesser (ed.), Handbook of Patristic Exegesis. The Bible in Ancient Christianity 2, Leiden 2004, 1395–1428.

Heither, Theresia, Schriftauslegung. Das Buch Exodus bei den Kirchenvätern (NSK.AT 33/4), Stuttgart 2002.

Herr, Moshe D., Church Fathers and the Aggadah, EJ 5 (1971), 554.

Hirshman, Marc, A Rivalry of Genius. Jewish and Christian Biblical Interpretation in Late Antiquity, Albany, N. Y. 1996.

Kessler, Edward, The Exegetical Encounter between the Greek Church Fathers and the Palestinian Rabbis, StPatr 34 (2001), 395–412.

Krochmalnik, Daniel, Schriftauslegung. Das Buch Exodus im Judentum (NSK.AT 33/3), Stuttgart 2000.

Kugel, James, Two Introductions to Midrash, Prooftexts 3 (1983), 131–155.

Langer, Gerhard, Midrasch, Tübingen 2016.

Langston, Scott M., Exodus through the Centuries (Blackwell Bible Commentary), Malden, Mass./Oxford 2006.

Lavee, Moshe, No Boundaries for the Construction of Boundaries. The Babylonian Talmud's Emphasis on Demarcation of Identity, in: R. Nikolsky/T. Ilan (ed.), Rabbinic Traditions between Palestine and Babylonia (Ancient Judaism and Early Christianity 89), Leiden 2014.

—, "Proselytes are as hard to Israel as a scab is to the skin." A Babylonian Talmudic concept, JJS 63 (2012), 22–48.

—, Rabbinic Literature and the History of Judaism in late Antiquity. Challenges, Methodologies and New Approaches, in: M. Goodman/P. Alexander (ed.), Rabbinic Texts and the History of Late-Roman Palestine (PBA 165), Oxford 2010, 319–351.

Lies, Lothar, Die "Gottes würdige" Schriftauslegung nach Origenes, in: G. Dorival/A. Le Boulluec (ed.), Origeniana Sexta. Origène et la Bible/Origen and the Bible, Leuven 1995, 365–372.

Maier, Johann, Jüdische Auseinandersetzung mit dem Christentum in der Antike (Erträge der Forschung 177), Darmstadt 1982.

McVey, Kathleen, The Anti-Judaic Polemic of Ephrem Syrus' Hymns on the Nativity, in: H. W. Attridge/J. J. Collins/T. H. Tobin (ed.), Of Scribes and Scrolls. Studies in the Hebrew Bible, Intertestamental Judaism, and Christian Origins, Lanham, Md. 1990, 229–240.

Miralles Maciá, Lorena, Judaizing a Gentile Biblical Character through Fictive Biographical Reports. The Case of Bityah, Pharaoh's Daughter, Moses' Mother, according to Rabbinic Interpretation, in: C. Cordoni/G. Langer (ed.), Narratology, Hermeneutics, and Midrash: Jewish, Christian, and Muslim narratives from the Late Antiquity until the Modern Times (Poetik, Exegese und Narrative, Studien zur jüdischen Literatur und Kunst 2), Göttingen 2014, 145–175.

Narinskaya, Elena, Ephrem, A "Jewish" Sage. A Comparison of the Exegetical Writings of St. Ephrem the Syrian and Jewish Traditions (StTT 7), Turnhout 2010.

Plietzsch, Susanne, "Dass jede einzelne Sache, für die Israel sein Leben gab, in seinen Händen Bestand haben sollte ..." Individuelle und regional unabhängige Religiosität in der Mekhilta des Rabbi Jischmael, JSJ 41,2 (2010), 244–285.

Reed, Annette Yoshiko/Becker, Adam H., Introduction. Traditional Models and New Directions, in: A. H. Becker/A. Y. Reed (ed.), The Ways that Never Parted. Jews and Christians in Late Antiquity and Early Middle Ages (TSAJ 95), Tübingen 2003, 1–33.

Shepardson, Christine, Anti-Judaism and Christian orthodoxy. Ephrem's hymns in fourth-century Syria, Washington, D. C. 2008.

—, Anti-Jewish Rhetoric and Intra-Christian Conflict in the Sermons of Ephrem Syrus, StPatr 35 (2001), 502–507.

Siquans, Agnethe, Die alttestamentlichen Prophetinnen in der patristischen Rezeption. Texte – Kontexte – Hermeneutik (HBS 65), Freiburg i.Br. 2011.

Stemberger, Günter, Mose in der rabbinischen Tradition, Freiburg i.Br. 2016.

—, Einleitung in Talmud und Midrasch, München, ^{8}1992.

—, Exegetical Contacts between Christians and Jews in the Roman Empire, in: M. Sæbø (ed.), Hebrew Bible/Old Testament. The History of Its Interpretation, vol. 1. From the Beginnings to the Middle Ages (until 1300), part 1. Antiquity, Göttingen 1996, 569–586.

—, Midrasch in Babylonien. Am Beispiel von Sota 9b–14a, Henoch 10 (1988), 183–203.

Tervanotko, Hanna, Denying her Voice. The Figure of Miriam in Ancient Jewish Literature (JAJSup 23), Göttingen 2016.

Visotzky, Burton L., Fathers of the World. Essays in Rabbinic and Patristic Literatures (WUNT 80), Tübingen 1995.

Bas ter Haar Romeny (University of Amsterdam)

Marking Boundaries in Antiochene Exegesis

It might come as a surprise that the title of this paper mentions "Antiochene" exegesis. It refers to the Antiochene School of exegesis, which is traditionally seen as standing in opposition to that of Alexandria. However, many recent publications question or even deny the existence of two separate schools of exegesis.[1] I am not entirely convinced by this new fashion. I think there is much confusion. Therefore this paper will begin with a justification of the title. I will discuss the delineation of boundaries between Antiochenes and Alexandrians in modern research; after this I will investigate what Antiochenes actually wrote in order to clarify what is correct exegesis and what is not: how did they mark the boundaries between correct and incorrect interpretations of the Bible?

The Boundaries between Antiochene and Alexandrian Exegesis in Modern Research

Thus we begin by examining modern research. In many recent studies about patristic exegesis one can read a statement of this sort:[2]

> Since the twentieth century, theological discussion of patristic exegetical practices has created an unnecessary bifurcation between Alexandrian and Antiochene hermeneutics, characterizing the former as mere allegorical and the latter as substantially literal. However, patristic scholars consider this dichotomy to be an oversimplification of ancient biblical interpretations. The standard contrast mistakenly presents allegorical and literal hermeneutics as separate methodologies. [...] The division between "Alexandrian" and "Antiochene" schools is a modern artificial construct that may have little relevance to fully understanding ancient patristic exegesis.

The supposition is that earlier scholars were either blind, not sincere, or led by presentist concerns, and that we now know better.

---

1 Note, for instance, the title of one of the workshops at the XVIII International Conference on Patristics Studies, held in Oxford in August 2019: "Behind and Beyond the Alexandria-Antioch Divide". One of the other workshops puts the reference to the two cities between quotation marks: "'Alexandrian' and 'Antiochene' Exegesis of the Bible: Exemplary studies on Eusebius of Caesarea and Severian of Gabala."

2 This particular formulation comes from Slade, Patristic Exegesis, 155–156.

The trouble with many of such statements is, first of all, that they are often not based on any study of the sources. Second, they caricature earlier research and then make an easy job of demolishing it. Let us look at one recent publication just to give a sample. I have chosen Donald Fairbairn's 2007 article 'Patristic Exegesis and Theology: The Cart and the Horse.'[3] Fairbairn is an evangelical Professor of Historical Theology from North Carolina. He states that the "typical view" of the Antiochene-Alexandrian dichotomy is based on three major assumptions.

The first assumption would be "that the Antiochene and Alexandrian schools were fairly uniform internally and were equally represented in the early church." I have read many earlier studies, such as the works by Diestel, Kihn, and Harnack in the nineteenth century,[4] and Bardy and Schäublin in the twentieth,[5] and none of them really suggest that the schools were uniform internally. It is a matter of course that within a school developments take place, and it would be a mistake to equate Origen and Cyril two centuries later, or Eusebius of Emesa in the early fourth century and Theodoret of Cyrrhus a century later. Earlier research is actually quite clear in maintaining that the Antiochene School was not a school in the sense of an institution, a *Lehranstalt*, but rather a direction of thought, a *Richtung*, as Diestel and Harnack previously wrote in the nineteenth century.[6] The idea that the two schools should be represented equally in the Church is not found in earlier research either. Fairbairn's discussion of this supposed assumption is rather surprising. I quote:[7]

> This assumption also leads scholars to ignore the church's rejection of certain people in this list. Given that Paul of Samosata, Theodore, Diodore, and Nestorius were all condemned by the church, how representative can one really claim the so-called school of Antioch to have been? Given that Origen was condemned by the church, what right do we have to call him the Alexandrian *par excellence*?

A statement like this is of course a total anachronism. Does Fairbairn know that Origen was condemned only 290 years after his death? Or that he had an enormous influence on Athanasius, the Cappadocian Fathers, and Jerome, to name but a few? He was, after all, one of the greatest minds of the Early Church. Erasmus wrote: "a single page of Origen teaches me more of Christian philosophy than

---

3 Fairbairn, Patristic Exegesis and Theology.

4 Diestel, Geschichte des Alten Testamentes; Kihn, Theodor von Mopsuestia und Junilius Africanus. For Harnack, see among others, Harnack/Möller, Antiochenische Schule.

5 Bardy, Recherches sur Saint Lucien d'Antioche, and Schäublin, Untersuchungen zu Methode und Herkunft.

6 Diestel, Geschichte, 126; Harnack/Möller, Antiochenische Schule, 592, and Harnack, Lehrbuch der Dogmengeschichte, 341 n. 1.

7 Fairbairn, Patristic Exegesis and Theology, 3.

ten of Augustine."[8] The fact that he mentions the condemnation of the exegetes Theodore and Diodore, likewise after their deaths, shows again that he is measuring the Church of the fourth century on the basis of later doctrinal standards. For a historian, this is a grave mistake. Such mistakes are made too frequently in recent research unfortunately. Thus John Behr's work on Theodore is a step backwards for scholarship.[9] The twentieth century, through the works of eminent Roman Catholic scholars such as Louis Pirot, Robert Devreesse, Marcel Richard, and Raymond Tonneau, saw a rehabilitation of Theodore of Mopsuestia, recognising that during his lifetime he had always been considered orthodox, and carefully placing his thought within the context of the debates of his time, including the struggle against Apollinarianism. The Eastern Orthodox scholar Behr again measures him against standards that did not apply during the period itself.

Let us move to Fairbairn's second assumption:[10]

> The second assumption is that the Antiochenes were the "good guys" who took Scripture seriously, and the Alexandrians were the "bad guys" who paid little attention to the text itself but instead treated the passage under consideration merely as a jumping-off point for philosophical speculation.

Fairbairn does not quote sources, but others who do invariably refer to a number of scholars who in the 1950s and 1960s embraced the Antiochene approach as the forerunner to historical criticism, which was then being adopted in Roman Catholic teaching and theology. Antiochene exegesis gave them an argument to accept historical critical exegesis. I am speaking for instance about Cardinal Jean Daniélou.[11] But Anglican scholars such as Geoffrey Lampe, Kenneth Woollcombe, and Richard Hanson also saw the Antiochenes in this way.[12]

In my opinion the use or abuse of a historical dichotomy cannot be used as an argument against its existence. Whether the dichotomy existed in history or not, is a question for historians and has nothing to do with presentist use of it. All this may seem very obvious, but unfortunately Fairbairn is just one of many scholars in our day who denies the Alexandrian-Antiochene dichotomy on the basis of the fact that the Antiochenes were seen by some as the champions of historical criticism in the 1950s and 1960s.[13] At least for Fairbairn, the background to his opinion

---

8 Erasmus, *Ep.* 844, ll. 251–253 (ed. P.S. Allen): 'Plus me docet Christianae philosophiae unica Origenis pagina quam decem Augustini.'

9 Behr, The Case against Diodore and Theodore.

10 Fairbairn, Patristic Exegesis and Theology, 3.

11 See, among others, his "Sacramentum futuri" and his "Essai sur le mystère de l'histoire."

12 Lampe/Woollcombe, Essays in Typology, and Hanson, Allegory and Event.

13 Cf. the statement by Frances Young: "The problems with the now traditional account lie, I suggest, in the assumption that Antiochene literalism meant something like modern historicism" (idem,

would seem to be that he is an opponent of historical criticism, and wants to free patristic biblical interpretation from the association with it.[14]

The third and last assumption Fairbairn sees behind the dichotomy is that the different theologies and homiletic emphases of Antioch and Alexandria were the result of different exegetical methods. Ignoring centuries of scholarship, including such detailed works as Christoph Schäublin's *Untersuchungen zu Methode und Herkunft der antiochenischen Exegese*, he states that there are differences between Antioch and Alexandria, but "to assert that these differences were produced by thoroughly distinct exegetical methods is to make an assumption, rather than to state a fact."[15]

Fairbairn continues by stating that the dichotomy is not useful for us because if we are exactly like the Antiochene "good guys" and completely different from the Alexandrian "bad guys," there will be nothing to learn for us in patristic exegesis. A piece of inimitable reasoning … Then his final argument is that there are "many anomalies that create problems for the model of an Antiochene-Alexandrian exegetical dichotomy."[16] He considers the fact "that fathers from the same school, allegedly using the same method, often come to vastly different conclusions" the most serious one. Again, this is a case where he makes a caricature of his opponents. None of them actually says that the methods preferred in Antioch together form a systematic method that in a scientific way should always produce exactly the same results.

Fairbairn then states:[17]

> Externally, the "schools" are not as distinct as they have been made out to be: the Alexandrians do not "allegorize away" the OT as much as has been thought, and the Antiochenes are not necessarily more literal in their methods than the Alexandrians.

Finally he lumps Chrysostom, John of Antioch, and Theodoret with the Alexandrians on the basis of their theology (rather Christology), and concludes that the others, Diodore, Theodore, and Nestorius, were all condemned by the Church. He writes:[18]

> Clearly, then, the Antiochene school was not a significant portion of the early church, nor were the Antiochenes the "good guys" in the mind of the church at that time. They were a tiny minority, and their thought was deemed to be heretical.

Biblical Exegesis, 166). This is, however, certainly not the assumption of all scholars who studied early Christian biblical interpretation in the nineteenth and twentieth centuries.

14 See Fairbairn, Patristic Exegesis and Theology, 18–19.

15 Ibid., 3.

16 Ibid., 6.

17 Ibid., 9–10.

18 Ibid., 15.

This leads him to the conclusion that the notion of an Antiochene School has to be laid aside altogether. Now we can of course say that Fairbairn's argument is anachronistic or even naïve. But this sort of reasoning finds its way into good peer-reviewed journals and into monographs published by presses of high repute. It has become a real fashion.

However, it is important to recognise that just as the Antiochenes were not all the same, also in the modern movement against the Antiochene-Alexandrian dichotomy there are many different voices. Thus that of Frances Young is much more sophisticated than that of Fairbairn. We also see a clear development in her work. Thus in her 1994 article on typology she still states that this term is a construct of twentieth-century scholars who wanted to see the roots of their own historico-critical method in the Antiochene School, and that both the term and the concept are modern: "Typology was never clearly distinguished as a method or procedure in patristic accounts of their own methodology."[19] For her 1997 book *Biblical Exegesis and the Formation of Christian Culture* she had evidently read more primary sources, and started to rethink the question.

The problem is that in her 1997 book, Young would seem not to have chosen between the options of simply saying that modern descriptions of the schools are deficient and saying that the whole opposition between the schools is a modern construct. When she writes that categories such as literal, historical, typological, and allegorical are not sufficient to describe the opposition between the schools, if only because our modern definition of these terms is not that of the ancient exegetes, one can only agree with her. For example, when one describes the Antiochene method as "literal," one would not expect the strong tendency to take moral lessons from the texts. This has much to do with our own preconceptions when hearing these terms. However, in other passages Young's book still reflects the stance of her 1994 article on typology.[20]

What has happened is that in contrast to some other authors, Young has realised the relevance of a number of recently rediscovered texts which show that the idea of typology and the contrast between the schools as such are not (or not only) twentieth-century constructs, but constructs of the fourth century. I am referring especially to methodical treatises and introductions in the Psalms commentaries of Theodore of Mopsuestia[21] and Diodore of Tarsus.[22] She actually discusses one of these texts in her 1997 book, but in my opinion she has not yet been able to reach

19 Young, Typology, 33.

20 The very long footnote 23 on pp. 194–195 of Young, Biblical Exegesis, in fact copies pp. 31–33 of her article "Typology", as she states on p. 192 n. 19.

21 Van Rompay, Théodore de Mopsueste.

22 Mariès, Extraits du commentaire de Diodore de Tarse sur les Psaumes, and Olivier, Diodori Tarsensis Commentarii in Psalmos 1.

a full new synthesis here. Thus in Chapter 8 she gives one of the most lucid explanations of the difference between allegory and typology, whereas elsewhere she still holds that "Typology is a modern construct" and that "Ancient exegetes did not distinguish between typology and allegory" (which are, as we shall see, errors of fact).[23] In any case, she has come to realise that a flat denial of the opposition between the schools is not borne out by the sources, especially since the publication of the newly discovered texts.

My position would be that our description of the distinction needs to be broadened through further mapping of the actual practice of Antiochene and Alexandrian hermeneutics. The way out is simple: the opposition between the schools may be a construct, but then it is a construct of the fourth century. It was taken seriously and was seen as essential at the time. Therefore Antiochenes did write commentaries which are different from the Alexandrian ones. The description of the differences should be done with care, and should also take the many points of agreement into account. We have to reach beyond the surface of the Antiochene and Alexandrian self-descriptions. Hagit Amirav has done precisely this in her book *Rhetoric and Tradition*, a study on the Antiochene John Chrysostom,[24] and I have done the same for Eusebius of Emesa.[25] In her ERC project Amirav is interested in the way the opposition was constructed. In other words: what is the *motivation* behind the establishment of the schools in question as a key element in the consolidation of Christian identities?[26]

Marking Boundaries in Antiochene Theoretical Statements

In the second part of this paper we will be looking at the way Diodore of Tarsus and Theodore of Mopsuestia are delineating the boundaries between acceptable exegesis and inacceptable forms of interpretation. Chronologically we should start with Diodore, and we will discuss the Prologue to the Psalms commentary attributed to him as well as the Preface to Psalm 118.[27] As the text by Theodore is incomplete, I will treat it more cursorily here.

Diodore begins his Prologue very significantly with a quotation from Paul, which summarises the Antiochene approach to the Old Testament: "All Scripture is inspired by God and profitable for teaching, for reproof, for correction, for training in righteousness" (2 Tim 3:16). For the Antiochenes the Old Testament

23 Young, Biblical Exegesis, 152.

24 Amirav, Rhetoric and Tradition.

25 Romeny, A Syrian in Greek Dress.

26 Amirav, The Christian Appropriation of the Jewish Scriptures.

27 The translations of Diodore quoted are by Froehlich, Biblical Interpretation, 82–94.

was indeed a source of moral instructions. It reports on God's pedagogic approach to humanity. As Diodore says: "Scripture teaches what is useful, exposes what is sinful, corrects what is deficient, and thus it completes the perfect human being." He explains that the Psalms can be used for thanksgiving, but also as a remedy for suffering, as the Holy Spirit "anticipated all kinds of human situations." Especially in such circumstances we come to understand the Psalms. He contrasts this with the situation in which "we are just chanting the Psalms." He stresses that he is giving an exposition of the Psalms precisely to make sure that "the brothers" would understand their meaning even when chanting them.

Diodore continues discussing the subject matter of the Psalms, which according to him "is divided into two categories: ethical and doctrinal." He then gives further subdivisions. For the doctrinal Psalms, there are two: "some Psalms argue against the idea that all beings are self-moved, others against the claim that not all beings are subject to divine providence." He adds that there are also other subjects, such as the Babylonian captivity and the times of the Maccabees.

For the Antiochenes the historical context of the authors was very important. Hence the following statement:[28]

> Let us begin now, following the order of items in the Book of Psalms itself, not the order of events which they reflect. For the psalms are not arranged in chronological order but in the order of their discovery. Numerous psalms will provide evidence of this, most strikingly a comparison of the inscription of Psalm 3, "A Psalm of David when he fled from the face of his son Absalom," with the inscription of Psalm 143, "A song against Goliath." Who does not know that the Goliath episode occurred much earlier than the events concerning Absalom? The psalms suffered much displacement because the book was accidentally lost during the Babylonian captivity. Afterwards, about the time of Ezra, it was rediscovered, though not the whole book at once but piecemeal—one, two, or perhaps three psalms at a time. These were then reassembled in the order in which they were found, not as they were arranged originally. Hence, even the inscriptions are mostly incorrect; more often than not, the collectors tried to guess the context of the psalms they found but did not treat them according to a scholarly method.

Here we find an interest in the chronology of events and a critical attitude towards the text as handed down to us. Is this historical criticism as we know it today? Perhaps not in the sense that the text is treated as a document providing data which could help us to reconstruct the historical reality of the events mentioned in it, but it is clear that the line between Diodore's statement and our historical criticism is thinner than for instance Frances Young would like to admit,[29] especially where we see that Diodore eliminates the inscriptions to the Psalms as later additions. Among Alexandrians there was also an interest in factual data, but it would be

28 Ibid., 85.

29 Cf. Young, Biblical Exegesis, 167.

hard to find a text matching this one. It is a typical early Antiochene trait to accept translation errors in the Septuagint, at least before Theodore.[30] Here Diodore goes even one step further, stressing the human hand in collecting the biblical texts and allowing for errors, not just of translation, but also in the addition of headings.

Diodore continues:[31]

> Nevertheless, with the help of God, we shall attempt an explanation even of these errors as far as this is possible. We will not shrink from the truth but will expound it according to the historical substance (*historia*) and the plain literal sense (*lexis*). At the same time, we will not disparage anagogy and the higher *theōria*. For history is not opposed to *theōria*. On the contrary, it proves to be the foundation and the basis of the higher senses. One thing is to be watched, however: *theōria* must never be understood as doing away with the underlying sense; it would then be no longer *theōria* but allegory. For wherever anything else is said apart from the foundational sense, we have not *theōria* but allegory.

This is one of the classic statements delineating the boundaries between good and bad exposition according to the Antiochenes. Let us look at it more in detail. Obviously the references to *historia* and *lexis* would seem to confirm the idea of a historical and literal reading. But the meaning of the terms should be clarified further. *Historia* is not history in our sense,[32] but rather refers to the narrative and its historical context. The sequence of events in the narrative and the fabric of the text as a whole, the *akolouthia*, were very important to Antiochenes. *Lexis* is here the plain text as opposed to the explanation. Behind the use of this term is the understanding that by way of principle, the text of the Bible is clear and has a single meaning.[33] This stands in marked contrast to Origen's approach. As Marguérite Harl has pointed out, obscurity was an essential element of the biblical text for him. According to Origen's theory of language "words are signs that refer to a reality without reaching it; the mystery is 'above what is written.'"[34] It was the divine Economy which inserted "stumbling-blocks, offences, and impossibilities" which disabled a literal understanding in order to point the reader to the higher sense, which is often hidden "*apo tōn pollōn.*"[35] A good illustration of this is found in the following striking passage from Origen's *On First Principles*:[36]

30 On this, see Romeny, A Syrian in Greek Dress, 100–139.

31 Froehlich, Biblical Interpretation, 85.

32 On this, see Young, Biblical Exegesis, 79–80.

33 See Romeny, A Syrian in Greek Dress, 99, 117–118, and also Fragment I.

34 Harl, La Septante, 253–266, and idem, Origène, 334–371. The quotation is from Origen's *Comm. Jo.* 13,31 (ed. Blanc, Commentaire, 48).

35 Origenes, *Princ.* 4,2,9: Crouzel/Simonetti, Origène, 334–340.

36 Origenes, *Princ.* 4,3,1: Crouzel/Simonetti, Origène, 340–344. English translation quoted here from Froehlich, Biblical Interpretation, 63.

What intelligent person can believe that there was a first day, then a second and third day, evening, and morning, without the sun, the moon, and the stars; and the first day—if this is the right term—even without a heaven [Gen. 1:5–6]? Who is foolish enough to believe that, like a human farmer, God planted a garden to the east in Eden and created in it a visible, physical tree of life from which anyone tasting its fruit with bodily teeth would receive life, and that one would have a part in good and evil by eating the fruit picked from the appropriate tree [Gen. 2:8–9]? When God is depicted walking in the garden in the evening and Adam hiding behind the tree, I think no one will doubt that these details point figuratively to some mysteries by means of a historical narrative which seems to have happened but did not happen in a bodily sense.

Let us return to Diodore. It is clear that he would never follow Origen in denying the reality of the Creation narrative. Nevertheless we have just seen that he does say: "At the same time, we will not disparage anagogy and the higher *theōria*." This is potentially confusing, as the term *theōria* was also used by Alexandrians for allegory. Therefore Diodore adds: "For history is not opposed to *theōria*. On the contrary, it proves to be the foundation and the basis of the higher senses. One thing is to be watched, however: *theōria* must never be understood as doing away with the underlying sense; it would then be no longer *theōria* but allegory." What is apparently the crucial difference between his conception of *theōria* and allegory is whether one recognises the underlying sense as something that has truly happened or discards it. This is a very clear boundary.

Next Diodore has to deal with the fact that Paul himself also uses the term allegory, that is, in Galatians 4:22–24 (nrsv):

22 For it is written that Abraham had two sons, one by a slave woman and one by a free woman. 23 But the son of the slave was born according to the flesh, while the son of the free woman was born through promise. 24 Now this is said by way of allegory, for these women are two covenants.

Diodore explains:[37]

Even the apostle did not discard history at any point although he could introduce *theōria* and call it allegory. He was not ignorant of the term but was teaching us that, if the term "allegory" is judged by its conceptual content, it must be taken in the sense of *theōria*, not violating in any way the nature of the historical substance.

In short: it is obvious that Abraham really had two sons, so Paul may have used the term allegory, but we have to understand that as *theōria*. On the other hand there are those who "have introduced allegory because they are careless about the historical substance, or they simply abuse it. They follow not the apostle's intention but their own vain imagination, forcing to take one thing for another." Diodore

37 Froehlich, Biblical Interpretation, 85–86.

also gives samples: they interpret the word "abyss" as demon and the word "dragon" as devil, in the sense that there is no real dragon, just the devil. "Responsible theorizing" is different according to him, and again an example follows:[38]

> We may compare, for example, Cain and Abel to the Jewish synagogue and the church; we may attempt to show that like Cain's sacrifice the Jewish synagogue was rejected, while the offerings of the church are being well received as was Abel's offering at that time; we may interpret the unblemished sacrificial lamb required by the law as the Lord. This method neither sets aside history nor repudiates *theōria.*

Here obviously Cain and Abel did exist, but they also point forward to what happened later with the synagogue and the church.

Frances Young speaks of "ikonic and symbolic mimesis," associating the former with Antiochene *theōria* and the latter with allegory.[39] She explains that in ikonic exegesis the text is taken as a coherent whole and the deeper meaning is a mirror image of it. In symbolic exegesis or allegory, however, words are symbols or tokens referring to other realities according to a code. The latter approach destroys the coherent narrative. The word we use for the Antiochene *theōria* is typology, which is less ambiguous. Despite her criticism of the term, even Young accepts it as useful to some extent.[40] And indeed, why would we reject it? The term as such is new, but the procedure to see an event described in the narrative as the foreshadowing of another event is described very clearly here by Diodore. Antiochenes also used the term *typos*, so why should we reject "typology"?

Finally Diodore adds a piece of rhetoric on the position of his own method:[41]

> Rather, as a realistic, middle-of-the-road approach which takes into account both history and *theōria*, it frees us, on the one hand, from a Hellenism which says one thing for another and introduces foreign subject matter; on the other hand, it does not yield to Judaism and choke us by forcing us to treat the literal reading of the text as the only one worthy of attention and honor, while not allowing the exploration of a higher sense beyond the letter also.

In other words: allegory is Hellenism and accepting only the letter of the text is Judaism. The conclusion is clear: Christians should stay clear from both extremes and follow the middle-of-the-road approach. I am calling this a rhetorical device as the association of allegory with Hellenism is only half the truth: Diodore's own method was based on the education of the pagan grammarians and rhetors and therefore not less Hellenistic. Likewise the association with Judaism is only half

38 Ibid., 86.

39 Young, Biblical Exegesis, 161–162.

40 Idem, Typology, 35, and idem, Biblical Exegesis, 193.

41 Froehlich, Biblical Interpretation, 86.

the story: the text can be taken at face value in Judaism, but the midrashim show very many examples of non-literal interpretations.

Interestingly both Diodore and his pupil Theodore of Mopsuestia also wrote Prefaces to the very long Psalm 118 in the Old Greek version, that is 119 in the Hebrew Bible. The reason for this, according to Diodore, is that it contains much figurative language. The Alexandrians often took such language literally, which forced them to allegorise it. The Antiochenes therefore found it important to recognise and classify figurative expressions, and to indicate again the boundaries between this sort of language and allegory. Diodore therefore starts by explaining, again with reference to the letter to the Galatians, that Scripture "knows the term allegory" but not its application. He also explains what allegory is:[42]

> The Greeks speak of allegory when something is understood in one way but said in another. […] The Greeks say that Zeus, changing himself into a bull, seized Europa and carried her across the sea to foreign places. This story is not understood as it reads but is taken to mean that Europa was carried across the sea having boarded a ship with a bull as figurehead. A real bull could not possibly swim such a distance across the ocean.

His second example is that Zeus called Hera his sister and his wife. According to the Greeks there was not really such an incestuous relationship, but the text is about ether mingling with air. These examples are significant in at least two ways: first of all, they allow him again to make a connection between allegory and the Greeks, that is, the pagans. Second, the point he makes clearly echoes the criticism of the pagan philosopher Porphyry, who wrote a fierce intellectual attack on Christianity just before the Diocletianic persecutions.[43] He states that allegory is a way to interpret myths, but as the Bible is history rather than mythology, allegory cannot be applied. Antiochenes took this seriously.

Returning to the text, we see that Diodore repeats again that the underlying prior history is never repudiated when a higher vision, a *theōria*, is developed, and explains:[44]

> The fact that the apostle[45] "theorizes" in this way does not mean that he repudiates the historical account. For who could persuade him to say that the story of Hagar and Sarah was untrue? With the historical account as his firm foundation, he develops his *theōria* on top of it; he understands the underlying facts as events on a higher level.

---

42 Ibid., 87.

43 It was quoted in full by Eusebius of Caesarea, *Hist. eccl.* 6,19,1–11 (Schwartz, Eusebius, 556–562); see also Romeny, Question-and-Answer Collections, 152.

44 Froehlich, Biblical Interpretation, 88.

45 Here he is again referring to Galatians 4.

Diodore then starts explaining about the forms of figurative language that we do find in the Bible. He mentions the example of Ps 79:9 OG: "You (God) removed a vine from Egypt." This he calls "tropologia." We would indeed call it a trope or metaphor. What is crucial, according to Diodore, is the fact that Scripture itself identifies the vine with the people. The next form he mentions is what he calls parabolic language (we would perhaps rather speak of a simile), which he says "is easy to recognize when it follows upon an introductory 'like' or 'as.'" Though "by way of ellipsis" this introduction may be omitted, as in "You have made my arm a brazen bow" (Ps 17:35 OG). Scripture also frequently calls a narrative a "parable" or sometimes "problem" or "enigma." He continues:[46]

> One would probably classify much of the material in the books of Moses as enigmas (*ainigmata*) rather than allegories. When the author writes: "The serpent said to the woman", "the woman said to the serpent"; "God said to the serpent", we have enigmas. Not that there was no serpent; indeed there was a serpent, but the devil acted through it. Moses speaks of the serpent as the visible animal but under this cover hints at the devil in a hidden way. If this was allegory, only the word "serpent" should be there [and no real serpent] as "we explained earlier. The truth is that there was both a reality and an enigma. The reality was the serpent but, since a serpent is by nature irrational and yet was speaking, it is obvious that it spoke empowered by the devil.

Thus he concludes his explanation of figurative expressions. He adds an important issue, namely that of prophecy. The Antiochenes saw in fact much of the Bible as prophecy. Thus he says: "this psalm accompanies generations of human beings, conforming itself to events both actual and on a higher plane." What he means is that a description of an event in the past may also refer to events in the future. An example: in Ps 29 Hezekiah says "you have brought up my soul from Hades," which applies in what he calls a hyperbolic way to the actual event of healing from his very serious illness, but it also fits in a non-hyperbolic way the situation in the future when he rises from the dead.

As indicated, I shall deal more briefly with Theodore of Mopsuestia, whose Preface to Psalm 118 came down to us under the secondary title "Treatise against the Allegorists." It has been preserved in a Syriac translation, but the copy which we have seems to go back to an original which was damaged, as several half lines have been kept empty, and it would also seem that the beginning is missing. Therefore it is not entirely clear whether the most conspicuous difference between this text and Diodore's Preface goes back to a conscious choice or is accidental. The thing is that the two Prefaces deal with the same issues, except that Theodore does not pay attention to the higher sense or *theōria*. This may be significant, as he actually limited the use of typology in this commentary: only four Psalms receive a

46 Froehlich, Biblical Interpretation, 90.

Christological interpretation. It also appears that he, in his explanation of the passage from Galatians, does not use the word type or *theōria*: he seems to think rather of a comparison.

Otherwise Theodore appears to deal with much the same issues as Diodore. He too discussed figurative speech, giving many examples, including some also given by Diodore. What is new is that he makes it explicit that the use of metaphors or enigmas is part of biblical language. The point he makes is that anyone who does not know the specific nature of biblical language could misunderstand an expression like "You have made my arm a brazen bow," but that to those in the know it is clear that we should understand "You have made my arm *like* a brazen bow." The concept of biblical language and the idioms of Scripture has its basis in Greek philology, which paid attention to the idioms and style of an author.[47] The first application among Antiochenes can be seen in Diodore's comments on the Psalms, but Theodore went much further and would seem to have given long lists of *idiōmata* in his lost introduction to the Psalms.[48]

Like Diodore, Theodore also stresses that by using allegorical interpretation the historical narrative is denied. There is a clear difference between recognising figurative language as part of the way the biblical authors expressed themselves, and allegorising interpretation which breaks the narrative and reads something different into the text, making it look, as Theodore says, "mendacious and false." Here he also mentions the fact that pagans applied allegorical interpretation to myths exactly because the myths were totally untrue and indecent. So by applying it to the Bible, one suggests the Bible is as false as those stories, whereas in reality it is useful and instructive. If ever it mentions anything indecent it is in order to teach us not to do it, he says. We find here a clear echo of Porphyry's criticism. In this context it is important to note that Theodore does not mention Hellenism and Judaism as the two extremes. He concentrates on refuting allegory and gives a historical outline of the application of allegory to the Bible, stating that it was Philo who first did this, after he had learnt this method from the pagans. It was then Origen who would have followed Philo and introduced it to the Church.

Here he also shows another reason why he deemed allegory dangerous: not only did Origen sometimes interpret this way and sometimes that way, he also used allegory to introduce false ideas. Here Theodore mentions the idea that we would rise from the dead in a different body, that our soul existed before our birth, and that the soul of God would be his Son. Also defenders of adoptionist and anomoian ideas about the relation between the Father and the Son would have found support in his works. One can hardly be mistaken in seeing here the influence of

---

47 Schäublin, Untersuchungen, 128. On the way Theodore used the recognition of *idiōmata* as an alternative to direct recourse to the original text, see Kamesar, Jerome, 175, cf. 158–159.

48 Devreesse, Essai, 58 with n. 2, and cf. 58–68.

the Origenist controversy, which began around Diodore's death. Though the fear that wrong doctrines could be introduced through allegorical interpretation may always have been an issue, it really becomes acute here. For Diodore and before him Eusebius of Emesa, Porphyry's criticism was still the major issue.

Epilogue

By way of conclusion we can say that the main boundary line we have come across is that according to the Antiochenes the texture and consistency of the narrative should not be broken. An interpretation which applies some sort of code to give different meanings to single words is what needs to be avoided. For Diodore there was still another line he did not want to cross: the risk of being too literal. Hence his instance on typology or, as he calls it, *theōria*. For Theodore, perhaps because of the Origenist controversy and the Christological debate, the risk of being too literal seems to have faded away. In practice we see that his application of typology is in fact rather limited. For both authors, however, it is clear that there is yet another boundary: that between the Old and the New Testament eras.

If we look at the respect paid to the main boundary line mentioned above, early Antiochenes such as Eusebius of Emesa, Diodore, and Theodore are rather consistent. It is important to see that problems in the text were often classified as follows: there were ambiguous or imprecise expressions, inconsistencies, obscurities, inappropriate expressions, and impossibilities.[49] The first categories was treated equally by Antiochenes and Alexandrians: with the help of the methods of the grammarians, applying the rule that the text can be explained on the basis of the text itself by looking at the context and similar passages, and by paraphrasing. The latter categories were those which Origen saw as the "stumbling-blocks" pointing to higher interpretations. Here the Antiochenes would not follow him. They often dealt with the same problems, but had to use other strategies. They had to use the methods of the grammarians more consistently. Sometimes they also pointed out that an impossibility was not really an impossibility, but an enigma. And Eusebius and Diodore also changed the text now and then on the basis of the Hebrew or the Syrian; Theodore stopped doing that, but was able to use the idea of biblical idioms.

Much of the confusion in modern research on Patristic exegesis may have to do with the fact that the developments within the two schools are overlooked. Thus it is important to recognise that Theodoret of Cyrrhus was much less strict than Diodore and Theodore. He also tended to see the Old and New Testaments as one single whole, which his predecessors had not done. On the Alexandrian side, however,

49 See Romeny, A Syrian in Greek Dress, 101–105 with n. 64.

Cyril was also really a different exegete than Origen. He is applying allegory much less, and from him one would not expect the sort of scathing statement that Origen made on God planting Paradise. It would seem that the schools were slowly growing in each other's direction and that boundaries had begun to become less divisive.

Literature

Sources

Allen, Percy S. (ed.), Selections from Erasmus: Principally from his Epistles Erasmus, New Rochelle, N.Y. [2]1983.
Blanc, Cécile (ed.), Commentaire sur Saint Jean 3 (SC 222), Paris 1975.
Crouzel, Henri/Simonetti, Manlio (ed.), Origène. Traité des principes 3. Livres III et IV (SC 268), Paris 1980.
Mariès, Louis (ed.), Extraits du commentaire de Diodore de Tarse sur les Psaumes. Préface du commentaire – Prologue du Psaume cxviii, RSR 9 (1919), 79–101.
Olivier, Jean-Marie (ed.), Diodori Tarsensis Commentarii in Psalmos 1. Commentarii in Psalmos I-L (CCSG 6), Turnhout 1980.
Schwartz, Eduard (ed.), Eusebius Werke 2. Die Kirchengeschichte 2 (GCS 9,2), Leipzig 1908.
Van Rompay, Lucas (ed. and transl.), Théodore de Mopsueste. Fragments syriaques du Commentaire des Psaumes (Psaume 118 et Psaumes 138–148) (2 vols.; CSCO 435–436, Script. Syr. 189–190), Leuven 1982.

Scholarly Works

Amirav, Hagit, The Christian Appropriation of the Jewish Scriptures: Allegory, Pauline Exegesis, and the Negotiation of Religious Identities, ASEs 28 (2011), 39–55.
—, Rhetoric and Tradition: John Chrysostom on Noah and the Flood (TEG 12), Leuven 2003.
Bardy, Gustave, Recherches sur Saint Lucien d'Antioche et son école (Études de theologie historique), Paris 1936.
Behr, John, The Case against Diodore and Theodore. Texts and Their Contexts (OECT), Oxford 2011.
Daniélou, Jean, Essai sur le mystère de l'histoire, Paris 1953.
—, Sacramentum futuri: études sur les origines de la typologie biblique, Paris 1950.
Devreesse, Robert, Essai sur Théodore de Mopsueste (Studi e Testi 141), Vatican City 1948.
Diestel, Ludwig, Geschichte des Alten Testamentes in der christlichen Kirche, Jena 1869.
Fairbairn, Donald, Patristic Exegesis and Theology: The Cart and the Horse, WThJ 69 (2007), 1–19.
Froehlich, Karlfried, Biblical Interpretation in the Early Church (Sources of Early Christian Thought), Philadelphia, Pa. 1984.
Hanson, Richard P. C., Allegory and Event, London 1959.

Harl, Marguérite, La Septante et la pluralité textuelle des Écritures. Le témoignage des Pères grecs, in: idem (ed.), La langue de Japhet. Quinze études sur la Septante et le grec des chrétiens, Paris 1992, 253–266, also in: Naissance de la méthode critique. Colloque du centenaire de l'École biblique et archéologique française et de Jérusalem (Patrimoines. Christianisme), Paris 1992, 231–243.

—, Origène et les interprétations patristiques grecques de l'«obscurité» biblique, VC 36 (1982), 334–371.

Harnack, Adolf, Lehrbuch der Dogmengeschichte 2. Die Entwickelung des kirchlichen Dogmas 1, Tübingen [4]1909.

—/ Möller, E. W., Antiochenische Schule, in Realencyklopädie für protestantische Theologie und Kirche 1, Leipzig [3]1896, 592–595.

Kamesar, Adam, Jerome, Greek Scholarship, and the Hebrew Bible. A Study of the Quaestiones Hebraicae in Genesim (OCM), Oxford 1993.

Kihn, Heinrich, Theodor von Mopsuestia und Junilius Africanus als Exegeten, Freiburg i.Br. 1880.

Lampe, Geoffrey W. H./Woollcombe, Kenneth J., Essays in Typology (SBT 22), London 1957.

Romeny, R. B. ter Haar, Question-and-Answer Collections in Syriac Literature, in: A. Volgers/ C. Zamagni (ed.), Erotapokriseis. Early Christian Question-and-Answer Literature in Context (CBET 37), Leuven 2004, 145–163.

Schäublin, Christoph, Untersuchungen zu Methode und Herkunft der Antiochenischen Exegese (Theophaneia 23), Köln/Bonn 1974.

Slade, Darren M., Patristic Exegesis. The Myth of the Alexandrian-Antiochene Schools of Interpretation, Socio-Historical Examination of Religion and Ministry 1 (2019), 155–176.

—, A Syrian in Greek Dress. The Use of Greek, Hebrew, and Syriac Biblical Texts in Eusebius of Emesa's Commentary on Genesis (TEG 6), Leuven 1997.

Young, Frances M., Typology, in: S. E. Porter/P. Joyce/D. E. Orton (ed.), Crossing the Boundaries. Essays in Biblical Interpretation in Honour of Michael D. Goulder (BiInS 8), Leiden 1994, 29–48.

—, Biblical Exegesis and the Formation of Christian Culture, Cambridge 1997.

Predrag Bukovec (KU Linz)

Auslegung in Abgrenzung

Antijüdische Bibelexegese bei Aphrahat dem Persischen Weisen

1. Aphrahat und seine Demonstrationen

Manche großen Geister der Alten Kirche treten völlig hinter ihr Werk zurück: Anders als bei Ps.-Dionysius Areopagita wissen wir wenigstens, dass Aphrahat sein richtiger Name war. Das einzige von ihm erhaltene Werk, die Demonstrationen (syr. ܬܚܘ̈ܝܬܐ), gibt nicht vor, aus apostolischer Zeit zu stammen, und wurde auch nicht so rezipiert: Es galt immer als Werk eines einzelnen Autors namens Aphrahat.

Doch wer war dieser Aphrahat? Kenntnisse über ihn erhält man allein aus interner Evidenz, d. h. aus Passagen, in denen der Autor der *Demonstrationen* über sich selbst spricht oder en passant Hinweise gibt: Aphrahat muss ein Gelehrter in einer leitenden Funktion gewesen sein, ein Geistlicher, aber kein ordinierter Kleriker.[1] Seine Autorität kann auch daran ermessen werden, dass er für sich die Bußgewalt in Anspruch nimmt und sein Werk als geistliche Führung in Erscheinung tritt, das auf die gestellten Fragen eines Mitbruders antwortet. Allerdings spricht hier nicht ein Bischof, sondern eine den Bundessöhnen nahestehende Respektsperson.[2]

1 Siehe Aphrahat, *Dem.* 14,25. Vgl. auch Lizorkin, Aphrahat's Demonstrations, 4.

2 Siehe Aphrahat, *Dem.* 6,4; 18,1. Die Bundessöhne und -töchter sind ein Phänomen des frühen syrischen Monastizismus: Es handelt sich um eine asketische Gemeinschaft, die als eigener Stand innerhalb der Gemeinden (d. h. nicht in der Wüste wie in Ägypten) ein evangeliumsgemäßes Leben führen wollte. Aphrahat widmet seine *Dem.* 6 den Bundessöhnen, aber auch andere Demonstrationen befassen sich mit Inhalten, die thematisch nahestehen, z. B. Aphrahat, *Dem.* 3 (Fasten), 4 (Gebet), 7 (Büßer) und 9 (Demut). Offenbar trat man in die Gemeinschaft im Zusammenhang mit der eigenen Taufe ein (Erwachsenentaufe): Sie wird als Eintritt in den eschatologischen Bund Christi verstanden, und auf diesen Bund vereidigt man sich bei der Initiation. Es ist zu beachten, dass das Wort für Bund, syr. ܩܝܡܐ, etymologisch und semantisch ein breites Spektrum an Bedeutungen bereithält: So hängt der „Bund" als Vereidigung und Stand sowohl mit den biblisch vorgegebenen Bedeutungsnuancen zusammen als auch durch die Verbalwurzel QWM „aufstehen" mit der Auferstehung. Die Taufe ist die realsymbolische Realisation dieser eschatologischen Seinsweise, als Sohn/Tochter des Bundes eröffnet sie (siehe Gal 3,28) die *Vita angelica* und die Einswerdung mit Christus (vgl. *Dem.* 6,19; 8,16; 18,5). Die Angleichung an den Herrn wird terminologisch durch die Alternativbezeichnung „Einzelne" (syr. ܝܚܝ̈ܕܝܐ) eingefangen, denn Jesus Christus ist der „Einzelne" (Einziggeborene) schlechthin und deswegen Prototyp für den Asketen, siehe auch Aphrahat, *Dem.* 6,6–8; 7,25. Siehe auch Greschat, Taten und Verkündigung der

Die 23 *Demonstrationen* sind alphabetisch gereiht, jede beginnt mit einem Buchstaben des syrischen Alphabets, bis die 23. Abhandlung wieder mit Ālaf einsetzt. Sie sind Antworten eines frühen syrischen Gelehrten auf die Probleme seiner Gegenwart und bezeugen eine Vielfalt von theologischen, ethischen und spirituellen Themen, die als geistliche Reflexionen Mitbrüdern und -schwestern Orientierung bei den Herausforderungen der syrischsprachigen Christen im Sassanidenreich geben sollten. Wir erfahren viel über das Christentum hinter der Grenze der römischen Oikumene, das seine eigene Ausprägung entwickelte[3] und eigene Diskurse hatte, welche manchmal wenig mit den westlichen Glaubensgeschwistern zu tun hatten. In den *Demonstrationen* kommen im Westen unbekannte Gruppen vor wie die genannten Bundessöhne und -töchter; gleichzeitig bekommt man alternative Antworten auf Fragen, die man sich im Römischen Reich auch stellte:[4] Wie soll man sich zum Staat und zum Krieg verhalten? Wie lebt man als guter Christ/gute Christin? Was entgegnet man Juden in der Nachbarschaft, wenn man mit ihnen über Religion diskutiert? Diese letzte Frage soll in diesem Beitrag im Vordergrund stehen.

Die *Demonstrationen* sind in zwei Schüben entstanden: Die ersten zehn Abhandlungen wurden 336/7 n.Chr. verfasst, wenn wir das in seleukidischer Zeitrechnung gegebene Datum in *Dem.* 10,9 übersetzen.[5] Da das Werk von Anfang an akrostichisch angelegt wurde (s. o.), scheint es auf Fortsetzung angelegt gewesen zu sein; die zweite Lieferung (*Dem.* 11–22) schreibt Aphrahat aber erst 344 n.Chr. nieder (vgl. auch *Dem.* 14,50). Ein Jahr später folgt, gleichsam als Postludium, die 23. *Demonstration*, die Kernthemen des Gesamtwerks zusammenführt.[6] Aphrahat sagt

zwölf Apostel, 399; Richter, Über die älteste Auseinandersetzung, 111; Lizorkin, Demonstrations, 4; Abouzayd, Iḥidayutha, 97; Brock, Early Syrian Asceticism; Griffith, Monks; Murray, The Features; Vööbus, History of Asceticism.

3 Auch liturgiegeschichtlich sind Besonderheiten zu verzeichnen, die Aphrahat als Referenzgröße wichtig erscheinen lassen: So hat etwa das Pascha, dem *Dem.* 12 gewidmet ist, einen quartadezimanischen Kontext und steht eindeutig unter „karfreitagstheologischen", passionschristologischen Vorzeichen. Interessant ist, dass trotz der semantischen Konnotationen in Richtung „Auferstehung", die die Taufe für die Bundessöhne/-töchter besitzt (siehe vorherige Anm.), an diesem Tauftermin das Kreuz und nicht die Auferstehung dominiert. Siehe auch Greschat, Taten, 410–412; Snaith, Aphrahat and the Jews, 243; Koltun-Fromm, Jewish-Christian Conversation, 141–147; Lizorkin, Demonstrations, 108, 131.

4 Aphrahat erwähnt das Konzil von Nizäa (325 n.Chr.) nicht und folgt in der Trinitätstheologie und Christologie der altsyrischen Terminologie, siehe auch Snaith, Aphrahat, 238; Lizorkin, Demonstrations, 3; Bruns, Das Christusbild Aphrahats. Er ist ganz oberflächlich über die Konstantinische Wende unterrichtet, da die Christenverfolgungen im Perserreich eine Reaktion auf den Status der Christen im Römischen Reich waren. Das letzte Ereignis, wovon er bessere Kenntnis besitzt, sind die Diokletianischen Verfolgungen, siehe Aphrahat, *Dem.* 21,23.

5 Aus Aphrahat, *Dem.* 5,1 geht ferner hervor, dass Aphrahat aus Anlass der Kriegsvorbereitungen der Perser gegen die Römer nach Konstantins Tod schrieb.

6 Greschat, Taten, 401.

selbst in *Dem.* 23,69, dass er nach der Abfassung von *Dem.* 1–22 als letztes einen Nachtrag geben wollte, der gleichzeitig Zusammenfassung ist.[7]

Da als Datierungsgrundlage nur die interne Evidenz in Frage kommt, weiß man auch nichts Konkretes über den Todeszeitpunkt des Autors. Die Annahme von Eliyahu Lizorkin, Aphrahat sei als Märtyrer gestorben, da mit *Dem.* 23 eine zweite Serie akrostichischer Traktate beginne, aber unvollendet blieb,[8] scheitert daran, dass der Autor doch selbst sagt, dass die letzte Demonstration eher als Summarium zu verstehen ist (s. o.). Wir wissen über das weitere Leben Aphrahats nach 345 n.Chr. nichts.

So harmonisch die alphabetische Abfolge von Traktaten auch aussieht, so ist jedoch die Zäsur zwischen den zwei Schaffensperioden nicht nur zeitlich gegeben, sondern spiegelt sich ebenfalls im Tonfall und der inhaltlichen Disposition wider. Erst ab 344 n.Chr. gerät das Judentum als Gegner derart stark in den Vordergrund,[9] während sich in *Dem.* 1–10 zwar auch polemische Passagen finden, aber die innerchristlichen Diskurse und Probleme vorherrschten. Ab *Dem.* 11 folgt eine kontroverstheologische Debatte nach der anderen: Was ist in der Zwischenzeit passiert?

Ein Interregnum ist – das lehrt die Geschichte – ein willkommener Kriegsanlass. Konstantins d. Gr. Tod (337 n.Chr.) und die folgenden innerdynastischen Wirren um seine Nachfolge destabilisierten auch in den Augen des Großkönigs das Römische Reich. Konstantins Brief an den Herrscher im Osten, der von Eusebius wiedergegeben wird (*Vit. Const.* 4,9–13), appellierte an einen guten Umgang mit den Christen im Perserreich; auf der anderen Seite gab es römische Kriegsvorbereitungen noch zu seinen Lebzeiten. Diese Signale lenkten die Aufmerksamkeit der persischen Regierung auf die Minderheit der Christen, deren Loyalität nun in Frage stand. Das für die Sassaniden geopolitisch relevante Geschehen im Kaukasus, wo Armenien bereits das Christentum als Staatsreligion angenommen hatte (traditionell um 301 n.Chr.), machte die Anhänger dieses Glaubens der Westbindung verdächtig. Großkönig Šāβuhr II. (309–379 n.Chr.) erhob eine eigene Kopfsteuer nur für Christen zur Refinanzierung seiner militärischen Anstrengungen gegen das christlich gewordene Rom. Bei Aphrahat spürt man den Loyalitätskonflikt, der durch diese Situation entstanden ist: Eine eschatologisch aufgeheizte Atmosphäre wurde spürbar, da Rom nach Dan 2 und 7 als letztes der Weltreiche verstanden wurde (vgl. *Dem.* 5).[10] Die Verweigerung des Bischofs Simeon bar Sabbaʿe im Jahr 338 n.Chr., die Kopfsteuer zu entrichten,[11] ahndeten die Autoritäten hart: Sein Martyrium wurde der Auftakt der sassanidischen Christenverfolgung. In diesem Klima schrieb Aphrahat.

---

7 In Aphrahat, *Dem.* 22,25 rekapitulierte er bereits das bislang Geschriebene.

8 Vgl. Lizorkin, Demonstrations, 6.

9 Vgl. Snaith, Aphrahat, 235.

10 S. auch Tubach, Die syrische Danielrezeption.

11 Vgl. Koltun-Fromm, Conversation, 65; Lizorkin, Demonstrations, 5.

Doch warum dann die Juden als Gegner? Anders als die Christen waren die Juden im Sassanidenreich als religiöse Minderheit vergleichsweise privilegiert,[12] obwohl im 3. Jahrhundert die Karter-Inschrift die Christen ebenso wie die Juden, Buddhisten, Manichäer und andere zu den religiös zu verfolgenden Untertanen zählt.[13] Im 4. Jahrhundert änderte sich offenbar die Situation zumindest für die jüdischen Bewohner des Perserreichs wieder. Die persische Herrschaft ist ferner im AT durchaus positiv konnotiert, wenn man sich das Kyros-Edikt Esr 6,2–5 vergegenwärtigt oder das Buch Ester. Jedenfalls wurde gerade in der Mitte des 4. Jahrhunderts n.Chr. die Situation für die Christen prekär, während sich für sie der Eindruck einstellen musste, dass die Juden ihrer Nachbarschaft in Ruhe leben konnten. In theologischen Kategorien stellte sich die Frage, ob die Verfolgungen als Zeichen des Gotteswillens zu deuten wären, wonach die christlich-neutestamentlichen Verheißungen womöglich doch irregehen. Dieses soziale und religiöse Klima ist in Aphrahats zweiter Schaffensperiode sehr deutlich spürbar:[14] Viele Stellen der Demonstrationen drehen sich darum, dass das Trauma der Verfolgung nicht in dem Sinne als Strafe Gottes verstanden werden darf, dass das Heil in Christus widerrufen wäre. In mehreren Anläufen bemüht er sich, durchaus mit bibelexegetischer Brillanz, einen theologischen Ausweg aus dem Dilemma zu eröffnen. Ihm geht es sowohl darum, jüdische Gegenargumente, wie sie wohl im Alltag vorgekommen sein mussten, zu entkräften, als auch darum, die christliche Identität und Sicht der Heilsgeschichte zu stärken.

2. Welches Judentum?

So eindeutig es ist, dass Aphrahat das christlich-jüdische Verhältnis theologisch angesichts der akuten Situation aufarbeitet, so uneindeutig ist bei näherem Hinsehen das Judentum, welches gemeint ist. Wie bei den biographischen Informationen über den Autor haben wir auch für diese Frage nur die interne Evidenz der *Demonstrationen* als Ausgangspunkt vor uns (s. 1.).

Ein rein literarischer, fiktiver Gegner ist das Judentum jedenfalls nicht. Auch wenn in vielen Schriften der altkirchlichen Adversos Judaeos-Literatur das Judentum oft mehr als imaginiertes Gegenüber erscheint, das auf die Identitätssicherung innerhalb eines genuin christlichen Diskurses abzielt, ist dies bei Aphrahat nicht der Fall,[15] da ein Austausch zwischen Juden und Christen aufgrund der

---

12 Vgl. Snaith, Aphrahat, 236 f.

13 Vgl. Jullien/Jullien, Aux frontières de l'Iranité.

14 Koltun-Fromm, Conversation, 137, bringt noch Apostasien von Christen ins Spiel, die dem Christentum deswegen den Rücken gekehrt haben. Siehe auch Becker, Anti-Judaism, 307.

15 Vgl. Koltun-Fromm, Conversation, 162: „Aphrahat indicates that he writes, not from isolation, but in response to Jewish polemicizing against Christianity." Siehe auch Aphrahat, *Dem.* 18,12, das ziemlich eindeutig ist (Aphrahat gibt seinem Glaubensbruder Argumentationshilfen).

Verfolgungssituation und alltäglichen Debatten zwischen Anhängern beider Religionen vorausgesetzt wird.

Die Streitpunkte, die in der zweiten Gruppe von Aphrahats *Demonstrationen* abgehandelt werden, betreffen allesamt *identity markers* des Judentums[16] ebenso wie des Christentums. Während *Dem.* 11–13 und 15 zentrale Pfeiler des Judentums diskutieren (die Beschneidung, das Pascha, den Sabbat und die Speisegesetze), verteidigt der Autor in *Dem.* 17–19 christliche Institutionen, Lebensformen und Erwartungen (Christologie, Askese, Eschatologie) gegenüber Kritik, die von Juden vorgebracht wird. Zwischen diesen beiden Untergruppen steht wohl nicht zufällig das Thema der Erwählung (*Dem.* 16), d. h. die Frage nach dem Volk Gottes: Diese Zuspitzung, auf die hermeneutisch alles – auch die Argumentation in den anderen genannten *Demonstrationen* – hinausläuft, ist die Schlüssel- und Gretchenfrage, welche den Heilsstatus von Juden- und Christentum in den Vordergrund rückt. Angesichts der historischen Situation (s. 1.) ist für die christliche Seite die Vergewisserung über die eigene Identität und das eigene Erwähltsein zu einer brennenden Frage geworden.[17]

Die argumentative Basis des Disputs ist die Schriftgelehrsamkeit, v. a. in den gemeinsamen Schriften des Alten Testaments. Aphrahat hat beeindruckende und profunde Kenntnisse des AT[18] und misst biblischen Stellen aus dem ersten Teil des christlichen Schriftenkanons erhebliches Gewicht bei, während neutestamentliche Passagen in diesem Kontext in den Hintergrund treten. Auch seine Scheu vor vorschneller Typologisierung und Allegorese ist ein Hinweis auf die faktische Relevanz des Religionsgesprächs und die Realität des Gegenübers. Für die Frage, welches Judentum Aphrahat kennt, ist es nicht unwichtig, dass Hinweise auf eine *mündliche* Tora fehlen.

Aphrahat deutet an, dass auf jüdischer Seite eine gewisse Kenntnis neutestamentlicher Aussagen besteht, wenn beispielsweise in *Dem.* 21,1 das Senfkorngleichnis (vgl. Mt 17,20; Lk 17,5 f) vom Gegenüber kritisch beleuchtet wird. Hier ist eine wenigstens orale Transmission anzunehmen, die Bekanntschaft mit dem neutestamentlichen Text selbst ist nicht zwingend. Aber ein gewisses, fragmentarisches Basiswissen über Glaubensinhalte des Christentums scheint in den religiösen Streitigkeiten argumentativ verwendet worden zu sein.

Eine messianische Erwartungshaltung der endzeitlichen Sammlung der Juden scheint in *Dem.* 19,2; 21,5 durch. Die Hoffnung auf den Wiederaufbau Jerusalems mit Hilfe des persischen Herrschers schließt nicht nur an alttestamentliche Vorbilder wie Kyros an, sondern offenbart ein antirömisches Einvernehmen, das die Juden

16 Vgl. ebd., 161.

17 Vgl. ebd., 80.

18 Vgl. Richter, Auseinandersetzung, 104: „Seine Kenntnis des AT ist im übrigen meisterhaft, zeigt höchste religiöse Anteilnahme und verrät genaueste Vertrautheit mit der jüdischen Auslegung."

bewogen hatte, ihre Erwartungen an den sassanidischen Großkönig zu richten. Dass im 4. Jahrhundert jüdischerseits durchaus wieder messianische Tendenzen auftraten, bestätigt indirekt einige Jahrzehnte später – nun im Römischen Reich – auch die Sympathie für die Politik von Kaiser Julian [Apostata] (reg. 360–363), der als Teil seiner antichristlichen Wende Hoffnungen bei den Juden auf den baldigen Wiederaufbau des Tempels weckte.[19] In jedem Fall ist die messianische Aufladung bei Aphrahats jüdischem Gegner bemerkenswert und fügt sich gut in die historische Situation des persisch-römischen Kriegsgeschehens ein.

Diese Beobachtungen aus dem Werk Aphrahats zusammengenommen, wird schnell deutlich, dass das rabbinische Judentum wohl nicht der Gesprächspartner der syrischen Christen Aphrahats gewesen sein dürfte. Lange Zeit galt diese Annahme unbesehen als Selbstverständlichkeit in der Forschung, da die Bedeutung der babylonischen Rabbinen für die Geschichte des Judentums und die Kollation des Talmud Bavli alle anderen Möglichkeiten außer Acht ließen. Anfang der 1970er Jahre erkannte aber Jacob Neusner, dass sich der akute Messianismus und das Fehlen jedweder mündlichen Tora oder explizit nachbiblischen halachischen Tradition in Aphrahats *Demonstrationen* wohl schwer mit den theologischen Schwerpunkten der Rabbinen vereinbaren lassen.[20] Und in der Tat erkennen wir heute immer mehr[21] – auch infolge der Abkehr von allzu früher Datierung der talmudischen Überlieferungen, wie sie lange gang und gäbe war –, dass Mitte des 4. Jahrhunderts das Judentum im Sassanidenreich nicht allein aus rabbinischen Gelehrten bestand: Auf der einen Seite ist zu berücksichtigen, dass die rabbinischen Schulen wie Nehardea, Sura und Pumbedita im Süden des Zweistromlands zu lokalisieren sind,[22] während die Gegend um Nisibis und Edessa als frühsyrisch-christliche Zentren im Norden liegen.[23] Dies veranlasste Neusner dazu, das schon bei Flavius Josephus in *A. J.* 20,2 erwähnte Königshaus in Adiabene (Königin Helena und ihr Sohn Izates), welche im 1. Jh. n.Chr. zum Judentum konvertiert war und sogar einen Palast in Jerusalem besaß, mit dem Judentum bei Aphrahat

---

19 Seit der Baupolitik Konstantins d. Gr. war die Jerusalemer topographische Symbolik darauf ausgerichtet, dass der Tempelberg als Erfüllung christlicher Verheißungen brachliegt, während die christlich geprägten Stätten wie die Grabeskirche den Sieg und die Wahrheit des christlichen Glaubens offenbaren. An dieser Stelle setzt Julian an: Durch den Wiederaufbau des Heiligtums und die Wiederaufnahme des Tempelkults wären dann die jesuanischen Vorhersagen über die Tempelzerstörung (Mk 14,58; Mt 26,61; Joh 2,19; Apg 6,13 f), aber auch die christologische Sühnekonzeption stark erschüttert worden. Zunächst verlangsamte ein Erdbeben das julianische Projekt, schließlich sein unerwarteter Tod.

20 Vgl. Neusner, Aphrahat and Judaism.

21 Vgl. Stemberger, Mischna Avot; ders., Judaistik und neutestamentliche Wissenschaft; Leonhard, Die Pesachhaggada; ders., Blessings over Wine and Bread.

22 Vgl. Koltun-Fromm, Conversation, 56.

23 Vgl. ebd., 53 f. Vorsichtiger ist Lizorkin, Demonstrations, 3, was wohl auch mit seiner Annahme der Nähe zu den Rabbinen zusammenhängt (s. u.).

in Verbindung zu bringen.[24] Auf der anderen Seite ist zu berücksichtigen, dass die Gelehrsamkeit der Rabbinen eine religiös-soziale Elite abbildet, die nicht zwingend mit anderen Schichten des mesopotamischen Judentums zusammenhängen muss: Die Funde magischer Texte zeigen, dass sich jüdische, christliche und mandäische Gläubige neben- und miteinander austauschen konnten und der Synkretismus der Magie gerne auch transzendente Entitäten aus all diesen Religionen verwenden konnte, sogar neubabylonische und persische Götter und Dämonen wurden bemüht.[25] Aphrahats *Demonstrationen* sprechen aber eher für ein schriftkonformes Judentum, doch mag der heutige Befund von adiabenitischen Juden einerseits und Magica andererseits ein wenn auch nur fragmentarisches Bild von der Vielfalt jüdischen Lebens im Sassanidenreich geben, das eine allzu voreilige Identifikation mit den Rabbinen verhindert. Wie Neusner also plausibel machen konnte, sind die Gelehrten des Babylonischen Talmuds nicht die Gesprächspartner des Persischen Weisen.

2012 hat Eliyahu Lizorkin eine Alternativthese vorgeschlagen, um Kontinuitätslinien im mesopotamischen Judentum einerseits und die Verbindung von Aphrahat und Rabbinen andererseits wiederaufzunehmen. Er spricht von „proto-Rabbinic" bzw. „para-Rabbinic" bzw. „pre-Rabbinic Judaism" und versucht, vermeintliche talmudische Parallelstellen zu Textpassagen in den Demonstrationen ausfindig zu machen.[26] Wie Lizorkins Terminologie schon andeutet, soll es sich bei den Juden, auf welche Aphrahat reagiert, um Vorläufer der späteren Rabbinen handeln; allerdings zeigt schon die Wortwahl, dass das offenbar eher ein Hilfskonstrukt ist: Die Präfixe „proto-", „para-" und „pre-" sind ja weder deckungsgleich noch einheitlich, was bei terminologischen Problemen auch methodisch geboten wäre. Inwiefern ist das gemeinte Judentum „vorrabbinisch" oder in dessen Umfeld anzusiedeln? Schwierig ist die Kategorie auch deswegen, weil es ein terminologisches Konstrukt ist, dem keine beweisbare soziologische Größe zugeordnet werden kann aufgrund fehlender externer Evidenz unabhängig von Aphrahats *Demonstrationen*. Ein „protorabbinisches Judentum" im Zweistromland müsste historisch und ideengeschichtlich plausibel und tragfähig zuallererst entfaltet und nicht zirkulär als *missing link* zwischen Aphrahat und den Rabbinen eingesetzt werden, um danach die angenommenen Parallelen zu erläutern. Die Parallelen, die Lizorkin bemüht,[27]

---

24 Vgl. Greschat, Taten, 399.

25 Siehe als erste Einblicke: Montgomery, Aramaic Incantation Texts; Müller-Kessler, A Mandaic Incantation; Bohak, Ancient Jewish Magic.

26 Vgl. Lizorkin, Demonstrations, 8, 19, 157, 163–165.

27 Der diskursive Austausch soll s. E. zwischen den Schülern der „Proto-Rabbinen" und denen Aphrahats verlaufen sein. Er imaginiert hier also einen akademischen Disput, wobei nur einmal in Aphrahats Schriften das jüdische Gegenüber als „Weiser" (*Dem.* 21,1) erwähnt wird; von Schülern ist keine Rede, und über die Anrede hinaus sollte man eher nicht die Aussage inhaltlich strapazieren, da der konkrete Kontext nicht gegeben ist.

sind aufgrund des narrativen Stils des Bavli wenig aussagekräftig, obwohl das Postulat eines „prärabbinischen Judentums“ exklusive und stringente Gemeinsamkeiten bräuchte; die Ähnlichkeiten lassen sich nämlich auch anders erklären (z. B. als nicht spezifisch rabbinische Gehalte, die in verschiedenen jüdischen Kontexten auftauchten *oder/und* als biblische Bezugnahmen). Hermeneutisch fragwürdig ist bei der These weiters die Nivellierung der Unterschiede zwischen den Juden bei Aphrahat und den Rabbinen, die auch Lizorkin nicht verkennen kann: Die Annahme einer „Vorstufe“ reicht als Interpretation des inhaltlichen Abstands nicht aus und die Kategorie „disagreement by omission“, die er einführt,[28] ist fragwürdig und stellt eine argumentative Schwäche dar (*argumentum e silentio*).

3. Die theologischen Grundlagen der Position Aphrahats

3.1 Das Volk aus den Völkern

Für den Persischen Weisen stehen Judentum und Christentum, wiewohl beide Völker Gottes, in einem speziellen Verhältnis, das durch Asymmetrie bestimmt ist: Das Volk Israel, das Aphrahat gerne unter Rückgriff auf Jes 1,10 als „Fürsten von Sodom, Volk von Gomorrha“ bezeichnet,[29] ist Gott untreu geworden und wurde entsprechend der alttestamentlichen Prophetie (in seinem Verständnis) abgelöst und verlor den Heilsstatus als Volk Gottes.[30] An seiner Stelle sammelt sich Gott in der Christenheit ein „Volk anstelle des Volkes“ (vgl. den Titel von *Dem.* 16!),[31] ein nicht mehr allein durch Abstammung definiertes Ethnos, sondern ein eschatologisches Volk, das gewissermaßen die gängigen Definitionen transzendiert und universalisiert. Dieser Wandel ist Aphrahat zufolge endgültig und unumkehrbar, er resultiert aus Israels eigener Verschuldung und bewahrheitet die Strafansagen

28 Die hermeneutische Annahme, dass die Rabbinen im Falle von ihnen bekannten Unterschieden in der Schriftauslegung (zwischen sich und den „Proto-Rabbinen“) diese Unterschiede bewusst verschweigen, ist methodisch mehr als schwierig. Aus einem vieldeutigen Schweigen der talmudischen Texte eine intentionale Ignorierung abzuleiten, obwohl die Kenntnis der (in ihrer Existenz unbewiesenen) „Proto-Rabbinen“ ein unbegründetes Postulat darstellt, gibt den Talmudpassagen einen Subtext, der keinesfalls zwingend ist. Er unterstellt den rabbinischen Gelehrten auch ein diskursives Monopolstreben, das sich wohl kaum vereinbaren lässt mit dem Sachverhalt, dass gerade der Talmud dafür bekannt ist, unterschiedliche Lehrmeinungen nebeneinander zu stellen und tolerant und pragmatisch abzuwägen. Ein solches Verschweigen wäre untypisch und auch unnötig gewesen. In Wirklichkeit dreht sich das „disagreement by omission“ im Kreis: Die Auslegung X der „Prae-Rabbinen“ wird getilgt. Woher weiß man, dass die Rabbinen sie kannten? Weil sie sie absichtlich gestrichen hätten. Beide Leerstellen bedingen einander, beide sind jedoch Vorannahmen.

29 Vgl. Aphrahat, *Dem.* 11,1; 12,11; 16,3; 21,3.

30 Vgl. Becker, Anti-Judaism, 310.

31 Vgl. auch Greschat, Taten, 414.

der Bibel. Umgekehrt symmetrisch referenzieren die alttestamentlichen Verheißungen auf die Christen.[32] Auch die jüngsten Verfolgungen im sassanidischen Gemeinwesen (s. 1.) können diesen Entschluss Gottes, der sich in den biblischen Schriften kundtut, nicht kippen. Mit dem ausdrucksstarken Begriff des „Volkes aus den Völkern" findet der syrische Theologe also ein assoziationsreiches Schlagwort für ein dahinterliegendes theologisches Programm, das auch als Hoffnungsbotschaft für seine Mitgläubigen gedacht ist.

3.2 Die Bibelauslegung Aphrahats

Die Lesehermeneutik, die er an die Heilige Schrift anlegt, ist durch sein heilsgeschichtliches Paradigma vorgeprägt und spiegelt die Asymmetrie des Verhältnisses von Juden und Christen: Verdammung und Ablösung auf der einen Seite, Verheißung und Erfüllung auf der anderen Seite. Da sein theologisches Programm auf eine heilsgeschichtliche Kernaussage abzielt, ist die Präferenz für eine Exegese entsprechend des Literalsinns kaum verwunderlich.[33] Die Allegorese ist die große Ausnahme in seinen Demonstrationen. Beachtet man die jüdisch-christlichen Auseinandersetzungen in seinem Umfeld, gestaltet sich das wörtliche, historische Verständnis des Bibeltexts auch als wohl alternativlose Hermeneutik, wenn es darum geht, eine gemeinsame Basis für den Disput mit dem Judentum zu finden. Dass dieser Kontext eine Rolle spielt, ergibt sich nicht nur aus *Dem.* 18,7, sondern ebenso aus der Beobachtung, dass Aphrahat vergleichsweise wenige Allusionen und Zitate aus dem Neuen Testament anführt, v. a. nicht in der Auseinandersetzung mit dem Judentum; insofern erscheint seine profunde Kenntnis des AT als bemerkenswert ebenso wie die Zurückhaltung bei der argumentativen Verwendung des dem Judentum fremden NT.[34] Aphrahat fügt sich damit aber

---

32 Ambivalent bleibt freilich, dass die alttestamentlichen Verheißungen und Prophetien für Aphrahat *eo ipso* im Fall der Verdammung auf Israel bezogen sind, im Fall der Erfüllung auf die Christen. Siehe auch Becker, Anti-Judaism, 317 f: „[...] in their exegesis of the Hebrew Bible Christians understand statements of judgment and condemnation as addressing Jews and statements of promise and exaltation in the same passage as referring to Christians."

33 Vgl. Snaith, Aphrahat, 246.

34 Was den gelehrten Disput betrifft, favorisiert Aphrahat gegenüber dem Judentum eine eigentlich faire Ausgangsbasis, wenn auch zu beachten bleibt, dass das Ergebnis der Auseinandersetzung für ihn *a priori* auf die Wahrheit der christlichen Theologie hinausläuft. Dennoch ist festzuhalten, dass angesichts der schwierigen Situation der Christen in Persien in seiner Gegenwart und ebenso angesichts des Antijudaismus in den verschiedenen Ansätzen der spätantiken Theologie diese methodische Prämisse Aphrahats herausgestellt und gewürdigt werden sollte. Für ihn steht außer Frage, dass das AT die Offenbarungsschrift an Israel ist und als Gottes Wort an Israel gerichtet war und ist; es ist ein Dokument historisch geschehener, wahrer Ereignisse und in seiner Autorität auch auf christlicher Seite ungebrochen. Und das gilt nicht nur im Religionsgespräch, sondern aufgrund des soziohistorischen Kontexts auch bei der Selbstvergewisserung des syrischen Christentums im 4. Jahrhundert.

auch organisch ein in die Auslegungskonventionen der syrischen Theologie des 4. Jahrhunderts: Sein etwas jüngerer Zeitgenosse Ephräm (306–373) ebenso wie die weiter westlich gelegenen, griechischsprachigen Gelehrten Antiochiens favorisierten den Literalsinn.

Aufbauend auf dieser vorrangig am Literalsinn orientierten Exegese bemüht sich Aphrahat dann jeweils um eine schrittweise vorgehende, systematische Widerlegung der jüdischen Position. Die Theologie des neuen Volkes aus den Völkern (s. o.) dient ihm dabei als eine hermeneutische Orientierungsplanke, die der christlichen, in Frage gestellten Position den nötigen Rückenwind verschafft. Die jüdische Auffassung wird dementsprechend durch die exegetische Arbeit dekonstruiert.

4. Die argumentative Strategie Aphrahats

Der Persische Weise verfährt in seiner Argumentation nach wiederkehrenden Mustern, die allerdings nicht im Sinn eines klar strukturierten Traktats missverstanden werden dürfen. Vielmehr liegen aufgrund der methodischen Prämissen (s. 3.) einige argumentative Bausteine auf der Hand. Im Folgenden soll anhand der *Demonstrationen* 11, 13 und 15 exemplarisch extrahiert werden, wie der syrische Theologe gegenüber dem Judentum auftritt; die Themen Beschneidung, Sabbat und Kašrût sind sicher nicht zufällig oder willkürlich von ihm gewählt (siehe *Dem.* 15,9!), da sie drei zentrale identity markers des Judentums im Unterschied zum Christentum thematisieren.

4.1 Jüdische These

Ausgangspunkt ist jeweils ein Hauptmoment des jüdischen Glaubens, das im Christentum nicht fortgesetzt wird. Die normative Aussage des Judentums steht als These zur Debatte, während der theologische Gehalt aus jüdischer Blickrichtung eine bleibende, d. h. auch in der Gegenwart gültige, soteriologische Implikation trägt. Beschneidung, Sabbat und Speisegebote werden eingehalten, weil sie Teil der Tora sind und im Bund Israels mit dem Herrn ihre Einhaltung zur Erlösung Israels nach sich ziehen. Das Halten der Gebote der Tora führt zum Leben. Auf die Einzelthemen angewandt, dürfte die jüdische, soteriologische These so skizziert werden:

<u>Beschneidung:</u> *Die Beschneidung ist das Zeichen der Zugehörigkeit zu Israel; die Nachkommenschaft Abrahams wird erlöst.*

<u>Sabbat:</u> *Das Halten des Sabbatgebots ist bindend und führt zum ewigen Leben.*

<u>Kašrût:</u> *Die Speisegebote sind dem Volk Gottes auferlegt und haben erlösende Wirkung; verbotene Speisen bewirken Unreinheit.*

4.2 Christliche Gegenthese

Dass die Christen diese alttestamentlichen Gebote nicht einhalten, ist begründungsbedürftig. Gleichzeitig gilt im Rahmen von Aphrahats Argumentation als Folge: Das christliche Argument resultiert immer in einer Gegenthese, die der jüdischen Auffassung entgegensteht[35] und sie in der einen oder anderen Weise obsolet sein lässt. Dabei arbeitet der Persische Weise im Fall von *Dem.* 11–13 mit dem heilsgeschichtlichen Verheißungsschema, das auf christlicher Seite eine Erfüllung des früheren Gebots sieht (Taufe als verheißene, eschatologische Beschneidung: *Dem.* 12,9)[36] bzw. eine Typologie entwickelt (alttestamentlicher Sabbat und eschatologischer Sabbat: *Dem.* 13,13). Bei den Speisegeboten hingegen dekonstruiert Aphrahat die soteriologische Auffassung als argumentativ-logisches Paradoxon: Essen hat mit Reinheit nichts zu tun, was vom Judentum missverstanden wird (vgl. *Dem.* 15,1.3). Das Ethos der Zehn Gebote macht rein. Reinheit wird hier moralisch, nicht primär als Kultreinheit aufgefasst, ähnlich wie der eschatologische Sabbat eine übertragene Bedeutung postuliert, die nicht auf die Arbeitsruhe im Wochenrhythmus zu reduzieren ist. Interessant ist, dass Aphrahat trotz der exegetischen Belege entlang des Literalsinns nicht umhinkommt, die christliche Auffassung zum betreffenden Thema oft in eine übertragene, im Kern eschatologische Interpretation umzumünzen; dies ist ihm als Christen natürlich neutestamentlich vorgezeichnet. Gerade darum spielt die Dekonstruktion jüdischer Theologie *mit Hilfe des Alten Testaments* eine so wichtige und willkommene Rolle für ihn, da er dort, wo er Gegenbelege findet (z. B. bei den Speisegesetzen), diese verwenden kann, um die neutestamentliche Umdeutung auf anderem argumentativem Weg zu stützen. Die Vorgegebenheit des Ergebnisses ist abzulesen, da die Gegenthese zwar am Ende der *Demonstration* aufscheint, sie aber in Wirklichkeit keine Schlussfolgerung ist, sondern von Anfang an als Regulativ feststand und Aphrahat die ganze *Demonstration* hindurch auf sie zusteuert und abhebt.

<u>Beschneidung:</u> *Die Taufe ist die alttestamentlich verheißene Beschneidung der Herzen. Das Heil gilt dem Neuen Bund, Abrahams Nachkommen im Glauben.*

<u>Sabbat:</u> *Das Sabbatgebot hat nur als Typos des eschatologischen Sabbats der Ruhe Geltung. Den Sabbat halten heißt, den Willen Gottes zu tun.*

<u>Kašrût:</u> *Essen bringt weder Nutzen noch Schaden, wie bei Jesus Christus und Paulus deutlich wird. Die Zehn Gebote halten rein.*

---

35 Die christliche Gegenthese ist dabei die gespiegelte Inversion der jüdischen Position.

36 Zur Taufe und Tauftheologie Aphrahats; vgl. Duncan, Baptism in the Demonstrations of Aphraates; ders., The Administration of Baptism; Lattke, „Taufen“ und „untertauchen“.

4.3 Gegenbelege im Alten Testament

Das Gros der exegetischen Arbeit leistet Aphrahat im Zusammenhang mit der Suche nach Belegstellen, die seine Auffassung untermauern oder wenigstens die jüdische Sicht relativieren oder hinterfragen. In der Regel bedient er sich einer ganzen Florilegienreihe von zusammengestellten Ausnahmen in Israels Geschichte und Schriften. In den *Demonstrationen* 11, 13 und 15 gehen die Zitate und Allusionen quer durch das AT, von Ex über Ri, die Königsbücher, Propheten bis zu Est. An dieser Stelle kann die jeweils auf das Thema zugeschnittene Argumentation nur für *Dem.* 11 im 5. Kapitel genauer analysiert werden. Es sei hier jeweils nur ein markantes Beispiel angeführt: Gegen die Beschneidung führt Aphrahat schlechte Könige Israels an wie Jerobeam, der, obwohl beschnitten, verworfen wird (siehe *Dem.* 11,2; vgl. 1 Kön 13,34). Den Sabbat hielten in Kriegszeiten weder Josua noch die Makkabäerbrüder ein (Jos 6,15; 1 Makk 2,41), d. h. das Gebot war niemals absolut bindend (vgl. *Dem.* 13,4–12). Was die Kašrût betrifft, wird auf Simson abgehoben, der Honig aus einem Löwenkadaver aß (siehe Ri 14,5–18), ohne dass ihm das zur Last gelegt wird (*Dem.* 15,5).

4.4 Chronologie der Bundesschlüsse, Posteriorität der Gebote

Da die Gesprächsbasis vom Literalsinn und damit der Heilsgeschichte ausgeht, fällt es Aphrahat nicht schwer, auf Brüche in der Chronologie hinzuweisen, die sich aus der Tora selbst ergeben: Die Beschneidung, die seit Abraham geübt wurde, findet sich im Buch Gen, also lange vor der Inkraftsetzung der Mose-Tora in Ex: Adam und Noah waren nicht beschnitten, Abraham und die anderen Patriarchen lebten vor dem Bund mit Israel am Sinai. Dies relativiert für ihn eine allzu enge Verquickung von Beschneidung und Gesetz. Umso mehr gilt dies für den Sabbat und die Speisegebote, die auch erst am Sinai zur Geltung kamen. Wenn also vor Mose Beschneidung, Sabbat und Kašrût nicht zwingend heilsrelevant waren, dann ist ihre absolute Bindekraft für Aphrahat deutlich in Frage gestellt.

4.5 „Rationalisierende" Erklärung des Gebots

Der exegetische Durchgang veranlasst Aphrahat dazu, sich einen pragmatischen Sinn für die Gebote zu überlegen und so zu zeigen, dass sie faktisch nicht heilsrelevant, sondern den Umständen geschuldet sind. Die Beschneidung hat den „profanen"[37] Sinn gehabt, Israel von Kanaan zu separieren bzw. diente der

37 NB sei angemerkt, dass eine solche „Rationalisierung" von jüdischen Geboten auch in der modernen Exegese nicht unproblematisch ist: Die Annahme einer Beschneidung aus angeblich ursprünglich nur hygienischen Gründen oder der Verzicht auf Schweinefleisch wegen Seuchengefahr werden

Überführung von Frevlern. Da der Sabbat auch für Tiere im Hauswesen gilt (*Dem.* 12,2), Tiere aber nicht moralisch belangt werden und die Gebote nicht von sich aus halten können, zielt das Gebot allein auf die Arbeitsruhe ab. Die Speisegebote sollten zur Mäßigung beim Essen führen und idololatrische Kontexte abwehren. Beschneidung, Sabbat und Kašrût haben für den Persischen Weisen daher keine soteriologische Bedeutung, sondern eine rein pragmatische – sei sie sozial, tierethisch, heilsgeschichtlich-kontextuell oder zur Absicherung der alleinigen Gottesverehrung.

Beschneidung: *Sie wirkte bei der Trennung Israels von Kanaan im Hinblick auf die Landnahme; sie überführte ebenfalls Sünder beim Bundesbruch.*

Sabbat: *Der Sabbat dient dem Ausruhen von der Arbeit bei Mensch und Tier.*

Kašrût: *Speisegebote (und Tempelopfer)*[38] *dienten der Mäßigung und Abwehr des Götzendienstes.*

5. Exemplarische Analyse von Aphrahats Argumentation: Die Beschneidung (Dem. 11)

Ganz eindeutig teilt Aphrahat zu Beginn von *Dem.* 11 den kontextuellen Anlass für seine folgende Argumentation mit: Seinem Adressaten (ܚܒܝܒܝ) gibt er eine Handreichung, die dem „beredten Zeichen" (ܢܝܫܐ ܕܡܡܠܠܐ) des Judentums, der Beschneidung also, gewidmet ist.[39]

Aphr., ***Dem. 11,1***
Parisot 468

ܫܡܥ ܢܝܫܐ ܕܡܡܠܠܐ ܘܫܬܐܣܬܐ ܕܕܪܫܐ ܕܙܕܩ ܠܡܬܐܡܪܘ ܠܘܩܒܠ ܥܡܐ ܗܘ ܕܩܕܡܝܢ ܕܡܬܟܠܝܢ ܥܠ ܢܦܫܗܘܢ ܕܙܪܥܗ ܐܢܘܢ ܕܐܒܪܗܡ	*Höre (über) das beredte Zeichen und das Fundament des Disputs, das zu recht gegen sie gesprochen wird, die sich vor uns darauf verlassen haben, Same Abrahams zu sein.*

der alttestamentlichen Theologie und dem Judentum nicht gerecht und nivellieren die soteriologische Bedeutung dieser *identity markers*. Diese „rationalen" und „vorausschauenden" Lösungen, die man unterstellt, haben nur auf den ersten Blick eine positive Komponente; dass dies auf Kosten der religiösen Tiefe geht und damit das Judentum letztlich relativiert wird, darf man nicht vergessen. Auch können unausgesprochen damit Instrumentalisierungen einhergehen, wenn diese Gebote auf die sozialpolitische Ebene heruntergebrochen werden, als wären der Sabbat eine Art Vorläufer des 1. Mai und die Speisegebote eine gesundheitsdirigistische Maßnahme gewesen. Die entsprechenden Gebote werden in der Tora theologisch gesetzt und begründet. Gerade darum kann man Aphrahat, der die theologische Perspektive nie verlässt, nur bedingt für solche Analogien verantwortlich machen.

38 Siehe Aphrahat, *Dem.* 15,7.

39 Die syrischen Zitate werden nach der Edition von Parisot, Patrologia Syriaca, zitiert. Die Übersetzung ist meine eigene und mit Bruns' Übertragung in FC 5 abgeglichen und an seine Zählung angepasst.

Auf die durch die Beschneidung sichtbar werdende Zugehörigkeit zu Israel, zum „Samen Abrahams“ (ܙܪܥܗ ܐܒܘܢ ܕܐܒܪܗܡ), verlassen sich die Juden in seinen Augen allzu sehr. Sie halten unerschütterlich daran fest:

Aphr., Dem. 11,2
ebd., 471

ܕܚܢܢ ܠܗ ܓܒܝܢ ܘܓܙܝܪܝܢ ܘܝܕܝܥܝܢ ܡܢ ܟܠܗܘܢ ܥܡܡܐ	*„Wir sind erwählt und beschnitten und mehr als alle Völker bekannt.“*

Diese Aussage gewinnt im Text einen unterschwelligen Vorwurf: Ist diese Heilsgewissheit wirklich so sicher? Reicht ein Zeichen am Körper aus, um gerettet zu werden? Ist sich das Judentum im Sassanidenreich zu vorschnell seiner sicher – oder verzichtet es gar auf weitere Anstrengungen und ruht sich auf der Beschneidung aus? Bei „alle Völker“ (ܟܠܗܘܢ ܥܡܡܐ) schwingt natürlich auch das Volk aus den Völkern, die Christen, mit.

Während diese jüdische These den Ausgangspunkt bildet, läuft die ganze Demonstration auf den Kontrapunkt der christlichen Gegenthese hinaus, die am Ende der Abhandlung kristallklar zusammengefasst wird:

Aphr., *Dem.* 11,11
ebd., 502

ܐܠܗܢ ܓܝܪ ܫܪܝܪ ܘܩܝܡܘܗܝ، ܛܒ ܡܗܝܡܢܝܢ ܘܟܠ ܩܝܡ ܒܙܒܢܗ ܫܪܝܪ ܘܐܬܗܝܡܢ ܘܓܙܝܪ̈ܝ ܠܒܗܘܢ ܚܝܝܢ ܘܡܬܓܙܪܝܢ ܬܢܝܢܘܬ ܥܠ ܝܘܪܕܢ ܕܫܪܪܐ ܡܥܡܘܕܝܬܐ ܕܫܘܒܩܢܐ ܕܚܛܗ̈ܐ	*Unser Gott ist nämlich treu und Seine Bundesschlüsse sind sehr verlässlich. Und ein jeder Bund war zu seiner Zeit fest und zuverlässig. Und die an ihren Herzen Beschnittenen leben und werden ein zweites Mal am wahren Jordan beschnitten, der Taufe zur Vergebung der Sünden.*

In der Tat ist dieses Summarium ein Kontrapunkt zur Ausgangsthese: Die jüdische Position ist geprägt von zwei Momenten, nämlich der Heilsgewissheit und der Beschneidung als Bundeszeichen. Beide Aspekte stehen in einem unlöslichen Zusammenhang: Aufgrund der Beschneidung und mit der Beschneidung als unumkehrbarem Heilszeichen ist die Verheißung Gottes an die Nachfahren Abrahams verknüpft, errettet zu werden und Sein Volk zu sein. In Aphrahats christlicher Wendung ist dieser Konnex völlig analog: Die christlichen Gläubigen vertrauen ebenfalls auf einen realsymbolischen Akt, der durchaus auch eine Beschneidung ist – die Taufe ist die zweite Beschneidung, und zwar in typologisch-übertragener Weise als die in Dtn 10,16; 30,6; Jer 4,4 verheißene Herzensbeschneidung,[40] die durch den Akt des Getauftwerdens stattfindet. Das Taufwasser ist hier, typisch für

40 Vgl. Snaith, Aphrahat, 243; Lizorkin, Demonstrations, 35.

die syrische liturgische Terminologie, der „wahre Jordan“ (ܝܘܪܕܢܢ ܕܫܪܪܐ), dessen Vollzug die Sündenvergebung bewirkt (vgl. Mk 1,4; Lk 3,3). Dass diese Analogie überhaupt aufgeht, liegt dem Persischen Weisen zufolge an der Zuverlässigkeit Gottes als Subjekt und Akteur des Heilshandelns; dass es aber eine Analogie ist und damit die jüdische Beschneidung und die christliche Herzensbeschneidung im Kontrast stehen, ergibt sich aus dem Zeitgefälle, denn „zu seiner Zeit“ (ܒܙܒܢܗ) war der jeweilige Bund fest, der Bund mit Israel ist aber – so die implizite Aussage – abgelaufen und wurde vom Bund mit den Völkern abgelöst.

Hochinteressant ist die *en passant* mitgeteilte Aussage, dass die Taufe eine zweite Beschneidung darstellt, was nur bedeuten kann, dass es eine erste Beschneidung, d. h. die jüdische Beschneidung, gab. Hier könnte mehr vorliegen als nur ein Seitenhieb auf konvertierte Juden, denn der Satz scheint eine universalere Perspektive einzunehmen. Gegebenenfalls könnte dies dafür sprechen, dass die syrischsprachigen Christen aus Aphrahats Umgebung zu einem guten Teil jüdische Wurzeln haben. Die alternative Annahme, dass vor der Taufe (z. B. eines ehemaligen Zoroastriers) eine Beschneidung (im christlichen Kontext!) durchgeführt worden wäre, wäre jedenfalls schwieriger zu begründen. Demgegenüber erscheint die jüdische Provenienz vieler Christen aus Aphrahats Umfeld näherliegend und dürfte die Intensität, die der Persische Weise auf die antijüdische Argumentation legt, unterstützen. Die Stelle bleibt zu einem gewissen Grad dunkel und bedarf nochmals gesonderter Betrachtung.

Dem erwähnten Spitzensatz gehen biblisch-exegetische Erwägungen Aphrahats voraus, die sich weitgehend auf das AT konzentrieren (s. 4.3). Um zu den zeitversetzten Bundesschlüssen zu gelangen und gleichzeitig das potentielle jüdische Gegenüber zu „überzeugen“ (jedenfalls aus christlicher Warte), bedient er sich alttestamentlicher Stellen, die eine Abwendung Gottes von Israel intendieren und welche er als prochristliche Verheißungen deutet. Jes 1,10 nimmt dabei eine Schlüsselstellung ein, da die „Fürsten von Sodom und Volk von Gomorrha“ (ܫܠܝܛܐ ܕܣܕܘܡ ܘܥܡܐ ܕܥܡܘܪܐ, s. קְצִינֵי סְדֹם [...] עַם עֲמֹרָה) zum einen das für Aphrahat entscheidende Wort „Volk“ mit sich bringt, zum anderen die in Gen 19,1–29 beschriebene endgültige Vernichtung der Frevelstädte in Erinnerung ruft. Er schlussfolgert: So wie die Bewohner Sodoms und Gomorrhas unwiderruflich vernichtet wurden, so ist der Bund mit Israel mit einer Verwerfung verbunden. Beide Städte dienen nun als Leitmotiv und werden parallelisiert mit anderen Erwähnungen: In Ez 16,48 wird Jerusalem als Schwester Sodoms angesprochen, in Dtn 32,32 ist das Volk ein „Weinstock Sodoms und [eine] Pflanzung Gomorrhas“ (ܓܦܬܐ ܕܣܕܘܡ ܡܢ ܫܬܠܬܐ ܕܥܡܘܪܐ, s. כִּי־מִגֶּפֶן סְדֹם גַּפְנָם וּמִשַּׁדְמֹת עֲמֹרָה). Kurz davor im selben Kapitel – in Dtn 32,21 – wird ein neues Volk verheißen. Die Zusammenschau der betreffenden Sodom-und-Gomorrha-Passagen erfolgt als eine Kollektion, die sich Aphrahats Argumentation passgenau einfügt.

Er setzt aber zur Stützung seiner Sicht nochmals anders an: Aus der jüdischen Beschneidung kann keine selbstverständliche Heilsgewissheit abgeleitet werden, da das AT bezeugt, dass etwa Jerobeam als König Israels durchaus schlecht war, obwohl er beschnitten wurde. Es gibt keine Garantie. Außerdem, so Aphrahat, ist die Beschneidung keine für Israel reservierte Einrichtung, denn auch Ismael und seine Nachfahren, die Araber, sind beschnitten (vgl. Gen 17,25), obwohl ihm und ihnen nach Gen 21,10–13 kein Anteil am Bund zusteht. Der Zusammenhang von Erlösung und Beschneidung kann daher nicht als zwingend und absolut gesehen werden. Ähnliches gilt für Esau und seine Edomiter oder für die Ägypter – allesamt beschnitten, allesamt partizipieren sie nicht am Bund (siehe auch *Dem.* 11,5.10).

In gewisser Weise steht und fällt die jüdische Ausgangsthese auch mit Abraham als Stammvater. Um dies zu belegen, bemüht der Persische Weise die „prä-abrahamitischen" Episoden der Heilsgeschichte, die vor Gen 17 liegen und eine chronologische Schrittfolge der Bundesschlüsse Gottes mit den Menschen vorzugeben scheinen. Da ist als Erstes der Erzählzusammenhang um Adam und das Gebot bezüglich des Baumes der Erkenntnis (Gen 2) zu nennen, der – trotz Strafe – eine Solidarität Gottes mit dem ersten Menschen impliziert. Auch Generationen später wird Henoch entrückt (Gen 5,24), obwohl er nicht beschnitten war. Aus der Sintflut wird allein Noach mit seiner Familie errettet (Gen 9), der vor der Beschneidung Abrahams gelebt hat und dennoch mit dem Regenbogen ein Bundeszeichen (vgl. Gen 9,12–17) erhielt. Schon diese drei Beispiele zeigen, dass die Beschneidung nicht *conditio sine qua non* des rettenden Handelns Gottes sein kann. Umso mehr wird dies anschaulich in der Biographie Abrahams: Wenn in Gen 14 Melchisedek auftritt, der Priester des höchsten Gottes war, dann gab es im unmittelbaren Lebensumfeld Abrahams Menschen, die als Unbeschnittene Gott nahestanden. Und die Pointe kommt zuletzt: Selbst Abraham ließ sich erst im satten Alter von 99 Jahren beschneiden (Gen 17), die ganze lange Lebensspanne zuvor war er unbeschnitten und dennoch ein Freund Gottes (vgl. *Dem.* 11,3 f). Aphrahat bemüht sich mit diesen Exempeln darum, den Konnex von Beschneidung und Heilsautomatismus *ad absurdum* zu führen.

Aber was ist die Beschneidung dann? Wenn Aphrahats bisherige Argumentationsführung von Gegenbeweisen dominiert wurde, muss nun eine Alternativerklärung kommen, die plausibel zu machen sucht, was es mit der Beschneidung auf sich hat:

Aphr., **Dem.** 11,6
ebd., 484

ܡܛܠ ܕܡܫܟܚܐ ܗܘܬ ܝ ܒܗܘܬܐ ܠܡܗܘܐ ܐܠܘ ܠܐ ܐܬܪܫܡܘ ܕܒܪ ܢܬܚܫܒܘܢ ܡܢܗܘܢ ܕܦܠܚܝܢ ܠܦܬܟܪܐ ܐܘ ܡܙܢܝܢ ܘܓܝܪܝܢ ܘܓܢܒܝܢ ܘܥܒܕܝܢ ܡܕܡ ܕܠܒܪ ܡܢ ܢܡܘܣܐ ܗܦܟܝܢ ܗܘܘ ܐܝܠܝܢ ܡܢܗܘܢ ܕܒܗܠܝܢ ܡܬܬܚܕܝܢ ܘܟܦܪܝܢ ܗܘܘ ܕܠܐ ܗܘܝܢ ܒܢܝ ܐܒܪܗܡ ܐܝܟ ܕܠܐ ܢܬܩܛܠܘܢ ܘܢܩܒܠܘܢ ܡܫܡ ܦܪܥܢܐ	*Denn es bestand die Möglichkeit, dass einige von ihnen, wenn sie nicht gekennzeichnet gewesen wären, Götzen verehrten oder hurten und die Ehe brachen und stahlen und sonstiges Gesetzloses trieben, dann aber, wenn sie bei solchem Treiben erwischt worden wären, es ablehnten und leugneten, Söhne Abrahams zu sein, um dem Tod zu entgehen und keine Strafe zu erhalten.*

Der Persische Weise geht von einem pragmatischen Nutzen der Beschneidung im AT aus: Insofern der Geltungsbereich der Tora allein das Volk Israel betrifft, muss s. E. die Sinnhaftigkeit des Gebots im sozialen Kontext gesehen werden. Hier geht es um die leichtere und unzweifelhafte Überführung von Frevlern, die gegen den Dekalog verstoßen haben. Für die gleichsam gerichtliche Evidenz und zur eindeutigen Identifikation des Täters wurde die Beschneidung eingeführt, da sich aufgrund der körperlichen Kennzeichnung der Beschuldigte nicht damit herausreden kann, nicht zu Israel zu gehören und damit nicht von den Dekalogbestimmungen betroffen zu sein. Zur Zugehörigkeit zu den „Söhnen Abrahams" (ܒܢܝ̈ ܐܒܪܗܡ) gehört nämlich die Befolgung der Tora; ihr Übertreten kann die Todesstrafe nach sich ziehen. Die Allusion auf die Zehn Gebote und das Fehlen von anderen Geboten der Tora (z. B. kultische Reinheitsbestimmungen) dürfte damit zusammenhängen, dass Aphrahat den Bund Israels stark aus der Perspektive der Lebensführung wahrnimmt (s. 4.2).

6. Abschließendes

So sehr es natürlich bei Religionsgesprächen klar ist, dass jede Seite von ihrer eigenen Position ausgeht und sie zu verteidigen sucht, d. h. die Lösung jeweils schon feststeht, so bemerkenswert ist es doch, dass Aphrahat nicht auf Polemik und Hass setzt, sondern auf eine gelehrte Disputation, in der die Argumente zählen. Aphrahat geht streng methodisch vor und beschränkt sich weitgehend auf den Literalsinn des Textes. Die Auseinandersetzung mit dem Judentum seiner Umgebung erfolgt mit argumentativen Mitteln, die zumindest methodisch auch von der Gegenseite akzeptiert sind. Der Persische Weise möchte aus dem Wortlaut der Bibel und dem Verlauf der Heilsgeschichte die Wahrheit erkennen und fordert sogar zur jüdischen Stellungnahme auf.

Natürlich spielt hier auch die Verfolgungssituation für die Christen im Perserreich eine Rolle: Anders als im Römischen Reich bestand gerade keine Allianz mit der Regierung. Es blieb allein das gesprochene Wort für den Religionsdisput und – noch wichtiger – für die Selbstvergewisserung der syrischen Christen, die angesichts der Martyrien und der Steuerlast (ver)zweifelten, ob ihre Religion überhaupt die Wahrheit sei.

Literatur

Abouzayd, Shafiq, Iḥidayutha. A Study of the Life of Singleness in the Syrian Orient, From Ignatius of Antioch to Chalcedon 451 A. D., Oxford 1993.

Becker, Adam H., Anti-Judaism and Care for the Poor in Aphrahat's Demonstration 20, JECS 10 (2002), 305–327.

Bohak, Gideon, Ancient Jewish Magic. A History, Cambridge 2011.

Brock, Sebastian P., Early Syrian Asceticism, Numen 20 (1973), 1–19.

Bruns, Peter, Das Christusbild Aphrahats des Persischen Weisen, Bonn 1990.

Duncan, Edward J., Baptism in the Demonstrations of Aphraates the Persian Sage, Washington, D. C. 1945.

—, The Administration of Baptism in the Demonstrations of Aphraates, in: J. Vellian (Hg.), Studies on Syrian Baptismal Rites, Kottayam 1973, 16–36.

Greschat, Katharina, Taten und Verkündigung der zwölf Apostel. Zitation und Rezeption der Apostelgeschichte bei Aphrahat, in: T. Nicklas/M. Tilly (Hg.), The Book of Acts as Church History. Text, Textual Traditions and Ancient Interpretations, Berlin/New York, N. Y. 2003, 399–422.

Griffith, Sidney H., Monks, „Singles", and the „Sons of the Covenant". Reflections on Syriac Ascetic Terminology, in: E. Carr (Hg.), ΕΥΛΟΓΗΜΑ (FS R. Taft), Rom 1993, 141–160.

Jullien, Christelle/Jullien, Florence, Aux frontières de l'Iranité. „Nāṣrāyē" et „Krīstyonē" des inscriptions du Mobad Kirdīr enquête littéraire et historique, Numen 49 (2002), 282–335.

Koltun-Fromm, Naomi, Jewish-Christian Conversation in Fourth-Century Persian Mesopotamia. A Reconstructed Conversation, Piscataway, N. J. 2011.

Lattke, Michael, „Taufen" und „untertauchen" in Aphrahats taḥwyātā, in: D. Hellholm/T. Vegge/Ø. Norderval (Hg.), Ablution, Initiation, and Baptism. Late Antiquity, Early Judaism, and Early Christianity, Berlin/Boston, Mass. 2011, 1115–1138.

Leonhard, Clemens, Die Pesachhaggada als Spiegel religiöser Konflikte, in: A. Gerhards/S. Wahle (Hg.), Kontinuität und Unterbrechung. Gottesdienst und Gebet in Judentum und Christentum, Paderborn u. a. 2005, 143–171.

—, Blessings over Wine and Bread in Judaism and Christian Eucharistic Prayers. Two Independent Traditions, in: A. Gerhards/C. Leonhard (Hg.), Jewish and Christian Liturgy and Worship. New Insights into its History and Interaction, Leiden/Boston, Mass. 2010, 309–326.

Lizorkin, Eliyahu, Aphrahat's Demonstrations. A Conversation with the Jews of Mesopotamia, Louvain 2012.

Montgomery, James A., Aramaic Incantation Texts from Nippur, Philadelphia, Pa. 1913.

Müller-Kessler, Christa, Dan(ḫ)iš – Gott und Dämon, in: J. Marzahn/H. Neumann (Hg.), Assyrologica et Semitica (FS J. Oelsner), Münster 2000, 311–318.

—, A Mandaic Incantation against an Anonymous Dew Causing Fright (Drower Collection 20 and Its Variant 43 E), ARAM 22 (2010), 453–476.

Murray, Robert, The Features of the Earliest Christian Asceticism, in: P. Brooks (Hg.), Christian Spirituality (FS G. Rupp), London 1975, 63–77.

Neusner, Jacob, Aphrahat and Judaism. The Jewish-Christian Argument in Fourth-Century Iran, Leiden 1971.

Parisot, Jean (Hg.), Patrologia Syriaca. Teil 1, Bd. 1, Paris 1894.
Richter, Gustav, Über die älteste Auseinandersetzung der syrischen Christen mit den Juden, ZNW 35 (1936), 101–114.
Snaith, John G., Aphrahat and the Jews, in: J. A. Emerton/S. C. Reif (Hg.), Interpreting the Hebrew Bible (FS E. I. J. Rosenthal), Cambridge u. a. 1982, 235–250.
Stemberger, Günter, Mischna Avot. Frühe Weisheitsschrift, pharisäisches Erbe oder spätrabbinische Bildung?, ZNW 96 (2005), 243–258.
—, Judaistik und neutestamentliche Wissenschaft, in: L. Doering/H.-G. Waubke/F. Wilk (Hg.), Judaistik und neutestamentliche Wissenschaft: Standorte – Grenzen – Beziehungen, Göttingen 2014, 15–31.
Tubach, Jürgen, Die syrische Danielrezeption, in: M. Delgado/K. Koch/E. Marsch (Hg.), Europa, Tausendjähriges Reich und Neue Welt. Zwei Jahrtausende Geschichte und Utopie in der Rezeption des Danielbuches, Freiburg i.Br. 2003, 105–138.
Vööbus, Arthur, History of Asceticism in the Syrian Orient. A Contribution to the History of Culture in the Near East, Bd. 1, Louvain 1958.

Günter Stemberger (University of Vienna)

Is (rabbinic) Judaism a Mosaic Religion?

The Place of Moses in Israel's Foundation Story

In modern times the designation "Mosaic" or "Mosaic Religion" has sometimes replaced the terms "Jewish" or "Jewish Religion," probably because Jewish is sometimes considered to have possible negative connotations. In 1806, on the instruction of Napoleon, an Assembly of Jewish Notables was convened "to transform Jews from a 'nation within a nation' to 'French citizens of the Mosaic faith.'"[1] The contemporary French texts dealing with this event generally use the expression "la loi de Moyse,"[2] obviously based on Mal 3:22 "Remember the teaching of my servant Moses" (תורת משה), as explicitly stated by Isaac Leeser:

> Whence is the name "Mosaic Religion" derived? From MOSES [...] through whom God communicated his law to the people of Israel. So also teaches the Bible: "Remember ye the law of Moses my servant, to whom I commanded on Horeb statutes and judgments for all Israel."[3]

In this paper I do not intend to enter the discussion as to the appropriateness of the term "religion" for Judaism, but shall limit myself to the adjective "Mosaic." May it be used as parallel to "Christian" or "Buddhist" religion or "Mohammedan" (now more commonly replaced by "Muslim")? Jews certainly do not "believe in" Moses as Christians "believe in" Christ. But can Moses be considered the founder of the Jewish religion? What is the place of Moses in Israel's foundation story or even more so in Jewish religion?

As to Israel's foundation story, the exodus from Egypt, the answer seems clear. Based on the biblical book of Exodus, Moses certainly was charged by God to lead his people out of Egypt to the Promised Land, not comparable to the biblical patriarchs, but in his time and role the undisputed leader of the people from the departure in Egypt up to the end of the journey of the people through the desert. For the rabbis, his leadership was not uncontested—he had his faults, he had not the sufficient respect for the people, he called them "fools," and therefore was not allowed to enter the Promised Land. He had to pass on the leadership to his servant and pupil Joshua already in his lifetime and had to see how Joshua taught the people Torah while he had to keep silent and to listen to his former pupil (*Tanhuma*

1 Goodman, A History, 442.
2 Schwarzfuchs, Napoleon, passim.
3 Leeser, Catechism, Chapter II.4.

Wa-ethanan 6).[4] Whereas Aaron passed on his priesthood to his sons, Moses did not found a dynasty; his descendants have no special role and disappear in history.

But there is one hint in the biblical text that might be regarded as proof of the permanent central position of Moses in Jewish religion, "the Torah of Moses," a phrase to which I shall turn in the first part of my paper.

1. The Torah of Moses (*torat Moshe*)

Thirteen times in the Bible we encounter the formula "the Torah (or: the law) of Moses" (*torat Moshe*), most frequently in the wording "as it is written in the book of the law of Moses" (e.g. Jos 8:32 כַּכָּתוּב בְּסֵפֶר תּוֹרַת מֹשֶׁה; "a copy of the law of Moses, which he had written": אֵת מִשְׁנֵה תּוֹרַת מֹשֶׁה אֲשֶׁר כָּתַב). The Israelites are admonished "to observe and do all that is written in the book of the law of Moses, turning aside from it neither to the right nor to the left" (Jos 23:6). Other texts enlarge the formula "as prescribed in the law of Moses the man of God" (Esr 3:2 כַּכָּתוּב בְּתוֹרַת מֹשֶׁה אִישׁ הָאֱלֹהִים), or "the law of Moses, the servant of God" (Dan 9:11 בְּתוֹרַת מֹשֶׁה עֶבֶד הָאֱלֹהִים): Moses is not independent, but active as the "man" or "servant" of God. Nevertheless, it may be astonishing how frequently the Torah is called the "Torah of Moses," equally distributed in the Former Prophets and in the Writings, never in the Torah. The only prophetic text (of the Later Prophets) needs to be mentioned because it is so frequently quoted in later times: "Remember the teaching of my servant Moses, the statutes and ordinances that I commanded him at Horeb for all Israel" (Mal 3:22 MT = 4:4 Vulg. זִכְרוּ תּוֹרַת מֹשֶׁה עַבְדִּי אֲשֶׁר צִוִּיתִי אוֹתוֹ בְחֹרֵב עַל כָּל יִשְׂרָאֵל חֻקִּים וּמִשְׁפָּטִים).

In the Dead Sea Scrolls the phrase "the Torah of Moses" is rather frequent, mainly in the Damascus Document and in the Rule of the Sect, both texts also in versions from 4Q: the members of the group take upon themselves "to return to the Law of Moses with a whole heart and with a whole soul" (CD 15:12 לשוב אל תורת משה בכל לב ובכל נפש; parallels with slight variations 15:9; 16:1; 16:3; see also 4Q 256 Col. IX (Frg. 4) 7, and several other occurrences in 4Q copies of CD and the Rule).

In early rabbinic literature the phrase "the Torah of Moses" occurs almost only in the context of the confession of the high priest in the liturgy of Yom Kippur:

> O God, I have committed iniquity, transgressed and sinned before thee, I and my house. O God, forgive the iniquities [...] as it is written in the Law of thy servant Moses (ככתוב בתורת משה עבדך): For on this day shall atonement be made for you to cleanse you; from all your sins shall ye be clean before the Lord (Lev 16:30) (Mishnah Yoma 3:8).[5]

---

4 For this rabbinic transformation of the biblical account (Deut 31:1–8.23) see Stemberger, Mose, 237–241.

5 Transl. Danby, The Mishnah; parallel in Tosefta *Yoma* 2:1, MS Vienna.

The high priest repeats this confession while laying his hands on his bullock (4:2), and again while laying his hands on the scapegoat (6:2). The text of the Tosefta is taken up again twice in *Sifra Ahare Mot* (the midrash on Lev 16) parashah 2, pereq 1 (Weiss 80d), Mishnah *Yoma* 4:2 in pereq 2 (Weiss 81a) and Mishnah *Yoma* 6:2 in parashah 4, pereq 1 (Weiss 82a), and then again in the Palestinian Talmud *Yoma* 3:7 40d (and also in the Babylonian Talmud *Yoma* 35b, 41b and 66a). Thus there are altogether twelve passages introducing Lev 16:30. Within the text of the high priest's confession the reference to what "is written in the Law of thy servant Moses" and the biblical passage may seem strange—it is rather the biblical basis for the liturgy, a kind of rubric; but it is present in all versions of the passage and might therefore be an actual remnant of the Second Temple liturgy. I hesitate.

Another passage in tannaitic literature clearly shows that the phrase "Torah of Moses" was considered problematic. In the *Mekhilta* (*Shira* 1) we read:

> There were three things to which Moses devoted himself with his whole soul and they were all named after him. He devoted himself with his whole soul to the Torah and it was named after him. For it is said: "Remember ye the law of Moses, my servant" (Mal. 3.22). But is it not the law of God, as it is said: "The law of the Lord is perfect restoring the soul" (Ps. 19.8)? Hence, what does it mean by saying: "The law of Moses, my servant?" Merely, that because Moses devoted himself with his whole soul to it, it is named after him. But where do we find that he devoted himself with his whole soul to the Torah? It is said: "And he was there with the Lord," etc. (Ex. 34.28). And it also says: "Then I abode in the mount forty days and forty nights," etc. (Deut. 9.9). Thus, since he devoted himself with his whole soul to the Torah, it is called after him.[6]

The oldest and generally best manuscript of the *Mekhilta* does not read the critical passage "But is it not the law of God, as it is said: 'The law of the Lord is perfect restoring the soul' (Ps 19:8)? Hence, what does it mean by saying: 'The law of Moses, my servant?'" One might think that this text, questioning the formulation "The Torah of Moses" has been added only later. But it is present in all other textual witnesses and clearly has been omitted by the copyist of MS Oxford by homoioteleuton, jumping from the first "my servant" to its next occurrence. There are many parallels with the three things which were named after Moses, but only the early texts (*Mekhilta de-Rabbi Shim'on* 15:1;[7] *Midrash Tannaim* 16:18[8]) include the objection that in reality the Torah is the law of God.[9]

6 Horovitz/Rabin, Mechilta, 117; transl. Lauterbach, Mekilta, vol. 2 f.–4.

7 Epstein/Melamed, Mekhilta, 71.

8 Hoffmann, Midrash Tannaim, 96.

9 Parallels without this objection: *Deut. Rab. Wa-ethanan* (ed. Lieberman, Midrash); *Tanhuma Buber Shoftim* 4; *Tanhuma Shoftim* 5; *Tanhuma Beshallah* 10; *Tanhuma Ki Tissa* 35; *Pesiqta Rabbati* 5:4 (Ulmer, Pesiqta 52); *Midr. Psalms* 30:4 (Buber, Midrash, 235).

A much later parallel is a little different: *Seder Eliyahu Rabbah* 7 makes it explicit that the forty days and nights that Moses spent on the mountain, do not refer to his first stay (Exod 24:18), but to his second stay without food and drink, the time of his intercession for Israel after the sin with the golden calf. No one of all the other prophets

> knew how to pour out [pleas for] mercy and utter supplications as did Moses. Hence it is said, "Remember the Torah of Moses my servant" (Mal 3:22). But is it Moses' Torah? Is it not Yours, kept by you for 974 generations before the world was created, was it not you who refined it, and then gave it to Israel Your servant? Why, then, is it said "Remember the Torah of Moses my servant"? Because on four and five occasions Moses stood up in prayer and saved Israel from death, the Holy One credited him with the writing of the Torah as though it had actually been wrought by him—as though, in fact, it belonged to him. Hence "Remember the Torah of Moses my servant."[10]

Here it is not so much Moses' effort to receive again the Torah the tables of which he had broken when discovering the sin of the Golden Calf. It is his intercession for the people which stands at the center. For this he receives as reward that the Torah is named after him, although in reality it belongs to God. This is somewhat incongruous, but in agreement with rabbinic thinking on the Torah (on this later). As the text emphasizes, God gave the Torah to Israel his servant; Moses his servant receives it only on behalf of Israel. Moses is only *credited* with the writing of the Tora, *as though* he had written it, although in reality he of course had not done it. In spite of this formulation, the Torah in reality is not the Torah of Moses.

Another explanation why the Torah could have been attributed to Moses is to be found in the Babylonian Talmud, *Shabbat* 89a:

> When Moses came down from before the Holy One, blessed be He, Satan came and said before him: Lord of the world, where is the Torah? He said to him, I gave it to the earth. He went to the earth and said to her: Where is the Torah? "God understands her way" (Job 28:23). He went to the sea, and it replied: It is not with me. He went to the deep, and it replied: It is not in me; for it is said, "The deep says, it is not in me, and the sea says, it is not with me, destruction and death say, we have heard a rumor thereof with our ears" (Job 28:14, 22).

> So he went back and said before the Holy One, blessed be He, Lord of the world, I have searched throughout the earth but not found it. He said to him: Go to the Son of Amram. He went to Moses. He said to him: The Torah that the Holy One, blessed be He, gave you—where is it? He said to him: So what am I, that the Holy One, blessed be He, gave me the Torah?

10 Friedmann, Seder Elyahu, 33; transl. Braude/Kapstein, Tanna debe Eliyahu, 117.

> Said the Holy One, blessed be He, to Moses: Moses, you're a liar! He said before him: Lord of the world, you have a precious thing stored up for yourself, with which you play every day. Am I going to hold on to the benefit of that for myself? Said the Holy One, blessed be He, to Moses: Since you have humbled yourself, it will be called by your name: "Remember you the Torah of Moses, my servant" (Mal 3:22).[11]

As this text underlines, Moses would never regard the Torah as his own; it belongs to God alone. But because he humbly accepted this fact, God rewarded him with this attribution. It clearly does not reflect reality, but is an honorary attribution. Here again we see how difficult it was for the rabbis to accept this biblical phrase.

Early rabbinic literature up to and including the Yerushalmi and the classical midrashim therefore rather avoid speaking of the *Torat Moshe*; the fact that this phrase never occurs in the Pentateuch makes it easy for them. The only other early quotation of the phrase is to be found in *Sifre Deuteronomy* § 41:

> Scripture says, *Thine eyes as the pools in Heshbon, by the gate of Bathrabbim* (Song 7:5): *thine eyes*—these are the elders appointed over the community, as it is said, *For the Lord hath poured out upon you the spirit of deep sleep, and hath closed your eyes; (the prophets ... hath He covered)* (Isa. 29:10); *pools*—just as one cannot know what is in a pool, so can he not fathom the words of the Sages; *in Heshbon*—in calculations (*hesbonot*) which result from consultation and thought; and where are these calculations made? In houses of study, by the gate of Bath-rabbim. What is meant by *Thy nose is like the tower of Lebanon, which looketh toward Damascus* (Song 7:5)? If you perform the Torah, you may hope for (the coming of) Elijah, to whom I had said, *Go, return on thy way to the wilderness of Damascus* (1 Kings 19:15), and I had also said, *Remember ye the Torah of Moses, My servant, etc., Behold, I will send you (Elijah the prophet before the coming of the great and terrible day of the Lord)* (Mal. 3:22–23).[12]

The passage offers an allegorical interpretation of a verse of Canticles, understanding it of the Torah, its study and performance. This will lead to the eschatological coming of Elijah, whom the rabbis consider a disciple of Moses (Tosefta *Sota* 4:7 etc.). Mal 3:22 is a central text for the rabbis when speaking of the forthcoming end of times (but here again most quotations are late). In this context the wording *Torat Moshe* is unavoidable, but not the real focus of the rabbinic sayings.

The Babylonian Talmud and later midrashim to some extent give up this reserve. In the Babylonian Talmud the phrase *Torat Moshe* is encountered more frequently. I give only the most important examples. In *Yoma* 71a we read:

> This matter we have not learned from the Torah of our lord, Moses (דבר זה מתורת משה רבינו לא למדנו), but from the teachings of Ezekiel b. Buzi we have learned it, "No alien, uncircumcised in heart and uncircumcised in flesh, shall enter

11 Transl. Neusner, Talmud.

12 Finkelstein, Sifre, 86 f; transl. Hammer, Sifre, 84 f.

> my sanctuary" (Eze. 44:9),—until Ezekiel came along and made that statement, how did we know the correct rule? Rather, it is a tradition that was handed on, and Ezekiel came along and supplied it with support from Scripture.[13]

This tradition appears eleven times in the Bavli—it seems to have been important for the redactors that a fundamental law regarding the temple is not found in the Torah, but only in Ezechiel. The emphasis on *Torat Moshe* is due to the contrast with the prophetic teaching, but not in order to qualify the Torah as belonging to Moses.

Somewhat different is the case of *Baba Batra* 74a (MS Hamburg 165). Rabba bar bar Hannah is led to a place in the desert where he encounters those associated with Korah who were swallowed up (Num 16:32 ff). Asked to listen closely at a crack that emitted smoke, he heard them say: "Moses and his Torah are truth, and we [lit. "they"] are liars" (משה ותורתו אמת והן בדאין; cf. *Sanhedrin* 110b). The followers of Korah denied that God had sent Moses; they said against Moses and Aaron: "All the congregation are holy, every one of them, and the Lord is among them. So why then do you exalt yourselves above the assembly of the Lord?" (Num 16:3). In the netherworld they must confess that Moses had truly spoken in the name of God; in this context they explicitly connect the Torah with Moses.

We may sum up this paragraph: The biblical phrase *Torat Moshe* is used by the early rabbis in a very restricted way. They are not really at ease with it. And even later when it becomes more common, the rabbis feel bound to explain it, why it is used in the Bible and how one may correctly understand it. Moses' special relationship with the Torah has to be explained.

2. The Law of Moses (*dat Moshe*)

Apart from the biblical phrase *Torat Moshe* the rabbis use another formula, "the Law of Moses" (*dat Moshe*). It occurs exclusively in the context of marriage law. In Mishnah *Ketubbot* 7:6 we read:

> These are they that are put away without their Ketubah: a wife that transgresses the Law of Moses and the Jews (העוברת על דת משה ויהודים;[14] Danby: "Jewish custom"). What [conduct is such that transgresses] the law of Moses? If she gives her husband untithed food [Num. 18:21 f], or has connexion with him in her uncleanness [Lev. 18:19], or does not set apart dough-offering [Num. 15:18 ff], or utters a vow and does not fulfil

---

13 Transl. Neusner, Talmud.

14 This is the reading of codex Kaufmann; the standard editions read: דת משה ויהודית, 'Moses' and Jewish law'; Danby's distinction between 'the Law of Moses' and 'Jewish custom' follows later understanding, but is not justified by the Hebrew text.

> it [Deut. 23:21]. And what [conduct is such that transgresses] the law of the Jews? If she goes out with her hair unbound, or spins in the street, or speaks with any man."[15]

The parallel in Tosefta *Ketubbot* 7:6 first turns to unacceptable behavior of the husband:

> [If] he required her by vow to give a taste of what she was cooking to everybody [who came by], or that she draw water and pour it out onto the ashheap, or that she tell everybody about things which are between him and her, he must put her away and pay off her marriage-contract.[16]

Thus far the text is parallel to Mishnah *Ketubbot* 7:5. But then the Tosefta alone adds: "because he has not behaved with her in accord with the law of Moses and of Israel" (מפני שלא נהג עמה כדת משה וישראל), exactly parallel to the following statement regarding the wife "for she has not behaved with him in accord with the law of Moses and of Israel" (מפני שלא נהגה עמו כדת משה וישראל). The Tosefta replaces in the formula "Jews" by "Israel," but *dat Moshe* is the same in both texts. The text does not speak of the "Torah of Moses", but of his *dat*—a Persian loanword, "law," which only much later is used in the meaning of "religion." In this formula "Moses and the Jews" (or "Israel") are a unit, something impossible with "Torah"—one never finds *Torat Yisrael*; *Torat Yehudim* occurs only seldom in early modern responsa. The Mishnah refers *dat Moshe* to biblical commandments, norms of Jewish behavior based on the Torah, *dat Yehudim* to accepted Jewish behavior not explicitly based on the Torah.

The formula is clearly traditional and not rabbinic. We first find it in Tobit 7:12 regarding Sara: "Take her to be your wife according to the Law and the ordinance written in the Book of Moses."[17] Unfortunately no Hebrew or Aramaic text for this verse has survived in Qumran. But we have this formula in Aramaic marriage contracts from the Dead Sea which are clearly pre-rabbinic. Papyrus Murabba'at 20 is the ketubbah of Babatha (probably 117 C. E.): [ד]י ההוא לי לאנתה כדין מ[שה ויהדא]; another ketubbah is Papyrus Yadin 10 (ca. 125–128 C. E.): "that you be to me as a wi[fe according to the la]w of Moses and the J[u]daeans" (כדי]ן מושה ויה[ו]דאי]).[18] It is the formula still used today in the Jewish marriage contract: "When you enter my house you shall be my wife according to the law of Moses and the Jews" (לכשתיכנסי לביתי תהויין לי לאינתו כדת משה ויהודאי: *Yevamot* 15:1, 14d; cf. Yerushalmi *Ketubbot* 4:8, 29a). Tosefta *Ketubbot* 4:9 reads "Israel" instead of

15 Transl. Danby, The Mishnah, adapted.

16 Transl. Neusner, Tosefta.

17 Transl. Fitzmyer, Tobit.

18 Papyrus Murabba'at: Cotton/Yardeni, Documentary Texts, 58 n. 4; Papyrus Yadin: Yadin et al., The Documents, 126–127.

"Jews": כשתכנסי לביתי תהוי לי לאנתו כדת משה וישראל. As we see, דין is considered equivalent to דת and may replace it, since it has nearly the same meaning.[19] In the same way "Jews" and "Israel" may be used indiscriminately.

The traditional formula does not go back to the rabbis, but has been accepted by them (even if they had wanted, they could not have abolished the established practice) in the strict limits of tradition. It does not teach anything about the attitude of the rabbis to Moses. It is even possible that the name of Moses was introduced only later into a formula like כנימוס יהודאי (cf. Tobit), as suggested by Menahem Kister.[20]

3. A Halakhah Given to Moses from Sinai (*halakhah le-Moshe mi-Sinai*)

Different from the two phrases discussed up to now is the statement that something is "a halakhah given to Moses from Sinai"—it is a phrase found only in rabbinic literature in many examples from the Mishnah onward throughout this literature and thus clearly rabbinic. I give only one example, Mishnah *Peah* 2:6 concerning details of Lev 19:9: "When you reap the harvest of your land, you shall not reap to the very edges of your field, or gather the gleanings of your harvest." A rabbi sowed his field with two kinds of wheat and wanted to know whether he had to give one Peah for the whole field or one for every kind of wheat. He went to the Chamber of Hewn Stone, a room in the Temple where according to rabbinic fiction a sanhedrin decided the halakhah. There Nahum the Scribe stated:

> I have received a tradition from R. Measha, who received it from his father, who received it from the Zugoth, who received it from the Prophets as a Halakah given to Moses from Sinai, that if a man sowed his field in two kinds of wheat and made them up into one threshing-floor, he grants one Peah; but if two threshing-floors, he must grant two Peahs.[21]

---

19 It may even be replaced by the transcription of the Greek νόμος, as in the Ketubbah of Cologne (from Antinoopolis, Egypt, dated 417 C. E.): כנימוס כל בית [בנת?] ישראל. See, Kister, Ke-dat Moshe, 203.

20 Idem, Ke-dat Moshe, 204.

21 Halivni, Revelation Restored, 55, states that of the three occurrences of the phrase in the Mishnah, only here "could the reference possibly be meant literally as an actual allusion to historical Mosaic tradition. The other two occurrences must certainly be hyperbole." "[T]he Tannaim made almost no use of the concept of Halakha le-Moshe mi-Sinai. Instead, scriptural verses appear as the bases of Tannaitic halakha" (ibid.). As ibid., 54 and 74, shows, the use of the phrase increases in the Amoraic period and even more so in the Middle Ages and in modern times, as the idea of an independent oral law more and more replaces exegesis based on hermeneutical principles. Hayes, Halakhah, in her detailed analysis of the rabbinic occurrences of the term comes to similar, but more differentiated conclusions. Against Halivni, for her the chain of tradition in Mishnah *Yadayim* 4:3 "implies a fairly literal understanding of the term" (Hayes, Halakhah, 71; equally for *Eduyot* 8:7, ibid., 72). But then she takes a step back: "It must be conceded, however,

The particular halakhah does not interest us in our context, but only the way the text tries to document by a chain of tradition back to the prophets, that a certain halakhic practice is extremely old and could go back even to Moses at Sinai. No biblical proof is needed, old tradition is enough. It is based on the claim, to be found above all in the Talmudim, that Moses on Sinai received many halakhot which are much more detailed than what is to be found in the biblical text. They all are included in "the statutes and ordinances and laws that the Lord established between himself and the people of Israel on Mount Sinai through Moses" (Lev 26:46 ביד משה).

Moses is not the author, but simply the mediator of these halakhot. There is a certain tension between this idea of a "halakhah for Moses from Sinai" and the understanding of Lev 27:34 at the end of *Sifra*: "These are the commandments that the Lord gave to Moses for the people of Israel on Mount Sinai." As the midrash understands it, "'These are the commandments': a prophet will not make anything new from now on" (אלה המצוות–שאין נביא עתיד לחדש דבר עוד מעתה) "These," and *only* these are the commandments revealed by God. The further development of the halakhah does not rely on revelation, but only on the rabbinic interpretation of the commandments handed on to Moses—and, as the notion of a "halakhah for Moses from Sinai" makes clear, on authoritative tradition. Moses himself no longer plays any role in it, in spite of the appeal to Moses—he is simply the starting point.

4. Moses Received Torah from Sinai (*Moshe qibbel Torah mi-Sinai*)

But what about Moses' role at Sinai? The probably best known passage of all rabbinic literature, the beginning of tractate *Avot*, states: "Moses received Torah from Sinai and handed it on to Joshua, and Joshua to the elders, and the elders to the prophets, and the prophets handed it on to the men of the Great Assembly etc." Does this sentence not express the self-understanding of the whole rabbinic movement and thus place Moses at its root and very center? If we accept the traditional date of this text at the time of the Mishnah (some would even claim that it goes back to the time before 70 and is an originally Pharisaic maxim), this might be correct, especially if we accept Amram Tropper's description that *Avot* was intended to instill

> virtues and practical wisdom through repetition and memorization [...] as elementary textbooks meant to introduce the novice to the school's world-view, while also providing the expert with wisdom that he might contemplate and attempt to realize in his behaviour and thoughts.[22]

---

that even in these cases the term may be primarily metaphorical, indicating that a law is certain, correct, or ancient." (74)

22 Tropper, Wisdom, 187.

If this description of *Avot* were correct, we might expect that it left its traces in all subsequent rabbinic literature. But in rabbinic literature this text is hardly ever quoted. There are only two passages where it occurs, both times without a quotation formula. We first encounter it in Yerushalmi Sanhedrin 10:1, 28a, commenting on Koh 12:11: "The sayings of the wise are like goads" (כדרבנות):

> That is, like this ball (כדור) between girls (בנות). Just as this ball goes from hand to hand, but in the end comes to rest in one hand, so Moses received Torah from Sinai and handed it on to Joshua, Joshua to the elders, the elders to the prophets, and the prophets handed it on to the Men of the Great Assembly.

If we did not know the passage by heart, we would not recognize it as a quotation. Neither does *Qohelet Rabbah* 12:11 (early ninth century), commenting on the same verse, introduce the passage as part of the Mishnah.

The formula לקבל תורה is not frequent in rabbinic literature, and has another meaning than in *Avot*: It is the high priest who in the ritual of Yom Kippur receives the material Torah scroll from the servant and after the reading returns it to him (Mishnah *Yoma* 7:1), or it is Israel or the proselyte "who takes upon himself all words of the Torah" (*Sifra Shemini Mekhilta de Milluim*, ed. Weiss 45d קיבל עליו כל דברי תורה; many parallels). One accepts the Torah as an obligation, not as an ideal value to be handed on over generations. The normal way to express the revelation of the Torah is in all early texts the passive formula "the Torah was given" (תורה ניתנה), used as a *passivum divinum*. לקבל את התורה is never said of a single person: It is Israel as a people who are to receive, i. e., to take upon themselves the Torah. We have to wait for the Babylonian Talmud to encounter the statement that Moses received the Torah: "When Moses came up on high, the ministering angels said before the Holy One, blessed be He, 'Lord of the world, what is one born of woman doing among us?' He said to them, 'He has come to receive the Torah'" (לקבל תורה בא, *Shabbat* 88b).

Only at this rather late stage do we find passages depicting Moses as personally receiving the Torah from heaven, taking it over for Israel. But the dominant idea of rabbinic literature is that Israel as a people directly, without a mediator, was given the Tora (ניתנה) and willingly took it upon itself. The role of Moses is limited to what is explicitly stated in the Torah. Only in the Babylonian Talmud and in late midrashim does he receive mythical features. For the rabbis Moses belongs to their own group, his most common title is Moshe Rabbenu, "our master."[23]

The end of *Sifra* is the only early text that speaks of Moses as "messenger" (שליח), but this passage is missing in the earliest manuscript (Vatican 31) and most probably is a later addition. All other early texts that mention a messenger polemically refute this idea. Thus we read in the *Mekhilta*: "'And I will smite (every first born)' (Exod 12:12). Might I infer that it is to be through an angel or a messenger? Scripture says,

---

23 For more detail see Stemberger, Moses received Torah; idem, Mose.

'And the Lord smote all the first born,' not through an angel or a or a messenger" (שומע אני על ידי המלאך או על ידי שליח ת'ל וייי הכה כל בכור לא על ידי מלאך ולא על ידי שליח) (*Pisha 7*[24]). (*Pisha 7*[25]). In *Mekhilta Shabbeta* 1 we read: "'And the Lord said to Moses' (Exod 31:12). Not through an angel nor through a messenger" (לא על ידי מלאלך ולא על ידי שליח). We find the phrase in several other passages and also in the Haggadah of Pesah; it is a polemical refrain that is repeated time and again in rabbinic literature. It emphasizes the direct relationship of Israel with God. Even Moses may not stand in between.

Thus the rabbis would certainly have rejected the idea that Judaism is a "Mosaic" religion. Moses certainly plays an important role in the history of Judaism, but he is never placed between God and Israel. We may go a step further and state that not only the rabbis would never have considered their Judaism as "Mosaic;" also in reality it no longer was defined exclusively by the five books of Moses. This is even more true of modern Judaism. As Martin Goodman writes of the growing ranks of *baalei teshuvah*, penitents, in our own time,

> The religion to which these Jews "return" bears little resemblance to the religion ascribed to Moses in the Bible from which it purports to derive. Polygamy has disappeared, as has slavery […] None of this is a concern to the *baalei teshuvah* for whom authentic Judaism is located not in the desert of Sinai over 3,000 years ago […] but in the yeshivot and *shtetls* of eastern Europe in the eighteenth or nineteenth centuries. For them as for most religious Jews, a return to worship as stipulated in the Torah must await the messianic age.[26]

But even if we disregard the historical development of Judaism (as of all other religions) over the centuries, so that it never represents an imagined ideal state of the very beginnings, of the time of Moses, we have to recognize that the rabbis—or Jewish religious leaders at any other time—would never have considered their Judaism a "Mosaic religion." It is a misnomer imposed from outside and taken over by some Jewish leaders for apologetic reasons.

---

24 Transl. Neusner, Mekhilta; again in Pisha 13.

25 Transl. Neusner, Mekhilta; again in Pisha 13.

26 Goodman, A History, 533.

Literature

Sources

Braude, William G./Kapstein, I. J. (ed.), Tanna debe Eliyahu, Philadelphia, Pa. 1981.
Buber, Solomon (ed.), Midrash tehillim, Vilna 1891, repr. Jerusalem 1966.
Danby, Herbert (transl.), The Mishnah. Translated from the Hebrew with introduction and brief explanatory, Oxford 1933, repr. 1974.
Epstein, Jacob N./Melamed, Ezra Z. (ed.), Mekhilta de-Rabbi Shim'on bar Yoḥai, Jerusalem 1955.
Finkelstein, Louis (ed.), Sifre 'al sefer devarim = Siphre ad Deuteronomium, Berlin 1939.
Fitzmyer, Joseph A., Tobit (CEJL), Berlin 2003.
Friedmann, Meir (ed.), Seder Elyahu rabah ve-seder Eliahu zuṭa = Seder Eliahu rabba and seder Eliahu zuta (Tanna d'be Eliahu); according to a Ms. edited with commentaries and additions, Wien 1902, repr. Jerusalem 1960.
Hammer, Reuven (transl.), Sifre. A Tannaitic Commentary on the Book of Deuteronomy, translated from the Hebrew with Introduction and Notes, New Haven, Conn./London 1986.
Hoffmann, David (ed.), Midrash Tannaim, Tel Aviv 1965.
Horovitz, Saul/Rabin, Yisrael Avraham (ed.), Mechilta d'Rabbi Ismael cum variis lectionibus et adnotationibus, Jerusalem 1960.
Lauterbach, Jacob Zallel (ed.), Mekilta de Rabbi Ishmael. A critical edition on the basis of the MSS and realy editions with an English translation, introduction and notes, 3 vol., Philadelphia, Pa. 1933–1935.
Lieberman, Saul, Midrash Debarim Rabbah, Jerusalem ³1974.
Neusner, Jacob, Mekhilta according to Rabbi Ishmael. An Analytical Translation, 2 vol., Atlanta, Ga. 1988.
—, The Talmud of Babylonia. An American Translation, Chico/Atlanta, Ga. 1984 ff.
—, The Tosefta. Translated from the Hebrew, 6 vol., New York, N. Y. 1977–1986.
Ulmer, Rivka (ed.), Pesiqta Rabbati. A Synoptic Edition of Pesiqta Rabbati Based upon All Extant Manuscripts and the Editio Princeps, Atlanta, Ga. 1997.
Weiss, Isaak, Sifra deve Rav hu sefer Torat kohanim = Sifra, Commentar zu Leviticus, Wien 1862.
Yadin, Yigael et al. (ed.), The Documents from the Bar Kokhba Period in the Cave of Letters. Hebrew, Aramaic and Nabatean-Aramaic Papyri, Jerusalem 2002.

Scholarly Works

Cotton, Hannah M./Yardeni, Ada (ed.), Aramaic, Hebrew and Greek Documentary Texts from Naḥal Ḥever and Other Sites (DJD XXVII), Oxford 1997.
Goodman, Martin, A History of Judaism, London 2017.
Halivni, David Weiss, Revelation Restored. Divine Writ and Critical Responses, Boulder, Colo. 1997, 54–74.

Hayes, Christine, Halakhah le-Moshe mi-Sinai in Rabbinic Sources. A Methodological Case Study, in: S. J. D. Cohen (ed.), The Synoptic Problem in Rabbinic Literature (BJS 326), Providence, R. I. 2000, 61–117.

Kister, Menahem, "Ke-dat Moshe v'Yehud'ae." Toldoteha shel nushah mishpatit-datit, in: D. Boyarin et al. (ed.) Atara le-Haim: Studies in Talmudic and Rabbinic Literature (FS H. Z. Dimitrovsky), Jerusalem 2000, 202–208.

Leeser, Isaac, Catechism for Jewish Children, Philadelphia, Pa. 1863 (Digital version: Jewish-American History Documentation Foundation, 2019).

Schwarzfuchs, Simon, Napoleon, the Jews and the Sanhedrin (The Littman Library of Jewish Civilization), London 1979.

Stemberger, Günter, Mose in der rabbinischen Tradition, Freiburg i.Br. 2016.

—, "Moses received Torah…" (mAv 1,1). Rabbinic Conceptions of Revelation, in: idem, Judaica Minora II (TSAJ 138), Tübingen 2010, 347–359.

Tropper, Amram, Wisdom, Politics, and Historiography. Tractate Avot in the Context of the Graeco-Roman Near East, Oxford 2004.

Constanza Cordoni (University of Utrecht)

Identity and Sense of Place in Rabbinic Literature

The Case of the Land of Israel*

> Religions mark this place as unlike others. Religions say: take off your shoes before you enter here. Religions say: walk no farther than this on the Sabbath, [...] Religions, in other words, involve homemaking. They construct a home—and a homeland. They delineate domestic and public space and construct collective identity. Religions distinguish us and them—and prescribe where and how both should live.
>
> (T. Tweed, *Crossing and Dwelling*)

The expression "sense of place" has its roots in early humanistic geography and is used in the social sciences (including different strands within geographical research) to refer to how individuals and groups or communities relate positively (or not) to particular places, especially to those where they live, how they value places as distinctive, and identify with them. The concept is also used in relation to the question of how and why people's attitudes to places change over the course of time—for clearly, people, places, and the connection between them are all subject to change. As Edward Relph points out, sense of place is an element of most social and cultural experiences and not simply less sacred than the formerly quite popular genius loci which it appears to have been pushing aside.[1]

The reasons why different individuals and groups perceive places as distinctive are varied, so that different senses of place are possible for one and the same place. Research into sense of place and the related concepts of place attachment or spatial identity in the social sciences tends to focus on contemporary phenomena. Flesh and blood human beings may be interviewed concerning the "specific

* This article has been written in the context of the project "Reconfiguring Diaspora: The Transformation of the Jewish Diaspora in Antiquity," directed by Leonard V. Rutgers and financially supported by the Dutch Research Council (NWO). I wish to thank Günter Stemberger and Lieve Teugels for their suggestions on an earlier version of this text.

1 For a brief treatment of "sense of place," see Wilkie/Roberson, Sense of place. Apart from Relph's blog entry on "sense of place" (http://www.placeness.com/sense-of-place-an-overview/, 06.06.2019), I am not aware of a research overview or survey article on the uses of the concept "sense of place." For the related idea of place attachment and its historical background see Low/Altman, Place attachment, and the literature cited therein. Although the expression has become commonplace, it continues to appeal as meaningful. See Malpas, Place and Singularity.

feelings, perceptions, and attitudes generated in [them] by the particular qualities of a locality, or the events that they experience there,"[2] and the locality in question may be a directly observable one. The present article is concerned with a sense of place of the past and relies exclusively on the evidence of written texts. Its purpose is to examine the rabbinic representation of the link between Jewish self and the large-scale place Land of Israel in late antiquity and the early Middle Ages in terms of sense of place.

The Rabbinic Land of Israel: A Historical Diasporic Sense of Place

Recent scholarship has demonstrated that rabbinic Judaism is polyphonic also when it comes to its conceptualization of the Land of Israel, not only as setting for events in mythical patriarchal narratives, but also in narratives set in rabbinic times and with rabbinic actors.[3] The rabbinic period—generally thought of as inaugurated with the revolts and repression in the first and second centuries C. E.—is seen as the timeframe in which a renewed instance of the Jewish diaspora[4] came into being. When compared to the situation assumed to have been predominant among Jews living in Judaea and in the Diaspora during the Second Temple period, the period after the Bar Kochva Revolt witnesses what may be referred to as a diasporization of ancestral homeland itself. One of the manifestations of this Jewish diasporization of Roman Palestine—apart from the notion that Jews become at least in part Romans—is the fact that a new way of relating to the Land finds its way into rabbinic statements. New about these statements is, as Isaiah Gafni has argued, that they express the need of an active commitment to the Land and that they address its superiority with respect to other locations of Jewish diasporic existence, for example, exalting the Land for its supernatural attributes.[5]

In the Amoraic period (220–550 C. E.), the discourse of the Babylonian sages or Amoraim entered into a rich dialogue with the discourse of the Palestinian sages of their time and of the Tannaitic period (70–220 C. E.), the Tannaim. The Babylonian and the Palestinian perspectives on the Land of Israel were conflicting at times and complementary at others. They were both diasporic perspectives on the aLand if we understand diaspora, following Daniel Boyarin, as "people who participate in a doubled cultural (and frequently linguistic) location, in which they

2 Castree/Kitchin/Rogers, Sense of place.

3 See Gafni, Land, Centre and Diaspora, ch. 2 and 3; Boyarin, A Traveling Homeland, ch. 2; Cordoni, Inheriting and Buying.

4 In the context of diaspora research, the classical or paradigmatic case of diaspora. See Cohen, Global Diasporas; Reis, Theorizing diaspora; and Rutgers, Next year in Sardis.

5 Gafni, Land, Centre and Diaspora, 14.

share a culture with the place in which they dwell but also with another group of people who live elsewhere, in which they have a local and a trans-local cultural identity and expression at the same time."[6] In what follows I will be concerned with a series of statements of rabbinic discourse that can be subsumed under the "law of residence" in the Land of Israel[7]—a commandment[8] that stands in conflict with a Jewish existence outside of the Land and which is especially conceivable as response to the phenomenon of the Jewish diaspora, understood as the type of Jewish existence outside of the Land which results from the dispersion from an original homeland.

Although the praise of the Land promised to the patriarchs is a leitmotiv in Scripture, it is nowhere explicitly stated that Jews are supposed to live exclusively there. Neither does the Mishnah, much of whose law is devoted to the Land and its institutions, spell out that Jews are meant to live only within the limits of the Land. No biblical or mishnaic commandment prescribes the residence in the Land.

In the writings of the Second Temple Period the answers given by Judaean and Diaspora Jews to questions such as where Jews were at home and how they should relate to the Land of Israel may differ. However, no full-fledged debate between the two parties with respect to these issues has been identified for this period.[9] When the sages of the rabbinic period deal with these questions, the answers they provide in Tannaitic, Amoraic and post-Amoraic sources reveal a changed perspective, including, as pointed out above, the emergence of an opposition of discourses within rabbinic Judaism on what the "Encyclopedia Talmudit" designates as "law of residence": To reside in the Land has become a precept and this precept is part of a broader discourse on the required attachment to the Land, on a *prescribed sense of place*, as it were.

The Precept in Tannaitic Times

The earliest rabbinic passages that are explicit in expressing the idea that Jews should dwell in the Land are three texts comprising a mishnah, four consecutive halakhot in the Tosefta and two consecutive narratives in the halakhic midrash *Sifre Deuteronomy*. These three texts preserved in Tannaitic documents constitute a sort of mishnah or base text for the Amoraic interpretive discourse on the precept to dwell in the Land of Israel. Before we turn to how one of the arguments these

6 Boyarin, A Traveling Homeland, 19.

7 The heading of the third section of the article Erets Yisrael in the Encyclopedia Talmudit reads "Residence in it, its settlement and its other laws" (ישיבתה, ישובה ושאר דיניה).

8 Encyclopedia Talmudit, art. Erets Yisrael, 223.

9 See de Vos, Heiliges Land und Nähe Gottes.

passages advance is expanded upon in Amoraic and post-Amoraic documents, I will first consider the Tannaitic traditions themselves.

The beginning of the last mishnah in tractate Ketubbot reads: "All may be compelled to go up to the Land of Israel, but none may be compelled to leave it." (*mKet* 13:11) The situation this mishnah is concerned with is that of a husband or a wife who does not wish to immigrate to the Land or does not wish to remain in the Land. It is as an exposition upon this mishnaic ruling that the lengthiest Amoraic elaboration on the duty to reside in the Land is based—*bKet* 110b–112a, the *Fundgrube* on statements on the Land in Günter Stemberger's words.[10]

When we turn to the Tosefta, we notice a sharper impetus. In the first halakhah of the toseftan passage *tAZ* 5:3–6,[11] an unattributed apodictic statement claims that living in the Land and being buried in the Land constitute the *summum bonum* for Jews as far as their place on earth is concerned:

> A person should live in the Land of Israel, even in a town in which the majority of residents are gentiles, and not abroad, even in a town in which all of the residents are Israelites. This teaches that dwelling in the Land of Israel is weighed against all the other commandments of the Torah and that whoever is buried in the Land of Israel it is as if he were buried under the altar [of the Temple in Jerusalem]. (*tAZ* 5:3)[12]

If living in the Land may be compared to the rest of the commandments, it is because, so the argument of the Tosefta, it is the weightiest among the commandments.[13] Correspondingly important and ideally the natural consequence of a life in the Land, is death and burial there. The latter, irrespective of the precise location of one's grave within the Land are comparable to what must have been understood as the most desirable among the possible burial locations within the land, the place where the altar of the Temple once stood. What concerns us now is not what the rabbis thought and said about the location of human remains, but about the rabbinically approved geographical settings of rabbinic lives. According to this toseftan statement, only

10 Stemberger, Bedeutung, 193. Although this sugya is of paramount importance in this context, mainly for scope reasons I will not deal with it here. See Rubenstein, Coping.

11 The passage is found in the fifth chapter of the tractate in the Vienna Codex of the Tosefta and in the fourth chapter of the tractate in the Erfurt Codex.

12 For the translations of the Tosefta I follow the Vienna Codex and make use of Neusner's English translation (Neusner, The Tosefta).

13 On the hyperbole implied in representing living in the Land as equal to all the commandments in the Torah, Gafni (Land, Centre and Diaspora, 77) comments: "The question, of course, is one of mathematical logic, or if you prefer, of weights and measures: If mitzva A weighs the equivalent of all other mitzvot, B, C and D included, how is it that elsewhere mitzva B suddenly assumes the same overwhelming position? It would appear that the phrase was a means of proclaiming that at any given period, a particular commandment might be in danger and thus warrants—for the moment—a disproportionate amount of devotion." The same hyperbole is used in *tPeah* 4:19 and in *bNed* 25a to exalt other commandments.

in the Land is it appropriate for a Jew to live. This is presented as valid, even if the Tosefta states that in the Land there are cities which are predominantly inhabited by non-Jews and claims (again hyperbolically) that abroad there are cities which are exclusively inhabited by Jews. This Palestinian statement does not convey an either-or question, it is not a matter of either living or being buried in the Land, as is the case in Babylonian interpretations of the dictum.[14] As far as this halakhah is concerned, there is no viable alternative to a life in the Land. The corresponding rhetorical strategy to convey this notion is to use a hyperbole to claim that dwelling in the Land weighs as all the commandments of the Torah, which is why dwelling in the Land is comparable to the weightiest imaginable precept.

In the apodictic statement that follows upon this first halakhah, emigration from the Land is presented as exceptionally permitted in case of dearth:

> A person should not leave [to settle] abroad unless wheat goes at the price of two seah for a sela. Said Rabbi Simeon: Under what circumstances? Only in a case in which he does not find any to buy even at that price. But if he finds some to buy at that price, even [if] a seah of grain [goes] for a sela, he should not go abroad. And so did Rabbi Simeon say: Elimelech was one of the great men of his time and one of those who sustained (one of the leaders of) the community. And because he went abroad, he and his sons died in famine. But all the Israelites were able to survive on their own land, for it is said, *[And when they came to Bethlehem,] the whole town was stirred because of them* (Ruth 1:19). This teaches that all of the town had survived, but he and his sons had died in the famine. (*tAZ* 5:4)

Only extreme scarcity justifies emigration. As the example given by the second century Rabbi Simeon is supposed to illustrate, not even in the case of Elimelech was emigration the right measure, especially in view of the fact that he was one of those in charge of others.[15] Evidence for the fact that Elimelech's choice was wrong are his and his sons' early deaths. He and his sons left the Land and Bethlehem (lit. "the house of bread") for Moab purportedly because of a famine and died precisely of famine, while the rest of the population of Bethlehem stayed alive. I will return to the rabbinic afterlife of Elimelech as archetypal émigré.

In the third halakhah of the toseftan passage, the anonymous governing voice of the Tosefta utters a midrashic statement that makes use of scriptural exegesis to exalt life in the Land:

> See, it [Scripture] says, *So that I come again to my father's house in peace* (Gen 28:21). For does Scripture not say, *Then the Lord will be my God* (Gen 28:21)? And it [Scripture]

14 See *bKet* 111a.

15 In a modern midrash, Elimelech and his sons are described as having "belonged to the aristocracy of the land." (Ginzberg, Legends, 30–31)

> says, *I am the Lord your God, who brought you forth out of the land of Egypt to give you the Land of Canaan, and to be your God* (Lev 25:38). So long as you are in the Land of Canaan, I am your God. [If] you are not in the Land of Canaan, it is as if I were not God for you. And so it [Scripture] says, *About forty thousand ready armed for war passed over before the Lord for battle to the plains of Jericho* (Jos 4:13). And would it ever enter your mind that the Israelites would conquer the Land before the Omnipresent? But the meaning is this: So long as they are located upon it, it is as if it were conquered. If they are not located upon it, it is as if it were not conquered. And so David says, *For they have driven me out this day, that I should have no share in the heritage of the Lord, saying, 'Go, serve other gods'* (1 Sam 26:19). Now would it ever enter your mind that David would go and worship idols? But David made the following exegesis: Whoever leaves the Land in a time of peace and goes abroad, it is as if he worshipped idols. And so it [Scripture] says, *I will plant them in this land in faithfulness, with all my heart and all my soul* (Jer 32:41): So long as they are located upon it, it is as if they were planted before me in faithfulness with all my heart and all my soul. If they are not located upon it, it is as if they were not planted before me in faithfulness with all my heart and all my soul. (*tAZ* 5:5)

The passage concatenates four midrashic units,[16] each of which consists of the quotation of a scriptural text and a commentary on it. The first unit, which links two verses and identifies "my father's house" (Gen 28:21) with "the Land of Canaan" (Lev 25:38), suggests in two parallel conditional clauses that God is unquestionably Israel's God whenever they are in the Land given them. Elsewhere, the midrash cautiously suggests by letting God speak these words, the relationship between Israel and God is different, as it were. It is "as if" God were not Israel's God. In the next midrashic unit the anonymous voice of the Tosefta takes over to interpret Jos 4:13 as metaphorically—again "as if"—meaning that Israel once conquered the Land. When they are not on the Land, in any case, this is "as if" never conquered. In the next two midrashic units, the rabbinic voice resorts to interpretations it attributes to king David and God. The midrash suggests that in speaking 1 Sam 26:19 (which suggests a causal relation between losing one's part of God's heritage and worshipping other gods), David equalled leaving the Land in times of peace with idolatry. In other words, renouncing the Land equals renouncing its one God. The fourth and last midrashic unit has God interpret Jer 32:41[17] along similar lines as those of the first midrashic unit: Again, it is here the case that only in the Land can the relationship between Israel and God be characterised as one of plenitude. Elsewhere, it is "as if" this were not the case.

Despite the repeated use of "as if," this toseftan halakhah states unequivocally that as long as Israel reside in the Land God is their God, they may perceive the

---

16 The double vertical lines indicate the limits of the first, second and third of these midrashic units. For the concept of midrashic unit, see Samely, Forms, 65–69.

17 Depending on the textual witness, either David or the anonymous governing voice of the Tosefta quotes Jer 32:41.

Land as acquired by conquest, and Israel remains faithful to their one God. Being in the Land, therefore, makes a substantial part of Israel being Israel, the midrashic interpretations of these sets of verses suggest. An existence elsewhere jeopardizes Israel's identity.

In order to depict the ideological implications of an existence somewhere other than in the Land this midrashic halakhah describes it in terms of an almost God-less existence, of an existence lacking in part of the people's history, and of an unfaithful relationship to God.

In the last halakhah of the toseftan segment, the second century Rabbi Simeon ben Eleazar compares living outside of the Land to idolatry but he goes a step further in that he dispenses with the particle "as if":

> Rabbi Simeon ben Eleazar says: Israelites who live abroad are idolaters in innocence: How so? A Gentile who made a banquet for his son and went and invited all the Jews who live in his town—even though they eat and drink their own [food and wine], and their own waiter stands over them and serves them, they nonetheless serve idolatry, for it is said, *[You shall not make a covenant with the inhabitants of the land, for when they prostitute themselves to their gods and sacrifice to their gods,] someone among them will invite you, and you will eat of the sacrifice* (Exod 34:15). (*tAZ* 5:6)

The tanna tells what we may call a hypothetical story—a rabbinic literary form referred to as *ma'aseh* or precedent. Participation in a banquet of Gentiles, no matter how strictly the Jewish guests observe the laws of kashrut, is viewed not as potential, but as actual idolatry. Even if this idolatry is softened by the qualification "in innocence."[18] While being abroad is compared to partaking of a Gentile banquet, it is left unsaid where the "abroad" referred to lies: Does the Tosefta mean Transjordan and Syria? Or are also enclave regions within the Land of Israel, such as Beth Shean, Beth Guvrin, and Caesarea, meant as places where Jews are abroad and only apparently at home?[19] If the latter is the case, may we surmise rabbinic criticism of actual involvement in the affairs of the Gentiles in Palestine?

The four halakhot of this toseftan passage constitute the most clearly prescriptive formulation of where Jews are supposed to live preserved in Tannaitic literature. In a less apodictic and more narrative style instead, but more importantly, with rabbis as characters, two narratives transmitted consecutively in the halakhic midrash *Sifre Deuteronomy* are further evidence of the emergence of the Tannaitic precept to dwell in the Land. Both stories are closed with the same statement found in the first halakhah of the toseftan passage:

---

18 The qualification "in innocence" is only preserved in the Vienna Codex of the Tosefta. It may be seen as one of those cases in which the Tosefta adopts readings of baraitot (Tannaitic readings not transmitted in the Mishnah) preserved in the Babylonian Talmud.

19 See Safrai, Seeking out the Land, 118–121.

> *When you have dispossessed them and live [in their land]* (Deut 12:29): It once happened that Rabbi Judah ben Betherah, Rabbi Mattiah ben Cheresh, Rabbi Chananiah, the nephew of Rabbi Yehoshua, and Rabbi Jonathan were going abroad. When they reached Platana and remembered the Land of Israel, they raised their eyes [heavenward] and letting their tears flow rent their garments and recited the verse, *And when you occupy it and live in it, you must diligently observe all these statutes* (Deut 11:31–32). They said: Dwelling in the Land of Israel is weighed against all the other commandments of the Torah.
>
> At another time Rabbi Eleazar ben Shammua and Rabbi Yohanan the Sandal-maker were going to Nisibis to study Torah under Rabbi Yehudah ben Betherah. When they got to Sidon, they remembered the Land of Israel, raised their eyes [heavenward] and letting their tears flow rent their garments and recited the verse, *And when you occupy it and live in it, you must diligently observe all these statutes and ordinances* (Deut 11:31–32). They said: Dwelling in the Land of Israel is weighed against all the other commandments of the Torah. Thereupon they returned to the Land of Israel. (*SifDev* 80)[20]

Twice upon a time a group of sages who have set out to leave the Land realize at liminal situations[21] that their actions amount to the transgression of a precept. Having reached these places triggers in them the awareness of their transgression and of their place attachment. Even though this *anagnorisis* moment is narrated verbatim in both stories, what the first group makes of it, whether they leave the Land or return, is not explicitly narrated. From other rabbinic contexts we know that the mentioned sages are major Tannaim who emigrated to different places and at different times in the second century, which makes of the narrative in *Sifre Deuteronomy* a didactic fiction, an exemplum that emphasizes the sages' ideal expression of regret upon leaving the Land.

The reader of the quoted text is led to assume that at least one of the first group, namely, Rabbi Yehudah ben Betherah, emigrated and established for himself a reputation in Nisibis in Upper Mesopotamia—which would have meant leaving not only the Land but also the Roman Empire and settling in the city when it was under Parthian rule. The fact that this rabbinic teacher is in Nisibis is the reason why the two scholars in the second narrative wish to emigrate.[22] Why the scholars in the *first* group emigrate and which their destinations are is not spelt out

20 Text quoted with minor modifications following Hammer, Sifre.

21 The two narratives which follow the same pattern appear to refer to places in more or less the same liminal area that brings to the rabbis' minds the crossing of boundaries. It is probable that with with פטלום of MSS Vat. ebr. 32 and Oxford, Bodl. 151 the redactors of *SifDev* 80 meant פלטנוס or "Platana in the territory of Sidon" mentioned by Josephus, *B. J.* 1,539. See Reeg, Die Ortsnamen, 514 (פלטנוס) and 533–534 (צי״דן).

22 The sage is assumed to have been a contemporary of Rabbi Akiva in the early second century. See Stemberger, Einleitung, 91; Neusner, The Parthian Period, 121–124.

in the midrash.[23] In both cases, the narrative couples the transgression not just with awareness but with certain almost ritual actions that may be interpreted as expression of a sentiment related to their sense of place. All the emigrating rabbis weep, rend their clothes, and looking in the direction of heaven quote a verse from Deuteronomy which is read as containing the precept they are on the point of transgressing. Either the collective voice of the emigrating sages or the governing voice of the midrash provides an interpretation of the quoted verse that claims that to dwell in the Land is equivalent to all the precepts, which amounts to suggesting that it is the weightiest imaginable precept.

Is the sentiment our source attributes to the emigrating rabbis "despair upon leaving one's land," as Gafni suggests?[24] Does the narrative let us understand that the rabbis are in any way forced to emigrate? Or does the narrative suggest that both groups of Tannaim were on the point of leaving the land voluntarily and the realization that they would eventually be judged for this decision led them all to express grief, and only the rabbis of the second group to change their minds and return to the Land? As previously pointed out, Gafni sees a radical change taking place in the expressions of attachment to the Land in the generation following the defeat of the Bar Kochva revolt, a theme that he sees as minimally represented in statements attributed to the sages of the earlier, so-called Yabnean period. However, the rabbinic authorities who are quoted in the Tosefta and whose deeds are narrated in the text of *Sifre Deuteronomy* are assumed to have been active not exclusively in the post-Bar Kochva period. We may see these texts as evidence of a rabbinic pro-Land of Israel discourse that may have existed prior to the Bar Kochva revolt, or as evidence that at the time of redaction of the Tosefta (fourth century) and the halakhic midrash (third to fourth century) such a discourse was projected back onto pre-Bar Kochva times, thereby idealising the sages of early Tannaitic generations.

The governing voices of the quoted mishnah, the toseftan halakhot, and the narratives in *Sifre Deuteronomy*, as well as the embodied Tannaitic voices of the speaking and acting sages are thus primarily concerned with the meaningfulness of residence in the Land and with the implications of transgressing the prohibition against leaving the Land. The statements in this minimal corpus may have represented for the sages both a way of taking position about *faits accomplis* and an attempt to prevent further emigration. The particular emigration of Elimelech, with which Rabbi Simeon clearly finds fault in *tAZ* 5:4, was expanded upon in Amoraic sources and it is to these that I would like to turn my attention now.

---

23 See Neusner, The Parthian Period, 122, fn. 1 on emigration of sages in the second century as recurrent motif in rabbinic literature.

24 Gafni, Land, Centre and Diaspora, 61, fn. 7.

The Amoraic Elaboration on the Archetypal Emigré

In Amoraic times the elaboration on the dwelling precept takes the form of an intertextual dialogue between anonymous and attributed Tannaitic dicta and Palestinian and Babylonian Amoraic dicta. Gafni has pointed out that the early Amoraic period witnesses an enhanced severity in the rabbinic demands for commitment to the Land.[25]

A strategy with which the problem of emigration is addressed in the rabbinic literature of the Amoraic period consists in an elaboration of the narrative material of scriptural precedents.[26] The scriptural émigré Elimelech was identified already in Tannaitic literature as archetype of a negative attitude towards the Land.[27] According to the first chapter in the book of Ruth, Elimelech left his native Bethlehem during a famine. Among the seven proems that precede the actual commentary in the exegetical midrash *Ruth Rabbah* (end of fifth century),[28] the sixth focuses on the character of Elimelech:

> [*And the name of the man was Elimelech* (Ruth 1:2):] [In the face of] trouble you abandoned them and went away, *and a certain man of Bethlehem in Judah went* (Ruth 1:1). *Our princes (alufeinu) are well cared for (mesubbalim). [There is no breaching and no leaving, and no wailing in our streets]* (Ps 144:14). Rabbi Yohanan said: *Our princes (alufeinu) are well cared for.* It is not written here but *Our princes are well cared for*: when the small care [for the great]; *there is no breach* (Ps 144:14): there is no breaking out of punishment, as you say, *And a plague broke out among them* (Ps 106:29); *no leaving* (Ps 144:14): there is no going forth of punishment, as you say, *and fire went forth from the Lord* (Lev 10:2); *and no cry* (Ps 144:14): there is no cry of the punishment, as you say, *All Israel around them fled at their cry* (Num 16:34). Rabbi Simeon ben Laqish interprets the verse the other way round: *Our princes (alufeinu) are well cared for.* Do not read but *Our princes (alufeinu) are well cared for*: when the great care for the small; *there is no breach*: there is no breaking out of exile, as you say, *Through breaches you shall leave* (Amos 4:3); *no leaving* (Ps 144:14): there is no going forth of punishment, as you say, *Dismiss them from my presence and let them go forth* (Jer 15:1);); *and no wailing* (Ps 144:14): there is no wailing of punishment, as you say, *And the outcry of Jerusalem rises* (Jer 14:2). Rabbi Lulianus bar Tavros said [in the name of Rabbi Isaac]: When the great care for the small and the small for the great, *There is no breach and no leaving, and no cry of distress in our streets* (Ps 144:14). *There is no breach*: neither of punishment nor of exile; *and no leaving*: neither of punishment nor of exile; [*and no wailing*: neither of punishment nor of exile]. Rabbi Huna in the name of Rabbi Joseph says:

25 Gafni, Land, Centre and Diaspora, 71–72.

26 Interestingly, the voices that disapprove of emigration from the Land are not exclusively Palestinian ones. See below e. g. the statements of the Babylonian by choice Huna (*Ruth Rab.* 1:4) and the Babylonian Rav Chanan bar Rava (*bBB* 91a).

27 See *tAZ* 5:4.

28 On *Ruth Rabbah* see Stemberger, Einleitung, 351.

> When the small care for the great but the great do not bear the burden of the small, of them it [Scripture] says, *The Lord will bring this charge against the elders and officers of His people* (Isa 3:14). And against Elimelech, [for] when trouble came you abandoned them and left[, *and a certain man of Bethlehem in Judah went*.] (*Ruth Rab.* Proem 6)[29]

The first two verses in the book of Ruth thus constitute the proem's lemma and are in the first place interpreted by an anonymous voice which speaks Aramaic and addresses Elimelech in the first person reprimanding him for having fled in the face of trouble and for having abandoned others. The lemma verse is then linked to a petichah verse from the Psalms and interpreted in its light by three Palestinian authorities of the Amoraic period.[30] In its original context the expression *alufeinu* in Ps 144:14 is understood as referring to "our cattle," which "are well cared for." In the midrash it is associated with the likes of Elimelech, men of high standing in their community, or "princes." Rabbi Yohanan reads the verse as meaning that the young care for the old (or the small tolerate and obey the great), so that they are cared for (or endured, part. *mesubbalim*). Rabbi Simeon ben Laqish reads the verse as conveying not a passive but an active meaning, so that the princes are not "cared for," but rather "take care of." In the midrash, both the noun and the verb in the psalm verse appear to be exploited for their polysemy. Even though in rabbinic Hebrew it came to denote "princes," the original meaning ("cattle") still appears to be at work in the midrash, considering that both interpretations are complementary and that the rabbis expect both the small to respect the great and the great to take care of the small. This is evident in the summarizing view of Rabbi Huna. Only if both the small and the great behave properly towards each other do they avoid exile and its manifestations in the acts of breaching, leaving, and crying.

Elimelech's archetypal emigration is also the focus of attention in the first chapter of the actual commentary in *Ruth Rabbah*. The first verse of the book of Ruth is expanded upon in the text below with traditions related to a list of ten famines:

> *That there was a famine in the land* (Ruth 1:1). [...] Of the famine which came in the days when the judges judged, however, Rabbi Huna said in the name of Rabbi Dosa: Forty-two seah would be [the normal produce], and only forty-one were done. But have we [not] learnt: Israelites should not leave the Land unless two seah [of grain] cost a shekel? Rabban Simeon ben Gamaliel said: When [is this valid]? When one does not find what to buy, but when one finds what to buy even one seah for a shekel, Israelites should not leave the land. But [then] we have learnt: In time of pestilence and in time of war, gather your feet, and in time of famine, spread your feet. Why was he [Elimelech] punished? Because he caused the heart of Israel to fall on themselves. It is like a councillor who resided in a province and the children of the province trusted him that if years of dearth came, [he would sustain the province during ten years with

29 For the translations of *Ruth Rabbah*, I follow Lerner, The Book of Ruth.

30 On the literary form of the petichah, see Samely, Forms, 74–76 and 187–188.

> food. When a year of dearth did come,] his maidservant went out and came to the market with her basket in her hand. The people of the province would say, This is the one whom we trusted and said that if a year of dearth came, he would be able to sustain us during ten years, and see his maidservant standing in the market place with her basket in her hand! Likewise with Elimelech, who was one of the notables in his province and one of the leaders of his generation. When years of famine came, he said, Now all Israel will be at my door, this with his basket and this with his basket. What did he do? He fled from them, for it is written, *And a man [from Bethlehem in Judah] went [to live (lagur) in the country of Moab]* (Ruth 1:1). (*Ruth Rab.* 1:4)

As in *Genesis Rabbah*, whence the ten famines passage may have been taken,[31] so also in *Ruth Rabbah*, the third century Rabbi Huna, who himself emigrated to Babylonia where he is known to have acted as Jewish exilarch, describes the situation of the time of the judges as *not* amounting to a real famine. The rabbinic emigrant Huna therefore condemns the conduct of the scriptural emigrant Elimelech. This verdict is confirmed with the quotation of *tAZ* 5:4: Only when one does not find two seah of grain to buy for a sela is emigration justified.[32] However, the midrash goes on to argue that if Scripture mentions a famine, then a real famine must have been and under such circumstances, an anonymous tradition states, leaving the Land is justified. So the fact that he left because of a famine cannot have been the reason for the punishment of Elimelech.[33] It is here that *Ruth Rabbah* innovates with respect both to *tAZ* 5:4 and the parallels in *Genesis Rabbah* illustrating Elimelech's transgression with a parable that emphasizes that it is the people rather than the Land that he forsook.

It has been argued that the book of Ruth was written in the post-exilic period and that it is in essence a tale of hope and return conceived as promoting the Jewish resettlement of the Land.[34] In this sense, whereas the Tannaitic sources discussed above resort to the figure of Elimelech to illustrate the ominous consequences of emigration from the Land, the Amoraic *Ruth Rabbah* is not only concerned with expanding on this condemnation of Elimelech, but also makes part of its agenda to praise Naomi's return to her homeland in Bethlehem and the Moabitess Ruth's solidarity with her mother-in-law which expresses itself in leaving her own homeland

---

31 Famines are said to have come to the world in the days of Adam, Lamech, Abraham, Isaac, and Jacob, at the time when the judges ruled, and the days of David, of Elijah and Elisha. Apart from these scriptural contexts, the list of ten famines includes a not further specified "traveling famine" and an eschatological famine. The ten famines passage has three parallels in *Genesis Rabbah*. See *Gen. Rab.* 25:3, 40:3 and 64:2. The different order in the treatment of the famines is determined by the hermeneutical agendas of the rabbinic documents.

32 This is the double price of what, according to *mPeah* 7:8, appears to have been the standard price paid for grain, namely four seah per sela.

33 The scriptural text does not state that Elimelech leaves the land to settle abroad, but to reside temporarily (*lagur*) in Moab. See Eskenazi/Frymer-Kensky, Ruth, 4.

34 See Zenger/Frevel, Das Buch Rut, 283–285; Fischer, Rut, 89–91; Eskenazi/Frymer-Kensky, Ruth, xvii–xx.

to settle in a foreign land. The midrash praises Ruth's archetypal immigration to the Land of Israel by linking it to and likening it to a conversion to Judaism, for example, in the words of the fourth century Palestinian Yehoshua bar Simon:

> *When Naomi saw that she was determined to go with her* (Ruth 1:18). Rabbi Yehoshua bar Simon said: She could die but was resolute and she ceased to talk to her. Rabbi Abbahu said: Come and see how precious in the eyes of the Holy One, blessed be He, are converts (*gerim*). When she decided to convert [to Judaism], [Scripture] compares her to Naomi, *So the two of them went on [until they came to Bethlehem.]* (Ruth 1:19) (*Ruth Rab.* 3:5)[35]

The statement concerning Elimelech in the Tosefta is also elaborated upon in the Babylonian Talmud in the context of a *sugya* concerned how to deal with measures of produce which also makes use of other halakhot of the same toseftan context:[36]

> Our Rabbis taught [in a baraita]: It is not permitted to go forth from the Land to a foreign country unless two seah [of grain] are at [the price of] one sela. Rabbi Simeon said: When [is it permitted to leave the country]? When one cannot find [anything] to buy, but when one can [find something to] buy, even if a seah is at a sela one must not leave. And so said Rabbi Simeon ben Yohai: Elimelech, Mahlon, and Chilion were among the great men of their generation, and they were leaders of their generation. Why were they punished? Because they left the Land of Israel for a foreign country, for it is said, *[And when they came to Bethlehem,] the whole town was stirred because of them and they said, Is this Naomi?* (Ruth 1:19). What [is the meaning of,] *Is this Naomi??* Rabbi Isaac said: They said, Have you seen what happened to Naomi who left the Land for a foreign country? And Rabbi Isaac said: On the day when Ruth the Moabitess came to the Land of Israel the wife of Boaz died. This is why people say: Only when the deceased has died, is the one in charge of his house appointed. (*bBB* 91a)[37]

35 The Vilna edition of *Ruth Rabbah* transmits a briefer version of this tradition in the name of Rabbi Yehudah ben Rabbi Simon. Ruth's immigration is also exalted in the following atomizing exegesis of Ruth 2:11, which is reminiscent of an interpretation of Gen 12:1 transmitted in *Gen. Rab.* 39:9 about all that Abraham leaves behind when he follows God's call: *But Boaz answered her, It has been fully told me (huged hugad li)* (Ruth 2:11): [The verb appears] twice: It has been told me (*hugad li*) in the house and it has been told me (*hugad li*) in the field; *all that you have done for your mother-in-law since the death of your husband* (ibid.): it is not necessary [for Scripture] to say "during his lifetime;" *and how you left your father and mother* (ibid.)—*your father*: your real father; *and your mother*: your real mother; *and your native land* (ibid.): [this is your country. Another interpretation: *and how you left your father and mother*: your idolatry [...] *and your mother* (ואמך): that is your people (אומתך); *and your native land*:] this is your neighbourhood; *and came to [a people] that you did not know before (temol shilshom)* (ibid.): If you had come before, we would not have been accepted, for the halakhah was not yet accepted: *Ammonite* (Deut 23:4), but not Ammonitess, *Moabite* (ibid.), but not Moabitess." (*Ruth Rab.* 5:3)

36 See *bBB* 88b–91b.

37 This and the next passage from the Babylonian Talmud are quoted with minor changes following Epstein, Baba Bathra.

The quoted passage gives us an alternative version of the traditions found in *tAZ* 5:4 and *Ruth Rab.* 1:4 on the conditions of dearth which justify emigration and on Elimelech as scriptural precedent.[38] Unlike the Tannaitic text we notice that the Talmud focuses not only on the figure of Elimelech, mentioning him by name, but also on his sons, on all of whom was the same responsibility for those depending on them. The first of Rabbi Isaac's statements, which explains the question of Ruth 1:19 as meaning that Naomi is not recognised in her former homeland, highlights in this context that the transgressions of men have implications for the lives of the women related to them. Ruth's immigration is worthy of comment in the second of Rabbi Isaac's statements because of its timeliness: She came to the Land just in time for Boaz to be able to marry her by becoming a widower.

So far the Talmud has let "exclusively" Palestinian voices speak and confirm the Tannaitic verdict on Elimelech's deeds as deserving punishment. From now on, named Babylonian authorities take on:

> Rav Chanan bar Rava said in the name of Rav: *Elimelech and Salmon and such a one* (Ruth 4:1), and the father of Naomi, all of these were the sons of Nahshon, the son of Amminadab? What does he tell us? That even one who counts with the merit of their ancestors, it is of no avail for them when they leave the Land for a foreign country. […] Rav Chiyya bar Abin said in the name of Rabbi Yehoshua ben Qorchah: God forbid [that Elimelech and his family should be condemned for leaving the Land]; had they found bran, they would not have left. And why were they punished? Because they should have asked for mercy for their generation and they did not do so; for it is said, *When you cry out, let your collection of idols deliver you! [The wind will carry them off, a breath will take them away. But whoever takes refuge in me shall possess the land and inherit my holy mountain.]* (Isa 57:13) Rabba bar bar Chana said in the name of Rabbi Yohanan: This was taught only with respect to times when money is cheap and fruit expensive, but when money is expensive, even if four seah are at a *sela*, they may leave. (*bBB* 91a–b)

After quoting the fourth century Rav Chanan whose position again is in accordance with the Palestinian disapproval of Elimelech's conduct, the Talmud comes back on the prohibition against leaving the Land and lets the younger Babylonian Rav Hiyya bar Avin revise the interpretation of Elimelech's emigration with the aid of a Tannaitic authority, Rabbi Yehoshua ben Qorchah. Together, as it were, they explain that the archetypal emigration on account of a famine (which is not in the least questioned) was not the reason for the punishment inflicted on Elimelech and his family, but rather the fact that they failed to seek God's help—after all, Scripture does not depict them in prayer before deciding to leave for Moab—not

38 Just as in *tAZ* 5:4 it is here the second century Rabbi Simeon and not his contemporary Rabban Simeon ben Gamaliel (II) or the first century Rabban Simeon ben Gamaliel (I) who expresses these ideas in *Ruth Rab.* 1:4.

just for themselves, but more importantly for the rest of their community. More explicit in the justification of emigration is the second statement uttered by the Palestinians Rabba bar bar Chana and Rabbi Yohanan (late third and early fourth centuries): Whenever there is produce, but no money to buy it, Jews may leave the Land of Israel.

The Precept in Post-Amoraic Sources

A different exegetical use of the scriptural narrative of the book of Ruth and a reorientation of the rabbinic theme of Elimelech's punishment is found in a treatment of the latter's emigration transmitted in both recensions of the later midrash *Tanhuma*.[39] In the passage of this post-Amoraic exegetical narrative quoted below the anonymous voice of the midrash focuses on Elimelech's transgression and punishment:

> Another interpretation: *Many times he delivered them* (Ps. 106:43). [These words] speak about the children of Adam. When trouble comes to one [of them] and he immediately repents, the Holy One, blessed be He, saves him. So it is the first time and the second. [If] he repents, it is good; but if not, [He] brings trouble upon him. Why? Because it is difficult for the Holy One, blessed be He, to raise His hand against a [lit. "this"] human being. So what does He do to them? When one of them sins, He begins by raising His hand against his assets. From whom have you learned it? From Naomi, her sons, and Elimelech, who was the head of [his] generation. When famine came, what did he do? He left the Land of Israel and went to the land of Moab. Now the Holy One, blessed be He, was angry with him because he was prince (*nasi*) of [his] generation. The Holy One, blessed be He, said to him: If my children had acted like this, they would have let the Land of Israel become a wilderness.[40] What is written there? *Elimelech, Naomi's husband, died* (Ruth 1:3), but his sons were unable to learn from their father to return to the Land of Israel. And what else did they do? *They married Moabite women* (Ruth 1:4), whom they neither baptised nor proselytised; *one named Orpah and the other Ruth* (Ruth 1:4). *Orpah* (ערפה): because she turned her back (עורף) on her mother-in-law; *Ruth* (רות), because she regarded (ראתה) the words of her mother-in-law. *And they lived there about ten years* (Ruth 1:4): All those ten years the Holy One, blessed be He,

39 The documents of the major genre of homiletical late midrash known as Tanhuma-Yelammedenu literature are all considered as having grown by accretion and therefore consisting of "several developmental strata," whereby the late stratum is dated to the eighth or ninth century (Bregman, Tanchuma-Yelammedenu, 4–5; Weiss, Pious Irreverence, 12). It also appears to be the case that while the first stages of redaction took place in Byzantine Palestine, the last stage has another geographical and cultural setting, in the diaspora within but also without the Islamicate world. See Ulmer, Pesiqta Rabbati, 33–34; Weiss, Pious Irreverence, 84–85.

40 *Tan Be-har* 3 reads here more explicitly: "Had my children left (עזבו), they would have let the Land of Israel become a wilderness."

would warn them. When He saw that they would not repent, He began to raise His hand against their camels and their cattle; and yet they did not repent. Because He saw that they did not return in repentance, immediately, *those two, Mahlon and Chilion, also died* (Ruth 1:5). This proves that it is difficult for the Holy One, blessed be He, to raise His hand against a [lit. "this"] human being. So what does He do to them? He diminishes them in their assets, so that they sell them.

[Concerning] the man who sins, what does the Holy One, blessed be He, do to him first? He brings poverty upon him so that he sells his field, for it is said, *If your kinsman falls into difficulty and sells a piece of property* (Lev 25:25). If he repents, it is fine; but if not, he sells his house, for it is said, *If anyone sells a dwelling-house* (Lev 25:29). If he repents, it is fine; but if not, he sells his daughter, for it is said, *When a man sells his daughter as a slave* (Exod 21:7). If he repents, it is fine; but if not, he sells himself, for it is said, *If a fellow Hebrew sells himself to you* (Deut 15:12). Why all this? Because they became poor through transgressions. *If your kinsman is in straits [and has to sell part of his holding,] his nearest redeemer shall come [and redeem what his kinsman has sold]* (Lev 25:25). Who was this? Boaz. When? When Naomi sold the field, for it is said, *Naomi must sell the piece of land which belonged to our kinsman Elimelech* (Ruth 4:3). This is meant by [the verse] *has to sell part of his holding* (Lev 25:25). Rabbi Simeon ben Yohai said: *Elimelech, Salmon, So-and-So* (Ruth 4:1), and Naomi's father were all descendants of Nahshon ben Amminadab. [In view of the fact that] Elimelech, Mahlon, and Chilion were leaders of the[ir] generation, for what reason were they punished? Because they went out of the Land of Israel, for it is said, *[And when they came to Bethlehem,] the whole town was stirred because of them and they said, Is this Naomi?* (Ruth 1:19). What [is the meaning of] *Is this Naomi*? You saw Naomi who went abroad from the Land of Israel and what has happened to her? (*TanB Be-har* 8 par. *Tan Be-har* 3)[41]

The quoted passage links a petichah verse from the Psalms to a lemma verse from the book of Leviticus 25:25. To provide a homiletical transition between these two poles, the post-Amoraic *Tanhuma* weaves the Amoraic traditions discussed previously with other traditions of *Ruth Rabbah* into an exegetical narrative.[42] While the first part of the quoted text may give the impression of focusing on the interpretation of Ps 106:43, the second is more explicitly concerned with showing how the events narrated in the book of Ruth are a case in point of what Lev 25:25

41 Quoted with minor modifications following Townsend, Midrash Tanhuma.

42 Anonymizing the tradents, *Tanhuma* resorts to the following tradition in *Ruth Rabbah*: "*Then those two, Mahlon and Chilion, also died* (Ruth 1:5). Rabbi Chunia and Rabbi Yehoshua in the name of Rabbi Avin and Rabbi Zabda, the son-in-law of Rabbi Levi [said]: The Merciful never punishes the lives of men in the first place. […] And also in the case of Mahlon and Chilion it was thus. First their horses and their asses and their camels died, after this Elimelech died and *Then those two, Mahlon and Chilion, also died; so the woman was left* (Ruth 1:5). Rabbi Chanina [said]: She was made into the remnants of the remnants." (*Ruth Rab.* 2:10) The interpretation of the question posed by the people of Bethlehem in Ruth 1:19 where the midrash contrasts the wealth Naomi once had to her destituteness on returning to Bethlehem is addressed in *Ruth Rab.* 3:6–7.

prescribes.[43] The second part preserves in reverse order the two exegeses of Ruth 1:19 and Ruth 4:1 transmitted in *bBB* 91a–b.

The entire passage seems to have Naomi, a biblical sister of Job,[44] in focus: It is how *her* assets and *her* status are diminished, it is how God finds it difficult to raise His hand against *her*, and how He ultimately delivers *her* and her daughter-in-law when Boaz redeems the land for them. Thus, while God is thought of as slow to anger with respect to Naomi, He appears to respond promptly to the transgressions of the men in her family—this, after all, the scriptural narrative requires. The man Elimelech has to die, the midrash argues, because unlike his ancestors (Abraham, the Israelites who conquered and settled the Land) he risked letting the Land turn into a wilderness and emigrated. Mahlon and Chilion, the sons, have to die not only because of their intermarriage with women of Moab but because in the course of ten years they would not leave this region of Transjordan and return to the Land of Israel proper.[45] Naomi, on the other hand, has seen her family and property diminished, has been forced to sell, but has not been punished with a premature death because of her timely return to the Land and, clearly, because a kinsman who has remained in the Land is willing to help her out.

It could also be argued that Naomi is punished with poverty, which in turn is the consequence of the improper conduct of her husband and sons. The last part of the quoted text insists on the notion that the punishment of Elimelech and his sons is in accord with their high social standing. The emigration of leaders is not to be tolerated. The narrative understands the behaviour of Elimelech and his sons as the cause of the women's poverty and gives the latter due to their proper conduct in leaving Moab for Bethlehem the chance to recover with the aid of the proper conduct of the kinsman Boaz.[46]

---

43 The quoted text is only the first part of the exegesis of this verse in this chapter of *Tanhuma* Buber. The rest of the chapter is concerned with explaining how Boaz with his actions puts into practice the halakhah of Lev 25 taking the role of the redeemer, i. e., the closest relative able to redeem the land referred to in that verse, showing solidarity to Naomi and Ruth. The book of Ruth, as Zakovitch, Das Buch Rut, 47, and Fischer, Rut, 81–85, have pointed out, may indeed be seen as pre-rabbinic halakhic midrash in that it deals with controversial issues of a post-exilic time (obligations towards the poor, intermarriage, levirate marriage) not only on the basis of Lev 25:25, but also of Deut 23:4–7 and Deut 25. See Zenger/Frevel, Das Buch Rut, 281–282.

44 Ibid., 279.

45 The status of Transjordan is a disputed issue in rabbinic literature. Whereas according to *mKet* 13:9, *mBB* 3:2, and *SifDev* 180, Transjordan is one of the regions of the Land, other Tannaitic sources, e. g. *mYad* 4:3, *mBik* 1:10, *Sifra Metsorah* parashah 5,1–2, *SifDev* 299, *SifDev* 301, question this assumption and consider Transjordan as outside the Land. Both positions are discussed in *yBik* 1:10 (64b). See Stemberger, Bedeutung, 182–183; Safrai, Seeking out the Land, 128–134.

46 On poverty as central theme of the book of Ruth, see Siquans, Foreignness and Poverty.

Conclusion

The collection of late ancient and early medieval rabbinic texts I have discussed share a concern with giving textual shape to a religious duty that is not found in the Hebrew scriptures or in the Mishnah. The closest rabbinic texts come to spelling out a "dwelling precept" is the apodictic statement of *tAZ* 5:3 and the two rabbinic precedents of *SifDev* 80: In both cases we read "dwelling in the Land of Israel is weighed against all the other commandments of the Torah." The Amoraic and post-Amoraic texts discussed above do not preserve the motif of the weightiest imaginable precept.

Our itinerary of sources had its starting point in a Tannaitic text (*tAZ* 5:3–6) which focuses on the notion of the inconceivableness of a life outside of the Land. Although it does resort to different literary forms, its general tone is set by the use of hyperbole and the apodictic character of the opening halakhah. The notion that dwelling in the Land is a precept reappears at the close of the two narratives about emigrating rabbis in *SifDev* 80. Late ancient rabbinic readers would probably have more easily identified with fellow rabbis of the recent past as these depicted in the halakhic midrash than with scriptural characters or with the more impersonal statements of the toseftan text.

To examine the attitude towards the Land in the Amoraic period a group of sources that elaborate on the problematic archetypal emigration of Elimelech was selected. These stem from genres that allow for more polyphony and narrativity than the Tannaitic sources.[47] Whereas the Palestinian *Ruth Rabbah* intensified the condemnation of Elimelech's conduct in emigrating as cowardly and unfitting for a prince or councillor—he flees—the Babylonian Talmud offers a more nuanced appreciation of Elimelech's emigration. This was justified, but his having failed to pray for his people is not defensible. At the close of the itinerary, a Palestinian Tanhuma tradition—primarily concerned with making explicit the scripturally implicit link of the book of Ruth with Lev 25 and its discussion of the redemption of land—retains or recovers the earlier Palestinian condemnation of Elimelech. He and his sons were all punished for leaving the Land.

Although the hermeneutical agendas and style of the sources vary depending on the documents' genre and period, all of the examined literary forms (apodictic statement, midrashic unit, petichah, precedent, parable) acknowledge the duty to deal with this duty. They involve for this purpose the voices of pre- and post-Bar Kochva Tannaim as well as Palestinian and Babylonian Amoraim as mouthpieces of a discourse on the meaningfulness of the Land which an anonymous voice orchestrates and updates. At times they also opt to make minimal use of named authorities and let midrash speak for itself. The engagement with the dwelling

47 In different ways Palestinian Amoraic midrash and the Babylonian Talmud are multi-layered.

precept across time and space is revealed in these texts as a prescribed sense of place and diasporic Jewish category of belonging.

In "Crossing and Dwelling," a book concerned with the spatial practices that religions involve, Thomas Tweed writes that religions both "situate the devout in the body, the home, the homeland, and the cosmos"—which is why they are about being in place—and "employ tropes, artifacts, rituals, codes, and institutions to mark boundaries, and they prescribe and proscribe different kinds of movements across those boundaries"—which is why they are also about moving and crossing.[48] The rabbinic texts examined in this paper may be seen as historical manifestations of such a pre- and proscriptive tendency of religion. They prescribe a religious sense of place for the Land of Israel as ancestral and rabbinic homeland, proscribe movement out of it, and also nuance both prescription and proscription.

Literature

Sources

Epstein, Isidor (ed.), Baba Bathra, vol. 2 of The Babylonian Talmud. Seder Nezikin, transl. M. Simon and I. W. Slotki, London 1935.

Ginzberg, Louis (ed.), Legends of the Jews, vol. IV. Bible Times and Characters from Joshua to Esther, Philadelphia, Pa. 1913.

Hammer, Reuven (transl.), Sifre. A Tannaitic Commentary on the Book of Deuteronomy, translated from the Hebrew with Introduction and Notes, New Haven, Conn./London 1986.

Neusner, Jacob (ed.), The Tosefta, Translated from the Hebrew, vol. 4: Neziqin. The Order of the Damages, New York, N. Y. 1981.

Townsend, John T. (transl.), Midrash Tanhuma (S. Buber Recension), Translated into English with Introduction, Indices and Brief Notes, vol. 2. Exodus and Leviticus, Hoboken, N. J. 1997.

Ulmer, Rivka (ed.), A Bilingual Edition Pesiqta Rabbati, vol. 1. Chapters 1–22, Berlin/Boston 2017.

Scholarly Works

Art. Erets Yisrael. Encyclopedia Talmudit 2, Jerusalem 1956, 199–235.

Boyarin, Daniel, A Traveling Homeland. The Babylonian Talmud as Diaspora, Philadelphia, Pa. 2015.

Bregman, Marc, The Tanchuma-Yelammedenu. Studies in the Evolution of the Versions, Piscataway, N. J. 2003 (English and Hebrew).

48 Tweed, Crossing and Dwelling, 123.

Castree, Noel/Kitchin, Rob/Rogers, Alisdair, Art. Sense of place, A Dictionary of Human Geography, Oxford 2013.
Cohen, Robin, Global Diasporas. An Introduction, London/New York, N. Y. ²2008.
Cordoni, Constanza, Inheriting and Buying a Homeland. The Land of Israel and the Patriarchs, Journal for the Study of Judaism 49 (2018), 551–580.
Eskenazi, Tamara Cohn/Frymer-Kensky, Tikva Simone, Ruth. The Traditional Hebrew Text with the New JPS Translation, Philadelphia, Pa. 2011.
Fischer, Irmtraud, Rut (HTKAT), Freiburg i.Br. et al. 2001.
Gafni, Isaiah, Land, Center and Diaspora. Jewish Constructs in Late Antiquity, Sheffield 1997.
Lerner, Myron B. (ed.), The Book of Ruth in Aggadic Literature and Midrash Ruth Rabbah, Jerusalem 1971 (text of Ruth Rabbah available in e-book platform Bar Ilan Responsa Project).
Low, Setha M./Altman, Irvin, Place Attachment. A conceptual inquiry, in: I. Altman/S. M. Low (ed.), Place Attachment, New York, N. Y./London 1992.
Malpas, Jeff, Place and Singularity, in: J. Malpas (ed.), The Intelligence of Place. Topographies and Poetics, New York, N. Y. 2015, 65–92.
Neusner, Jacob, The Parthian Period, vol. 1 of A History of the Jews in Babylonia, Leiden 1965.
Reeg, Gottfried, Die Ortsnamen Israels nach der rabbinischen Literatur (BTAVO), Wiesbaden 1989.
Reis, Michele, Theorizing Diaspora. Perspectives on "Classical" and "Contemporary" Diaspora, International Migration 42 (2004), 41–60.
Rubenstein, Jeffrey, Coping with the Virtues of the Land of Israel. An Analysis of Bavli Ketubot 110b–112a, in: I. Gafni (ed.), Center and Diaspora. The Land of Israel and the Diaspora in the Second Temple, Mishna and Talmud Period, Jerusalem 2004, 159–188.
Rutgers, Leonard V., Next year in Sardis. Reflections on whether the Jewish Diaspora of the Roman Era was Diasporic at all, in: C. Cordoni/G. Langer (ed.), "Let the Wise Listen and Add to Their Learning" (Prov 1:5) (FS Günter Stemberger), Berlin 2016, 167–195.
Safrai, Ze'ev, Seeking out the Land. Land of Israel Traditions in Ancient Jewish, Christian and Samaritan literature (200 BCE–400 CE), Leiden/Boston 2018.
Samely, Alexander, Forms of Rabbinic Literature and Thought, Oxford 2007.
Siquans, Agnethe, Foreignness and Poverty in the Book of Ruth, JBL 128 (2009), 443–452.
Stemberger, Günter, Die Bedeutung des Landes Israel in der rabbinischen Tradition, Kairos Salzburg 25 (1983), 176–199.
—, Einleitung in Talmud und Midrasch, Munich ⁹2011.
Tweed, Thomas A., Crossing and Dwelling. A Theory of Religion, Cambridge, Mass. 2006.
Vos, Jacobus Cornelis de, Heiliges Land und Nähe Gottes. Wandlungen alttestamentlicher Landvorstellungen in frühjüdischen und neutestamentlichen Schriften, Göttingen 2012.
Weiss, Dov, Pious Irreverence. Confronting God in Rabbinic Judaism, Philadelphia, Pa. 2017.
Wilkie, Richard/Roberson, George F., Art. Sense of place, SAGE Encyclopedia of Geography 4, Thousand Oaks, Calif. 2010, 2533–2534.
Zenger, Erich/Frevel, Christian, Das Buch Rut, in: E. Zenger et al. (ed.), Einleitung in das Alte Testament, Stuttgart ⁹2016, 278–288.
Zakovitch, Yair, Das Buch Rut. Ein jüdischer Kommentar (SBS 177), Stuttgart 1999.

Elisabeth Birnbaum (Wien)

Hieronymus und die Anderen

Rhetorik und Polemik im Koheletkommentar

Einleitung

Sophronius Eusebius Hieronymus von Stridon († 420 n. Chr.), einer der vier lateinischen Kirchenväter, unterscheidet sich von den anderen dreien – Ambrosius von Mailand († 397 n. Chr.), Augustinus von Hippo († 430 n. Chr.) und Gregor dem Großen († 604 n. Chr.) – in mehrerer Hinsicht:

Während Ambrosius und Augustinus einflussreiche Bischöfe waren und Gregor der Große es sogar zum Papstamt brachte, erlangte Hieronymus nie höhere kirchliche Ehren – was jedoch die Nachwelt nicht daran hinderte, ihn später sogar als Kardinal darzustellen.[1]

Anders als die drei anderen lebte er den größten Teil seines Lebens nicht in bedeutenden Städten wie Rom oder Mailand, sondern am Rande der lateinischen Welt, in Betlehem – was ihn nicht davon abhielt, bedeutende Schriften und Bibelübersetzungen zu verfassen.

In Sachen Eigenwerbung war Hieronymus offensichtlich erfolgreicher als die anderen drei. Mithilfe seines ausgeprägten rhetorischen Talents schuf er ein Bild von sich, das seiner Stellung auf der kirchlichen Karriereleiter nicht entsprach und dennoch die Nachwelt entscheidend prägte.

Das Selbstbild, das er dabei offenbar hatte, ähnelt dem berühmten Bild Caravaggios „Der Heilige Hieronymus" (1606, Villa Borghese): Es könnte mit „Der gelehrte Asket" betitelt werden.[2] Ein halbbekleideter, ausgezehrter alter Mann mit Bart ist darauf zu sehen, der allein in seiner Schreibstube sitzt. Seine einzige Bekleidung ist ein roter Umhang. Er schreibt in ein großformatiges aufgeschlagenes Buch an einem einfachen Holztisch. Ein weiteres, ebenfalls aufgeschlagenes, liegt auf einem geschlossenen und darauf ein Totenschädel. Damit verknüpft Caravaggio zwei Bildtraditionen:[3] Die eine, eher im protestantischen Bereich angesiedelte Darstellungsweise sieht Hieronymus als humanistischen Gelehrten.[4] Die andere, katholisch favorisierte

---

1 Das bekannteste Beispiel dafür ist das Gemälde von Rubens: „Hl. Hieronymus in Kardinalstracht", ca. um 1625; Kunsthistorisches Museum Wien.

2 So die Überschrift des Blogs von Norbert Schnabel, Stendhal-Syndrom.

3 Vgl. Schnabel, Stendhal-Syndrom.

4 Ein Beispiel dafür ist die Darstellung Albrecht Dürers, „Hieronymus im Gehäus", 1514; British Museum.

Darstellung zeigt einen asketischen Hieronymus als Büßer in der Wildnis, begleitet nur von einem Löwen.[5]

Im Selbstbild des Hieronymus sind diese beiden Seiten wie im Gemälde von Caravaggio vereint. Er sieht sich als Exeget und Asket, als gebildeten, asketisch lebenden Menschen. Und dieses Selbstbild profiliert und präsentiert Hieronymus besonders in seinem Koheletkommentar – mittels einer rhetorisch geschickten Unterscheidung zwischen „Wir" und „die Anderen".

Rhetorik und Polemik als Abgrenzung von „Wir" und „die Anderen"

Hieronymus erlernte seine rhetorischen Fähigkeiten beim bedeutenden lateinischen Grammatiker Aelius Donatus (310–380 n. Chr.). Bei ihm studierte er bei seinem ersten Rom-Aufenthalt (358–366 n. Chr.), noch vor seiner Taufe, Grammatik und Rhetorik. Auch die Liebe zu paganen Autoren, wie Vergil oder Horaz, nahm er von dort mit. Dass Hieronymus seine Rhetorik oftmals zu Polemik geraten ließ, verdankte er wohl einerseits seinem Sinn für Satire und Sarkasmus, andererseits aber seinem genuin cholerischen Temperament.

Beides nützte er, um seine Anhänger/innen zu beeinflussen und seine Gegner/innen zu attackieren. Die folgenden Ausführungen sollen am Beispiel des Koheletkommentars zeigen, wie Hieronymus mit Identität und Andersheit umgeht, wie er das „Wir" und das „Ihr" definiert und anwendet. Dabei soll deutlich werden, dass Hieronymus im Grunde nur ein „Wir" im Sinn hat: Und dieses „Wir" nennt sich Hieronymus.[6]

Der Koheletkommentar[7]

Hieronymus schreibt seinen ersten großen alttestamentlichen Kommentar 388/389 in Betlehem.[8] Das gewählte Buch ist Kohelet. Das mag auf den ersten Blick

---

5 Z. B. Tizian, „Der hl. Hieronymus in der Wildnis", um 1575; Escorial, Madrid. Weitere Beispiele siehe Schnabel, Stendhal-Syndrom.

6 Damit soll nicht gesagt werden, dass Hieronymus in späteren Jahren nicht zu milderen und differenzierteren Urteilen gekommen wäre. In der Tat stellt der Koheletkommentar einen Sonderfall dar, der von persönlicher Betroffenheit und von der Notwendigkeit, sich selbst zu rechtfertigen und profilieren, geprägt ist.

7 Die hier verwendete Textgrundlage ist Hieronymus, *Comm. Eccl.* (CCSL 72) in der Revision durch Michael Margoni Kögler in: Birnbaum, Koheletkommentar.

8 Davor verfasste er kleine Kommentare zu Epheser, Galater, Titus und Philemon (alle 386), später folgten dann noch Kommentare zum Matthäus-Evangelium (398/399) und zur Offenbarung des Johannes (399).

überraschen, zählt das Buch Kohelet doch gemeinhin nicht zu den alttestamentlichen Schriften, die vorrangig zu behandeln sind. Augustinus etwa schrieb Kommentare zu Genesis und den Psalmen,[9] ähnlich Ambrosius.[10] Auch Hieronymus schreibt später sowohl zum Buch Genesis als auch zum Psalter ausgedehnte Werke,[11] bevor er sich den Propheten zuwendet, die er, vermutlich als einziger christlicher Exeget seiner Zeit, allesamt kommentiert. Die Wahl des Koheletbuches begründet Hieronymus im Vorwort seines Kommentars so:

> Ich erinnere mich, dass ich vor ungefähr fünf Jahren, als ich noch in Rom war, der heiligen Blesilla Kohelet vorlas, um sie zur Verachtung dieser Welt aufzufordern und zur Geringschätzung all dessen, was sie auf Erden sah, und dass sie mich damals bat, alles Unklare in Form eines kleinen Kommentars zu erörtern, damit sie das, was sie las, auch ohne mich verstehen könne.[12]

Die Zeilen geben einige Hinweise auf die Entstehungsgeschichte des Kommentars:[13] 1) Hieronymus verweist auf Rom, wo er vor seinem Weggang nach Betlehem lebte. 2) Er erwähnt Blesilla, eine junge Frau, die von ihm unterrichtet werden will. Und: 3) Es ist das Buch Kohelet, nach dem sie verlangt.

Schon hier zeigt sich das hervorragende rhetorische Talent des Hieronymus: Geschickt vermag er es, die Umstände seines Weggangs aus Rom anzusprechen und gleichzeitig zu verschleiern. Hieronymus verließ Rom nicht freiwillig. Er war dazu gezwungen worden. Der Grund dafür war die erwähnte Blesilla. Sie war im Alter von nur zwanzig Jahren an Magersucht infolge übersteigerter Askese gestorben. Hieronymus als ihr geistlicher Lehrer war es gewesen, der sie zu dieser exzessiven asketischen Praxis ermutigt und für ihren Eifer gelobt hatte:

> In jener Zeit [vor ihrer „Bekehrung"; Anm. E. B.] schienen ihr weichliche Federbetten noch zu hart, kaum konnte sie auf den aufgestapelten Polstern liegen. Jetzt erhebt sie sich eilig zum Gebete, nimmt mit ihrer melodischen Stimme den anderen das Alleluja vorweg und fängt als erste an, ihren Herrn zu loben. Sie kniet sich auf die bloße Erde, und mit reichlichen Tränen reinigt sie ihr Antlitz, das sie einst mit Bleiweiß besudelt

---

9 Vgl. Siquans, Art. Augustinus.

10 Neben Schriften zu Genesis und zu Psalmen verfasste Ambrosius auch zu Jesaja eine längere Auslegung, vgl. Wriedt, Art. Ambrosius. Dort der Verweis auf Dassmann, Ambrosius.

11 *Quaestionum hebraicarum liber in Genesim* (391/92); *Commentarioli in Psalmos* (vor 393).

12 *Memini me ante hoc ferme quinguennium, cum adhuc Romae essem et Ecclesiasten sanctae Blesilla legerem, ut eam ad contemptum istius saeculi provocarem et omne quod in mundo cerneret, putaret esse pro nihilo, rogatum ab ea, ut in morem commentarioli obscura quaequae dissererem, ut absque me posset intellegere quae legebat.* Hieronymus, *Comm. Eccl.*, Vorwort; Birnbaum, Koheletkommentar, 48–49.

13 Vgl. dazu Birnbaum, Koheletkommentar/Einführung aus bibelwissenschaftlicher Perspektive; zur Funktion von Vorworten bei Hieronymus im Allgemeinen und bei seinem Koheletkommentar im Besonderen vgl. auch Cain, Apology.

> hat. Ist sie mit dem Gebete der Psalmen zu Ende, so versagen der müde Nacken und die wankenden Knie den Dienst, aber den vor Müdigkeit zufallenden Augen gönnt der fromme Eifer kaum Ruhe.[14]

Nach Blesillas Tod wurden daher schnell Vorwürfe laut, Hieronymus habe ihren Tod verschuldet. Erschwerend kam hinzu, dass Blesillas Mutter und Schwester zwei der hingebungsvollsten spirituellen Schülerinnen des Hieronymus waren. Die Gefahr einer Entfremdung zwischen Schülerinnen und Lehrer stand im Raum. Wenn aber die römische Öffentlichkeit zum Schluss gekommen wäre, dass sich die angesehene und wohlhabende Paula von der Askesebewegung abgewandt habe, wäre dies fatal für Hieronymus und sein Anliegen geworden. Das war Hieronymus sehr bewusst, wie sich am „Trostbrief" ep. 39 an Paula zeigt. Da sein eigenes Ansehen und das Ansehen der Askese auf dem Spiel standen, fiel der Ton des Briefes sehr harsch aus:

> Ich kann nicht, ohne zu seufzen, aussprechen, was ich jetzt sagen will. Als man Dich ohnmächtig mitten aus dem feierlichen Leichenbegängnis hinwegtrug, da fing die Menge an zu raunen: „Haben wir es nicht oft genug gesagt, daß es so kommen wird? Sie weint um ihre Tochter, die ein Opfer des Fastens geworden ist. Sie ist untröstlich, daß sie nicht wenigstens aus deren zweiter Ehe Enkel zu sehen bekam. Wie lange mag es noch anstehen, bis man das abscheuliche Geschlecht der Mönche aus der Stadt vertreibt, mit Steinen zu Tode wirft oder in das Wasser stürzt? Sie haben die arme Frau verführt; denn jetzt zeigt es sich, daß sie keine Nonne sein wollte. Hat doch niemals eine heidnische Mutter so wie sie ihre Kinder beweint."[15]

Hieronymus benötigte die Unterstützung Paulas in Bethlehem sowohl in geistiger als auch in finanzieller Hinsicht, war er doch nicht dorthin gekommen, um sich vor der Welt zu verbergen, sondern um seine mit Paulas Geld neu gegründeten Klöster als spirituell-intellektuelle Zentren der Gelehrsamkeit bekanntzumachen. Die geistlichen Schüler/innen erwartete man vor allem aus Rom. Und gerade weil

---

14 Hieronymus, *Epist.* 38,4: *Illo tempore plumarum quoque dura mollities uidebatur et in extructis toris iacere uix poterat; nunc ad orandum festina consurgit et modulata uoce ceteris alleluia praeripiens prior incipit laudare dominum suum. flectuntur genua super nudam humum et crebris lacrimis facies psimithio ante sordidata purgatur. post orationem psalmi concrepantet lassa ceruix, poplites uacillantes in somnum que uergentes oculi nimio mentis ardore uix inpetrant, ut quiescant* (CCSL 54, 292); Übersetzung: Schade, Briefe, 43 f.

15 Hieronymus, *Epist.* 39,6: *Non possum sine gemitu eloqui, quod dicturus sum, cum de media pompa funeris exanimem te referrent, hoc inter se populus mussitabat: „nonne illud est, quod saepius dicebamus? dolet filiam ieiuniis interfectam, quod non vel de secundo eius matrimonio tenuerit nepotes. Quousque genus detestabile monachorum non urbe pellitur, non lapidibus obruitur, non praecipitatur in fluctus? Matronam miserabilem seduxerunt, quae quam monacha esse noluerit, hinc probatur, quod nulla gentilium ita suos umquam filios fleuerit"* (CCSL 54, 306); Übersetzung: Schade, Briefe, 27.

Hieronymus dort, im Zentrum der lateinischen Welt, nicht wirken konnte, war es umso notwendiger, positiv auf sich aufmerksam zu machen.

Im Vorwort des Koheletkommentars hatte Hieronymus also mehr als eine schwierige Aufgabe zu erfüllen: Er musste sein ungebrochen positives Verhältnis zu Blesillas Angehörigen beweisen, um seine Beziehung zu Rom nicht zu verlieren. Er musste glaubhaft machen, dass seine Niederlage in Rom in Wahrheit ein Erfolg war, um seinen Ruf zu wahren; er musste sich selbst als geistlicher Lehrer und begnadeter Schriftsteller etablieren, hier am Rande der Welt, um nicht in Vergessenheit zu geraten; und er musste die Askese angesichts des Todes von Blesilla als dennoch lebensförderlich darstellen, um seine Lehre zu verteidigen.

Daher verbindet er in einem ersten Schritt sich und den Kommentar mit Rom und Blesilla. Die Erwähnung Blesillas, die in aller Augen als unschuldig, fromm und angesehen galt, hat dabei mehr als eine Funktion: Zunächst wertet Hieronymus mit ihr sich selbst auf. Dazu überhöht er Blesillas Ruf sogar noch und nennt sie „sancta" (Heilige). Eine Heilige, eine unbefleckte sündenlose Person hat ihn, Hieronymus, zum geistlichen Lehrer erwählt. Auch der Kommentar selbst war demnach ihre Idee. Damit betont Hieronymus, dass es Blesilla war, die wollte, dass er a) ein spiritueller Lehrer, b) der Verfasser eines Bibelkommentars und c) ein Lehrmeister in Sachen Kohelet sein solle. Und nicht zufällig Kohelet:

In Hieronymus' Augen ist das Buch Kohelet Teil eines spirituellen Programms in drei Stufen. Das zentrale Stichwort lautet hier: Verachtung der Welt (*contemptus mundi*). Ausgehend von Origenes unterscheidet Hieronymus zwischen Anfängern (*incipientes*), Fortgeschrittenen (*proficientes*) und Vollkommenen (*perfecti*) auf dem spirituellen Weg. Jede dieser Gruppen benötige eine andere Lehrmethode: Für die Anfänger sei das Buch der Sprichwörter geeignet. Es lehre zwischen Gut und Böse zu unterscheiden, diene demnach als ethische Bildung, ähnlich wie im griechischen Bildungssystem. Das Buch Kohelet sei für die Fortgeschrittenen auf dem spirituellen Weg gedacht. Sie hätten das Wesen der Dinge zu erfassen, die „Physik". Kohelet lehre sie das Wesen der Welt zu erkennen, und dieses sei, wie in Koh 1,2 beschrieben, „nichtig und flüchtig" (*vanitas vanitatum*).[16] Die Fortgeschrittenen müssten daher lernen, sich nicht an irdische vergängliche Dinge zu halten, sondern an das Unvergängliche, Dauerhafte, Ewige, an Gott. Wer das gelernt habe, erfahre die Vereinigung mit dem Göttlichen, die *unio mystica*.

> Dieser [Salomo, Anm. E. B.] […] gab also drei Bücher heraus: Sprichwörter, Kohelet und Hohelied. In den Sprichwörtern belehrt er das Kind und klärt es durch die Sprüche gleichsam über seine Pflichten auf; daher wiederholt sich seine Rede häufig an seinen Sohn. In Kohelet wiederum lehrt er den Mann schon reiferen Alters, in den Dingen der Welt nichts für dauerhaft zu halten; vielmehr sei alles, was wir wahrnehmen, vergänglich

16 Hebräisch: הבל הבלם.

> und kurzlebig. Zuletzt vereint er im Hohelied den bereits vollkommenen und durch Verachtung der Welt vorbereiteten Mann mit den Umarmungen des Gemahls. Wenn wir nämlich nicht zuerst von den Lastern lassen und uns durch Verzicht auf weltlichen Prunk ungehindert auf die Ankunft Christi vorbereiten, können wir nicht sagen: Er küsse mich mit den Küssen seines Mundes (Hld 1,2 LXX).[17]

Das Buch Kohelet gilt demnach als geeignet, den Fortgeschrittenen auf dem spirituellen Weg die Vergänglichkeit und Nichtigkeit der Welt zu lehren und die Bedeutung einer Ausrichtung an unvergängliche Güter deutlich zu machen. Damit enthält es alles, was Hieronymus benötigte, um sein asketisches Programm zu verkünden und zu unterstreichen. Insbesondere seinen Kritikern konnte er mithilfe dieses biblischen Buches Paroli bieten.

Das Vorwort setzt fort:

> Als wir uns mit Vorarbeiten zu diesem Werk befassten, wurde sie uns durch plötzlichen Tod entrissen – wir waren [wohl] nicht würdig, liebe Paula und Eustochium, eine solche Gefährtin unseres Lebens zu haben – und infolgedessen verstummte ich, erschüttert durch den so schweren Verlust.[18]

Mit diesen Zeilen bezweckt Hieronymus zweierlei: Zunächst erklärt sich daraus, warum der Kommentar erst nach fünfjährigem Schweigen geschrieben wurde: Es sei die Erschütterung über den schweren Verlust gewesen, die ihn verstummen ließ. Andererseits, und noch bedeutsamer: Er kann damit die Schuld an Blesillas Tod zurückweisen. Indem er vom „Ich" auf das „Wir" schwenkt, bezieht er einerseits bei der Erwähnung der Vorarbeiten zum Kommentar Blesilla mit ein, andererseits bei der Schilderung von Blesillas Tod die Mutter und Schwester der Toten, Paula und Eustochium: „Wir" waren nicht würdig, Blesilla bei uns zu haben: Das Unwürdig-Sein betrifft damit nicht nur ihn allein, sondern auch die über allen Zweifel erhabenen Angehörigen der Toten. Hieronymus kann dadurch Teil des allgemeinen „Unwürdig-Seins" werden und zugleich die spezifischen Anschuldigungen an ihn persönlich zurückdrängen.

---

17 *Is itaque […] tria volumina edidit: Proverbia, Ecclesiasten, Canticum canticorum. In Proverbiis parvulum docens et quasi de officiis per sententias erudiens, unde ad filium ei crebro sermo repetitur; in Ecclesiaste vero maturae virum aetatis instituens, ne quidquam in mundi rebus putet esse perpetuum, sed caduca et brevia universa quae cernimus; ad extremum iam consummatum virum et calcato saeculo praeparatum in Cantico canticorum sponsi iungit amplexibus. Nisi enim prius reliquerimus vitia et pompae saeculi renuntiantes expeditos nos ad adventum Christi paraverimus, non possumus dicere: Osculetur me ab osculo sui.* Hieronymus, *Comm. Eccl.* I,1,2; Birnbaum, Koheletkommentar, 50–51.

18 *Itaque quoniam in procinctu nostri operis subita morte subtracta est et non meruimus, o Paula et Eustochium, talem vitae nostrae habere consortem tantoque vulnere tunc perculsus obmutui, […];* Hieronymus, *Comm. Eccl.*, Vorwort; Birnbaum, Koheletkommentar, 48–49.

„Jetzt, wo ich in Betlehem, einer erhabeneren Stadt bin.“[19] Mit dieser kleinen Bemerkung vermittelt Hieronymus den Eindruck, er habe Rom freiwillig verlassen. Betlehem sei die „heiligere“ oder „erhabenere“ Stadt – der Komparativ zielt dabei selbstverständlich auf Rom. Die erzwungene Ausreise von Rom wird so zu einem aus eigener Überzeugung getätigten Schritt, gewissermaßen zu einem asketischen Karrieresprung. Da die Kritiker des Hieronymus hauptsächlich in Rom zu finden waren, war der Bezug zu Blesilla, der jungen angesehenen Römerin, umso wichtiger. Und nicht nur das: „[…] löse ich das ein, was ich ihrem Andenken, aber auch euch schuldig bin“.[20]

Durch diesen nächsten Satz stellt Hieronymus klar, dass das Schreiben des Kommentars, der sein asketisches Programm beinhaltet, nichts anderes als eine heilige Pflicht gewesen sei, die Pflicht den letzten Willen einer Märtyrerin zu erfüllen. Blesilla, die römische Heilige, in gewissem Sinn also Rom, der Mittelpunkt der Welt, wünschte, dass er einen Kommentar über Askese schrieb.

Weiters widmet er diese *commentarioli* auch Blesillas Mutter und Schwester. Das war notwendig, um den Verdacht abzuwehren, Paula hätte sich nach dem Tod ihrer Tochter von ihm entfremdet. Das Vorwort des Kommentars diente dazu, zu untermauern, dass die enge Verbindung und die ungebrochen gute Freundschaft nie gelitten hätten.

Andrew Cain stellt in seinem Aufsatz: „Apology and Polemic in Jerome's Prefaces to his Biblical Scholarship“ fest:

> […] in this short preface, Jerome accomplishes many goals at once: he consoles Paula and Eustochium for the loss of their loved one to whom he pays tribute in the form of a biblical commentary; he emphasizes his status as the spiritual advisor to their ascetic family dynasty; he affirms the superiority of Bethlehem over Rome, which is implied to be the seat of worldliness; and he defends Hebraica veritas as a superior exegetical and text-critical methodology.[21]

Hinzuzufügen wäre: Er rechtfertigt sein spirituelles Programm als Verpflichtung, die er zu erfüllen hatte. Er weist die Schuld für Blesillas Tod zurück. Und er empfiehlt sich selbst als erfolgreicher Exeget. So richtet sich das Vorwort zwar vordergründig an Paula und Eustochium, dient jedoch in Wahrheit dazu, seinen römischen Widersachern zu kontern und für seinen Weg Werbung zu machen.

---

19 […] *nunc in Bethlehem positus, augustiori videlicet civitate*; Hieronymus, *Comm. Eccl.*, Vorwort; Birnbaum, Koheletkommentar, 48–49.

20 […] *et illius memoriae et vobis reddo quod debeo*; ebd.

21 Cain, Apology, 127.

Polemik im Kommentar selbst

Während Hieronymus im Vorwort mit Paula, Eustochium und Blesilla ein „Wir" geformt hat, befasst er sich im Kommentar immer wieder mit „den Anderen".

Im Umgang mit diesen „Anderen" ist Hieronymus kein diskreter Verkündiger seiner Botschaft. Als rhetorisch gebildeter Mann mit spitzer Zunge und cholerischem Temperament scheut er weder Übertreibungen, Beleidigungen, Abwertungen noch Sarkasmus, um seine Überzeugungen weiterzugeben. Er ist ein brillanter Demagoge, der weiß, wie er seine Fähigkeiten in den Dienst seiner Sache stellen kann. Es überrascht daher kaum, dass er polemisch ist. Eher verwundert es, wenn er es einmal nicht ist.

Im Koheletkommentar richten sich seine Attacken gegen unterschiedliche Gruppen, als da sind: andere Auslegende des Koheletbuches; Frauen; Juden; Häretiker; Philosophen; andere geistliche Lehrer; Kleriker, vor allem solche höheren Ranges, wie Bischöfe. Das Ausmaß der Polemik hängt dabei von der jeweiligen Gruppe ab.

Andere Auslegende des Koheletbuches

Überraschenderweise spricht Hieronymus über andere Exegeten nicht immer abwertend. Oft erwähnt er sie und ihre Auslegungen sogar ohne jeden weiteren Kommentar. Nur vereinzelt nennt er sie überhaupt mit Namen. So erwähnt er hin und wieder Origenes, jedoch ohne jede Polemik. Meist beschränkt er sich darauf, sie unter „einige", „gewisse Leute" oder „andere" zu subsumieren. Nur zweimal widerspricht er einer Auslegung explizit. Dann jedoch macht er sich über den Ausleger lustig, wie zum Beispiel im Kommentar zu Koh 3,5: „Ich staune, was ein beredter Mann Lächerliches über diese Stelle gesagt hat [...]"[22] Nach der Beschreibung der Auslegung fügt er scheinbar unterwürfig hinzu: „Ob er das zu Recht oder zu Unrecht gesagt hat, überlasse ich dem Urteil des Lesers."[23]

Eine andere Auslegung wird mit folgenden einleitenden Worten vorgestellt: „Ich weiß, dass ich in der Kirche einen, von dem man annahm, dass er Kenntnis der Schriften habe, diese Verse so erläutern hörte."[24]

Hier kann man sich des Eindrucks nicht erwehren, dass die Polemik weniger der Auslegung selbst geschuldet ist, sondern der Tatsache, dass der kritisierte Ausleger

---

22 *Miror, quomodo vir disertus rem ridiculam in hoc loco dixerit*; Hieronymus, *Comm. Eccl.* III,5,1; Birnbaum, Koheletkommentar, 94–95.

23 *Hoc utrum recte an perperam dixerit, lectoris arbitrio derelinquo*; Hieronymus, *Comm. Eccl.* III,5,1; Birnbaum, Koheletkommentar, 94–95.

24 *Scio me audisse in ecclesia ab eo, qui putabatur habere scientiam scripturarum, ita hos versiculos edissertos*; Hieronymus, *Comm. Eccl.* VII,15.1; Birnbaum, Koheletkommentar, 150–151.

eine offensichtlich hochgeachtete kirchliche Persönlichkeit ist. Im Allgemeinen scheint sich Hieronymus hingegen nicht persönlich von anderen Auslegungen angegriffen gefühlt zu haben.

Polemik gegen Frauen

Misogyne Äußerungen des Hieronymus stellen einen besonderen Fall im Koheletkommentar dar. Hier scheinen sich „die Anderen" mit dem „Wir" zu überschneiden oder zu konterkarieren.

Dennoch (oder deshalb?) spielt Frauenfeindlichkeit eine bemerkenswert große Rolle im Koheletkommentar, vor allem angesichts der Tatsache, dass Hieronymus in Betlehem von Frauen unterstützt wird. Er ist in der Lage, Klöster zu gründen und sich als geistlicher Lehrer zu profilieren, weil Frauen dafür die finanziellen Mittel aufbringen. Offenbar hält er es gerade deshalb für notwendig, sich dafür zu rechtfertigen, dass er seinen Kommentar Frauen widmet. Möglicherweise fürchtet er als *Womanizer* zu gelten.

Interessanterweise sind seine misogynen Äußerungen kaum offen polemisch. Anders als in Schriften wie *Adversus Jovinianus* und anderen verzichtet Hieronymus auf seine dort übliche scharfe Rhetorik. Gerade dieser Verzicht auf Übertreibungen und Bösartigkeiten lässt die Frauenfeindlichkeit jedoch noch perfider werden. Misogyne Ansichten werden dadurch zu einer unemotionalen nüchternen Tatsache, zu einer objektiven Wahrheit, die nicht weiter diskutiert werden muss.

Ein Beispiel: Koh 7,25–29 enthält den berühmten Ausspruch: „Und ich finde bitterer als den Tod die Frau, die ein Fallstrick ist, und Schleppnetze sind ihr Herz, Fesseln ihre Hände. Der Gute vor Gott wird ihr entrissen werden und der Sünder durch sie gefangen werden."[25]

In seiner Auslegung setzt Hieronymus nun, wie Feichtinger-Zimmermann aufgezeigt hat,[26] eine interessante Verschiebung der sprechenden Personen in Gang. Zunächst zitiert er den biblischen Text, danach paraphrasiert er Kohelets Worte noch einmal, mit wiederholtem Hinweis darauf, dass hier Kohelet selbst spreche. Tatsächlich jedoch vereindeutigt er in seiner Paraphrase die Worte Kohelets und spitzt sie, insbesondere was ihre Frauenfeindlichkeit angeht, noch einmal zu. Während Hieronymus sonst dazu neigt, Texte anderer Autoren zu zitieren ohne das explizit zu erwähnen, was ihm als Plagiat vorgeworfen wird, geht er hier also den

---

25 *Et invenio ego amariorem morte mulierem, quae est laqueus, et sagenae cor eius, vincula manus eius. Bonus coram Deo eruetur ab ea et peccator capietur in ea*; Hieronymus, *Comm. Eccl.* VII,26/27; Birnbaum, Koheletkommentar, 160–161.

26 Feichtinger-Zimmermann, Paula, bes. 196–201.

umgekehrten Weg. Er legt seine eigene Interpretation des Textes in den Mund der biblischen Autorität und gibt sie so als unanfechtbares Bibelwort aus.

Gesteigert wird dies noch dadurch, dass Hieronymus den Text mit anderen Bibeltexten verbindet, die seine frauenfeindliche Auslegung unterstützen. Es sind Texte aus dem Neuen Testament. Wie Agnethe Siquans[27] ausführt, zeigt Hieronymus dadurch, dass nicht nur alttestamentliche Autoren, sondern auch der „Heilige Paulus" im Neuen Testament vor Frauen warnen. Indem die Bibeltexte auf diese Weise verbunden werden, scheint es, als ob die Bibel einhellig und einstimmig über das problematische „schwächere" Geschlecht spreche. Danach bietet Hieronymus noch andere wichtige Zeugen auf: die Aquila-Tradition, eine jüdische Septuaginta-Rezension. Auch hier vermittelt er den Eindruck, christliche und jüdische Tradition seien in diesem Punkt einmütig. In einem letzten Schritt zitiert Hieronymus dann auch noch einen paganen Autoren, Vergil.[28] Feichtinger-Zimmermann meint dazu:

> Heidnische (Vergil/Merkur) wie christliche Autorität (Paulus) werden offenbar als Gewährsmänner für eine generelle fragilitas animi der Frau aufgerufen, die sie grundsätzlich versagensanfälliger macht, ohne dass der prätextuelle Kontext tatsächlich eine große Rolle spielt. Eher scheint die Einbettung des eigenen Urteils über die Sündenaffinität der Frau in einen autoritativen Mainstream die Intention des Hieronymus zu sein.[29]

So resümiert Barbara Feichtinger-Zimmermann:

> Zusammenfassend lässt sich also konstatieren, dass der Kommentartext die ambivalenten Aussagen des Bibeltextes über die Frau als Misogynismus vereindeutigt, durch Akkumulation der Motive ausweitet, aus asketischer Perspektive verschärft bzw. ergänzt und durch die Zitierung christlicher wie heidnischer Autoritäten wissenschaftlich fundiert, somit objektiviert und mit einer neuen Qualität von Allgemeingültigkeit ausstattet.
>
> Zugleich wird diese affirmative Steigerung in einer überindividualisierten Erzählhaltung des Textes gleichsam verborgen: Der Interpres-Erzähler, der mit dem Autor den unmittelbarsten Zusammenhang aufweist, spricht beinahe nur in textkritischen Passagen eindeutig selbst, ansonsten diffundiert er hinter anderen personae. Diese spezifische Sprechweise erhöht die Tendenz zur Objektivierung und Verallgemeinerung

---

27 Siquans, Frauenfeindlichkeit.

28 Das Zitat stammt aus Vergils Aeneis, ein kurzes Zitat aus dem Didobuch (Aen. 4,569 f): Feichtinger-Zimmermann, Paula, 199 und Fn. 24: Das Vergilzitat rekurriert auf die – mit der allgemeingültigen Sentenz endenden – Warnung des Gottes Merkur, der Aeneas im Traum erscheint, um ihn vor Didos Rache zu warnen und zur raschen Flucht aus Karthago – und somit vor Dido – zu mahnen. Im 2. Brief an Timotheus warnt Paulus dagegen vor Irrlehren (Häresien), die offensichtlich bei Frauen auf besonders fruchtbaren Boden fallen.

29 Ebd., 199 Fn. 24.

> der Negativaussagen über die Frau – und macht diese – paradoxerweise – nachhaltig wirksamer, aber eben weniger anstößig.[30]

Das Ziel des Hieronymus ist es also, die eigene Interpretation als allgemein anerkannte Tatsache darzustellen. Daher verzichtet er in diesen Fragen auf polemische Attacken.

Polemik gegen Juden

Hieronymus unterscheidet strikt das Judentum vor Christus und das Judentum nach Christus. Während er das Alte Testament und hebräische Traditionen schätzt und verteidigt, wertet er die Juden seiner Zeit ab. Er beschuldigt sie der Missachtung ihres religiösen Erbes, der Fehldeutung ihrer Heiligen Schriften und des Mordes an Jesus Christus. Doch ist er in seiner Verurteilung nicht durchgehend konsequent, hält er doch eine allgemeine Errettung Israels am Ende der Zeiten für möglich.[31]

Dazu kommt, dass Hieronymus oft auf die jüdische Schriftauslegung Bezug nimmt, die er angeblich von einem Juden gelernt haben will. Dieser „Hebraeus meus"dürfte zwar kaum im Umfeld des Hieronymus anzusehen, sondern vielmehr Teil der von Origenes importierten Auslegungen gewesen sein – also in Wahrheit der Zeit und Person des Origenes angehören[32] –, dennoch fällt auf, dass er auf diese Weise jüdischer Tradition und einem jüdisch(-christlich)en Lehrer offen Respekt bezeugt.

Zielscheibe seiner Polemik sind also nicht die Juden vergangener oder künftiger Tage, sondern hauptsächlich das Judentum seiner Zeit. Dabei bleiben seine antijüdischen Äußerungen inhaltlich sehr in allgemein üblichen Stereotypen haften. Er geht ähnlich vor wie bei seinen misogynen Äußerungen und bleibt hinter anderen Autoritäten verborgen. Eine gewisse Unbeteiligtheit könnte daraus ebenfalls gelesen werden. So sind seine Plädoyers für eine Wertschätzung des Alten Testaments wesentlich eindringlicher als seine abwertenden Bemerkungen über die Juden seiner Zeit.

Zu Koh 11,2 etwa: „Gib sieben einen Anteil und sogar acht[en], denn du weißt nicht, welches Übel auf der Erde sein wird", stellt er fest:

> Die Juden gaben sieben einen Anteil, indem sie an den Sabbat glauben, aber sie gaben ihn nicht acht[en], weil sie die Auferstehung am Herrentag leugnen. Im Gegensatz dazu geben die Häretiker Markion und Mani und alle, die das alte Gesetz mit wildem

30 Ebd., 202.

31 Vgl. dazu Lössl, Wahre Kirche.

32 Zur Diskussion vgl. Leanza, Gerolamo, bes. 18 f; optimistischer Stemberger, Hieronymus und die Rabbinen, 89 f.

> Maul zerfetzen, den Anteil acht[en], indem sie das Evangelium anerkennen, aber sie gestehen diesen nicht der Siebenzahl zu, indem sie das alte Gesetz verschmähen.[33]

Seine Anschuldigungen gelten sowohl Juden als auch solchen christlichen Häretikern, die nicht beide Testamente wertschätzen. In der Diktion ist jedoch die Kritik an Letzteren schärfer: Das wilde Maul, mit dem das alte Gesetz zerfetzt wird, hat emotionaleren Duktus als der Angriff auf die Juden. Das hängt auch mit der persönlichen Hinwendung des Hieronymus zum Alten Testament zusammen und da vor allem zur hebräischen Originalsprache, die er der Septuaginta gegenüber bevorzugt. Die „Anderen" sind somit auch hier nicht nur die Juden und die Markion-Anhänger, sondern alle, die nicht wie er in der hebräischen Textform die *hebraica veritas* erkennen wollen.

Polemik gegen „Philosophen"

Angriffe gegen Ansichten griechischer Philosophen sind im Koheletkommentar in unterschiedlicher Weise zu finden, einerseits in Form von inhaltlich fundierten Auseinandersetzungen mit philosophischen Strömungen, andererseits in Form von pauschalen Abwertungen. Hieronymus selbst war kein großer Philosoph. Er dürfte die griechischen Philosophen auch nicht gelesen haben.[34] Seine Interessen waren eher linguistischer und literarischer Natur. Die römischen Dichter und Literaten standen ihm näher als die griechischen Philosophen. Anders als Origenes oder Augustinus griff er auch nie maßgeblich in philosophische oder theologische Kontroversen ein.

Die inhaltlich fundierten philosophischen Auseinandersetzungen lassen sich daher auch wenig überraschend auf Origenes und Didymus zurückführen, während die allgemein gehaltenen Verunglimpfungen die Handschrift des Hieronymus aufweisen. Inhaltlich wenden sich die Angriffe im ersteren Fall gegen Ansichten, die Epikur zugeschrieben wurden. Ein „hedonistisches" Grundverständnis des Koheletbuches lehnt Hieronymus mit den einleitenden Worten ab: „Zu Unrecht also meinen manche, […]"[35] oder: „Daher werden wir nicht, wie gewisse Leute meinen, zum Überfluss und Vergnügen und zur Verzweiflung getrieben […]"[36]

---

33 *Iudaei dederunt partem septem, credentes sabbato, sed non dederunt octo, ressurectionem diei dominica denegantes. Econtrario haeretici, Marcion et Manichaeus et omnes qui veterem legem rabido ore dilaniant, dant partem octo suscipienties evangelium, sed eandem septenario numero non tribuunt legem veterem respuentes*; Hieronymus, *Comm. Eccl.* XI,2,1; Birnbaum, Koheletkommentar, 218–221.

34 Vgl. Conring, Hieronymus, 232 f.

35 *Male igitur quidam opinantur*; Hieronymus, *Comm. Eccl.* I,1,5; Birnbaum, Koheletkommentar, 52–53.

36 *Ex quibus non, ut quidam aestimant, ad luxuriam et delicias et ad desperationem* […] *provocamur*; Hieronymus, *Comm. Eccl.* II,12/13,1; Birnbaum, Koheletkommentar, 100–101.

Andere Kritikpunkte an „Epikur" sind die Negierung einer Vorsehung Gottes und – dies fälschlicherweise – der Glaube an immer wiederkehrende Welten und Ereignisse. In all diesen Punkten paraphrasiert Hieronymus die Argumente des Origenes,[37] wobei er dessen Aussagen manchmal ungenau wiedergibt,[38] sie ansonsten aber verkürzt und polemisch verschärft.

Daneben werden Philosophen immer wieder gemeinsam mit „Häretikern" pauschal verunglimpft.

Polemik gegen (christliche) Häretiker

Als „Häretiker" werden im Koheletkommentar Christen bezeichnet, die einen anderen Standpunkt bezüglich gewisser christologischer Aspekte einnehmen – wobei die Christologie in dieser Zeit noch bei weitem nicht abgeschlossen war. In seinen Angriffen bleibt Hieronymus äußerst vage, und wenn er doch auf einen konkreten Punkt eingeht, ist die Passage meist von Origenes übernommen. Sehr kurz nur diskutiert er die Frage, ob Jesus göttlicher oder menschlicher Natur war, oder in welcher Form die beiden Naturen verbunden sein könnten.[39]

Im Kommentar zu Koh 1,15[40] weist er eine Vorform der Prädestinationslehre zurück, wenn er den Gedanken abwehrt, dass manche Menschen infolge eines Mangels an Vernunft nicht für ihre Sünden zu verurteilen seien. Stattdessen hebt er die Bedeutung des freien Willens hervor und die beständige Möglichkeit und Verpflichtung zu Reue und Umkehr. Eine weitere Ansicht, die Hieronymus ablehnt, ist die, dass der neutestamentliche Gott der Liebe von einem bösen Schöpfergott, einem Demiurgen, zu unterscheiden sei. Damit in Zusammenhang steht auch die schon erwähnte Attacke gegen Marcion oder Mani, die das Alte Testament ablehnen.

Weitaus öfter sind die Attacken gegen die „Häretiker" sehr allgemein gehalten und eher Beschimpfungen als inhaltlich gefüllte Kritik. So wirft er ihnen wiederholt vor, „falsche Lehren" zu vertreten. Zu Koh 8,1 führt er aus: „Jeder Häretiker und Verteidiger eines falschen Lehrsatzes hat ein unverschämtes Angesicht."[41] Die in Koh 9,12 erwähnten Fische, die in einer schlimmen Falle festgehalten werden,

37 Vgl. ebd., 272–273.

38 So schreibt er auch den Glauben an exakt wiederkehrende Welten Epikur zu, während Origenes dafür korrekterweise die Stoiker kritisiert.

39 Vgl. Hieronymus, *Comm. Eccl.* II,8,6; XII,14,4; beachtlich dabei ist, dass seine Sicht einer vermischten Natur Jesu zwar zu Zeiten des Hieronymus noch nicht prekär, in späterer Zeit jedoch heftig diskutiert und scharf zurückgewiesen wurde.

40 Hieronymus, *Comm. Eccl.* I,15,1.

41 *Omnis haereticus et falsum dogma defendens impudenti vultu est*; Hieronymus, *Comm. Eccl.* VIII,1,3; Birnbaum, Koheletkommentar, 166–167.

bezieht er auf Menschen, die auf Häretiker hereinfallen: Diese hätten ein Netz, mit dem sie Fische/Menschen ins Unheil stürzten: „Ihr Netz ist die umgängliche Rede, das schmeichelnde Gespräch, simuliertes oder erzwungenes Fasten, ein alltägliches Gewand und die Nachahmung von Tugenden."[42] Sie sprechen zu viel, weil sie nichts verstehen (*Comm. Eccl.* X,13/14,2). Sie verirren sich und finden niemals zum Ziel (*Comm. Eccl.* X,15,2) und: „Die Häretiker sind unfruchtbare Hölzer und ein Stück Land ohne nützliche Früchte."[43]

Es fällt auf, dass die Vorwürfe, zieht man einmal die Polemik ab, Tätigkeiten anzielen, die denen des Hieronymus ähneln: lehren, fasten, tugendsam leben und Anhänger um sich sammeln. Es ist also nicht ausgeschlossen, dass Hieronymus unter die Häretiker auch spirituelle Askese-Lehrer zählt, die er als Konkurrenz ansieht.[44]

Hieronymus verwendet also allgemeine Sätze des Koheletbuches über Unheil, das über die Menschen hereinbricht, und über „Toren" oder „Dumme" und konkretisiert sie auf Häretiker, Philosophen und andere Widersacher. Im Koheletbuch werden diese „Dummen" meist mit den „Weisen" oder mit Kohelet selbst kontrastiert, die unter den „Dummen" leiden müssen. Bei diesem Thema wird Hieronymus in seiner Auslegung besonders leidenschaftlich und es wird schnell klar, wen er mit „den Weisen" identifiziert: In Koh 2,18/19 etwa klagt „König" Kohelet darüber, dass er die Frucht seiner Mühen nach seinem Tod einem Anderen überlassen muss und nicht weiß, ob dieser es wert ist. Hieronymus gibt in der Auslegung zwar zunächst zu, dass sich dieser Satz auf Reichtum und Besitz zu beziehen scheint, doch dann führt er aus:

> Aber mir scheint, da ich es höher betrachte, dass er von geistiger Mühe spricht: Dass sich der weise Mann bei Tag und Nacht an den Schriften abmüht und Bücher verfasst und eine Erinnerung an ihn der Nachwelt hinterlässt und sie [die Bücher] trotzdem in die Hände von Toren gelangen, die entsprechend der Verderbtheit ihres Herzens häufig Samen für Häresien daraus gewinnen und fremde Mühen verleumden.[45]

---

42 *Sagena eorum est sermo affabilis, blandum eloquium, simulata aut coacta ieiunia, vestis humilis, virtutum imitatio*; Hieronymus, *Comm. Eccl.* IX,12; Birnbaum, Koheletkommentar, 194–195.

43 *Haeretici ligna infructuosa sunt et saltus absque utilitate pomorum*; Hieronymus, *Comm. Eccl.* X,9; Birnbaum, Koheletkommentar, 206–207.

44 Vgl. dazu auch die besonders scharfe Attacke in Hieronymus, *Epist.* 22,14, gegen das sogenannte Agapetentum, der Sitte, dass gottgeweihte Jungfrauen eine durch Keuschheitsgelübde gebundene männliche Person in ihren Haushalt aufnahmen, die ihr Vermögen verwaltete und ihre weltlichen Interessen vertrat.

45 *Sed mihi altius contemplanti de labore videtur dicere spiritali, quod diebus et noctibus vir sapiens in scripturis laboret et componat libros et memoriam sui posteris derelinquat et nihilominus in manus stultorum veniant, qui frequenter secundum perversitatem cordis sui semina inde haereseon capiant et alienos labores calumnientur*; Hieronymus, *Comm. Eccl.* II,18/19,2; Birnbaum, Koheletkommentar, 86–87.

In Passagen wie diesen kann man sich des Eindrucks nur schwer erwehren, Hieronymus spräche über niemand anderen als sich selbst.[46]

Polemik gegen Kirchenmänner

Es überrascht kaum, dass Hieronymus seine schärfste Polemik gegen Kirchenmänner richtet: gegen Kleriker, die ihn aus Rom vertrieben haben, einerseits und gegen solche, die er wegen ihres Ansehens oder ihrer Stellung beneidet, andererseits. Ein zentrales Kriterium bei der Bewertung der Kollegenschaft ist dabei deren Einstellung zur Askese. Da die asketische Bewegung bei manchen erfolgreichen Klerikern mit Argwohn betrachtet wurde und Hieronymus von dort keine Unterstützung, sondern Anfeindungen erlebte, dürfte sein Groll auf solche askesefeindlichen Kleriker erheblich gewesen sein. Andererseits waren Kleriker, die Askese hochhielten und dennoch erfolgreich waren, für ihn Rivalen und ebenso wenig erwünscht.

Das Koheletbuch bietet für eine Abrechnung genügend Anknüpfungspunkte. Kohelet klagt über Mächtige, die unverdient zu Ansehen und Macht gekommen sind, über Gottlose und Toren. Hieronymus spitzt das noch zu und deutet die Aussagen auf seine Feinde.

Während sich die Aussagen Kohelets jedoch wie in Koh 10,16–19 an weltliche Machthaber, an Könige richten, genauer an junge, unerfahrene Könige, die es sich gut gehen lassen, nur an Geld interessiert sind und dabei ihr Reich verwahrlosen lassen, wendet Hieronymus diese Texte, insbesondere die Verse 10,18–19, auf die Kirchenobrigen an und nützt sie für eine fundamentale Kritik an denselben: Die Kirchenleitenden zerstören die Kirche durch ihre Nachlässigkeit, so sein Vorwurf. Einerseits würden sie dort nicht sprechen, wo sie lehren sollten, und sich für ihr Schweigen bezahlen lassen. Andererseits würden sie, wenn sie lehren, nur die Sünder in ihren Lastern bestärken und allen nach dem Mund reden.

Auch bei den im Koheletbuch sehr allgemein erhobenen Vorwürfen – etwa Irrlehren zu verbreiten, in Laxismus und Scheinheiligkeit zu leben und Schmeichelei zu betreiben – kommt Hieronymus schnell auf die Lehrer in den Kirchen zu sprechen.[47]

Und wenn Kohelet davon spricht, dass „das Brot nicht den Weisen […] und die Gnade nicht den Wissenden" gehört (Koh 9,11), klingt persönlicher Groll durch, wenn Hieronymus das sofort auf sich und den Klerus bezieht:

---

46 Dafür spricht auch, dass sich diese Auslegung nicht in früheren Kommentaren findet, die Hieronymus benutzte. Vgl. dazu auch Lössl, Wahre Kirche, 178.

47 Vgl. Hieronymus, *Comm. Eccl.* III,7,2; VII,5; VII,6/7.

> Was er aber sagt: DAS BROT GEHÖRT NICHT DEN WEISEN, wird täglich durch das Beispiel Vieler bewiesen, die, obwohl sie sehr weise sind, das Nötige entbehren. Und DIE GNADE GEHÖRT NICHT DEN WISSENDEN: Du kannst nämlich in der Kirche gerade die größten Nichtskönner glänzen sehen; und weil sie die Unverfrorenheit ihrer Mienen pflegen und sich Zungenfertigkeit erwarben ohne zu bedenken, was sie sagen, halten sie sich für klug und gebildet – besonders, wenn sie die Gunst der Masse haben, die mehr durch Geschwätz erfreut und bewegt sind. Und im Gegensatz dazu siehst du den gebildeten Mann im Dunkeln verborgen sein, Verfolgungen erleiden und nicht nur beim Volk keine Gunst haben, sondern sich in Not und Armut verzehren.[48]

Bei den so als „Nichtskönnern" diffamierten Klerikern könnte Hieronymus unter anderem an Papst Siricius, an Helvidius und an Johannes II. von Jerusalem gedacht haben. Papst Siricius war sein Rivale um den Papststuhl und ein großer Gegner der asketischen Bewegung; Mit dem Kleriker Helvidius führte Hieronymus eine heftige Debatte über Jungfräulichkeit und Ehe (vgl. *Adversus Helvidium*), und die Beziehung zu Johannes II. von Jerusalem war geprägt von Konkurrenz um die Vormacht im Heiligen Land, die später zu einem offenen Bruch und sogar zur zeitweiligen Exkommunikation des Hieronymus führte (vgl. *Contra Iohannem*).

Noch schärfer wird die Attacke im Kommentar zu Koh 8,9–11. Hier scheint Hieronymus an eine bestimmte Person zu denken – seine ausgesprochen scharfe Polemik verrät persönliche Involviertheit.

Koh 8,9–11 spricht von Gottlosen, denen ein ehrenvolles Begräbnis zuteil wird, und die in der Stadt gepriesen werden. Hieronymus deutet nun diese „Gottlosen" (*impios*), zunächst allgemein auf Bischöfe:

> Wir können dieses Zeugnis gegen die Bischöfe verwenden, die in der Kirche Macht erlangt haben und diejenigen eher zum Bösen verführen, die sie [eigentlich] belehren und zum Besseren anspornen sollten. Sie werden nach ihrem Tod oft in der Kirche gelobt und von ihren Nachfolgern oder vom Volk öffentlich als selig gepriesen für das, was sie an nicht Rühmenswertem getan haben. Und das ist somit nichtig, denn weil sie nicht nach dem gelten, was sie taten, und nicht sofort in ihrer Sünde getadelt werden – niemand wagt einen Höheren anzuklagen –, deshalb vermehren sie als Pseudo-Heilige und -Selige, die in den Geboten des Herrn wandeln, Sünden um Sünden.[49]

---

48 *Quod autem ait: Non est sapientibus panis, multorum cotidie probatur exemplo, qui cum sapientissimi sint, necessariis indigent. Et non est Scientibus gratia: Videas enim in ecclesia imperitissimos quosque florere; et quia nutrierunt frontis audaciam et volubilitatem linguae consecuti sunt, dum non recogitant quid loquantur, prudentes se et eruditis arbitrantur, maxime si favorem vulgi habuerint, quid magis dictis levioribus delectatur et commovetur; et econtrario eruditum virum latere in obscuruo, persecutiones pati et non solum in populum gratiam non habere, sed inopia et egestate tabescere* Hieronymus, *Comm. Eccl.* IX,11,2; Birnbaum, Koheletkommentar, 192–193.

49 *Possumus hoc testimonio uti adversum episcopos, qui acceperunt in ecclesia potestatem et scandalizant magis eos, quos docere et ad meliora debuerant incitare. Hi frequenter post mortem laudantur*

Dann wechselt er in die Einzahl:

> Schwierig ist eine Anklage gegen einen Bischof. Denn auch wenn er gesündigt hat, wird es nicht geglaubt, und wenn er überführt worden ist, wird er nicht bestraft.[50]

Diese hier angesprochene Person könnte Ambrosius sein. Hieronymus stand ihm aus mehreren Gründen sehr misstrauisch gegenüber. Einerseits war Ambrosius ein Konkurrent: Er war ebenso wie Hieronymus asketisch engagiert und daneben ebenfalls als Übersetzer griechischer Autoren tätig. Andererseits erfreute sich Ambrosius jedoch weitaus größeren Ansehens: Als berühmter Bischof von Mailand, im Zentrum der römischen Welt, wurde er sogar von weltlichen Herrschern hochgeschätzt. Hieronymus dagegen musste sein Dasein ohne öffentliche Stellung am Rande der Welt fristen.[51]

Kein Wunder, dass Hieronymus ausführlich über „fähige und gelehrte Männer" spricht, denen nicht erlaubt ist, „sich in den Gemeinden zu zeigen", während „der noch so Ahnungslose in der Kirche die Leitung innehat".[52] Diese Ungerechtigkeit schreibt er dem Wirken des „Fürsten der Welt", des Teufels, zu.[53]

Die folgenden Worte sind denn auch zwar in „Wir-Form" formuliert, aber in Wahrheit wohl an sich selbst gerichtet:

> Seien wir daher nicht traurig, wenn wir in dieser Welt niedrig zu sein scheinen, wissen wir doch, dass es vom Gesicht des Teufels ist, wenn die Dummen erhoben und die Reichen gestürzt werden.[54]

Zusammenfassung

Hieronymus verwendet seine Rhetorik und Polemik kunstvoll und gezielt. Er bewirkt damit in seinem Koheletkommentar mehreres:

---

in ecclesia et beati in his, quae non probabiliter fecerant, publice sive a successoribus sive a populis praedicantur. Et hoc itaque vanum est; quia enim non ut egerunt, sic audiunt, nec statim corripiuntur in peccato suo – nemo quippe audet accusare maiorem –, propterea quasi sancti et beati et in praeceptis domini ambulantes augent peccata peccatis; Hieronymus, *Comm. Eccl.* VIII,9/11,2; Birnbaum, Koheletkommentar, 172–173.

50 *Difficilis est accusatio in episcopum. Et si enim peccaverit, non creditur, et si convictus fuerit, non punitur*; ebd.

51 Vgl. Rebenich, Jerome, 39; Grützmacher, Hieronymus, 74–78.

52 *Et imprudens quisque in ecclesia teneat principatum […] dum potentes quosque et doctos viros premat nec eos in populis apparere permittat*; Hieronymus, *Comm. Eccl.* X,5/7,2; Birnbaum, Koheletkommentar, 202–205.

53 *Princeps mundi*; vgl. Hieronymus, *Comm. Eccl.* X,4,1; Birnbaum, Koheletkommentar, 202–203.

54 *Non simus itaque tristes, si in hoc saeculo humiles esse videamur, scientes a facie diaboli et stultos sublevari et divites deici*; Hieronymus, *Comm. Eccl.* X,5/7,5; Birnbaum, Koheletkommentar, 204–205.

1) Er bewirbt sein Askese-Programm.
2) Er weist Anschuldigungen im Zusammenhang mit Blesillas Tod zurück.
3) Er beschönigt seine Anwesenheit in Betlehem und seine wenig erfolgreiche kirchliche Karriere.
4) Er wertet seine Widersacher und Gegner ab.
5) Er entwirft von sich selbst das Bild eines gelehrten Asketen, und das äußerst erfolgreich.

In seiner Unterscheidung von „Wir" und „die Anderen" stellen „die Anderen" die erheblich größere Gruppe dar: Es sind alle Auslegungen, die seiner nicht entsprechen; Philosophen und Häretiker ganz generell; Frauen im Allgemeinen, bis auf gelegentliche (taktisch motivierte) Ausnahmen; Juden, mit Ausnahme seines (fiktiven oder realen) Gewährsmannes; andere geistliche Lehrer, denen er pauschal Unredlichkeit vorwirft, und alle Kirchenmänner, vor allem jene, die in der Kirche erfolgreich sind.

Das „Wir" wiederum stellt keine feste Größe dar, es hängt von den jeweiligen Zielen des Hieronymus ab. Dieses „Wir" können andere Auslegungen sein, solange sie der seinen nicht widersprechen. Das „Wir" kann ihn und bestimmte Frauen umschließen, wenn es der Hebung seines Ansehens nützt; das „Wir" kann Hieronymus und seinen „*Hebraeus meus*" meinen, wenn es dazu dient, seine Auslegung zu bestätigen. Im Grunde könnte man sagen: Für Hieronymus gibt es im Koheletkommentar nur ein feststehendes „Wir", und das besteht ausschließlich aus ihm selbst.

Der Koheletkommentar ist ein wichtiger Schritt hin zu jenem Hieronymus, den die Nachwelt kennt. Hieronymus gelingt es, durch seine rhetorischen und polemischen Fähigkeiten seine selbstgewählte Selbstdarstellung zu profilieren und zu verbreiten: die Selbstdarstellung als gelehrter Asket, die ihn zu dem werden ließ, als den ihn die Nachwelt kennt: als frommen Büßer, bedeutend(st)en Bibelübersetzer, als Kirchenvater und als (nie geweihten) Kardinal.

Literatur

Quellen

Birnbaum, Elisabeth, Der Koheletkommentar des Hieronymus. Einleitung, revidierter Text, Übersetzung und Kommentierung; Revision des lateinischen Textes durch M. Margoni-Kögler (CSEL extra seriem), Berlin/Boston 2014.

Hieronymus, Commentarius in Ecclesiasten (CCSL 72; M. Adriaen, Hg.), Turnhout 1959.

Hieronymus, Epistulae 1–70 (CSEL 54, I. Hilberg; editio altera supplementis aucta curante M. Kamptner), Wien 1996.

Schade, Ludwig, Des heiligen Kirchenvaters Eusebius Hieronymus ausgewählte Briefe, in: Des heiligen Kirchenvaters Eusebius Hieronymus ausgewählte Schriften Bd. 2–3; (BKV, 2. Reihe, Band 16 und 18), Kempten/München 1936–1937.

Forschungsliteratur

Birnbaum, Elisabeth, Der Koheletkommentar des Hieronymus. Eine Einführung aus bibelwissenschaftlicher Perspektive, in: E. Birnbaum/L. Schwienhorst-Schönberger (Hg.), Hieronymus als Exeget und Theologe (BETL 168), Leuven 2014, 11–40.

Cain, Andrew, Apology and Polemic in Jerome's Prefaces to his Biblical Scholarship, in: E. Birnbaum/L. Schwienhorst-Schönberger (Hg.), Hieronymus als Exeget und Theologe (BETL 168), Leuven 2014, 107–128.

Conring, Barbara, Hieronymus als Briefeschreiber. Ein Beitrag zur spätantiken Epistolographie, Tübingen 2001.

Dassmann, Ernst, Ambrosius von Mailand. Leben und Werk, Stuttgart 2004.

Feichtinger-Zimmermann, Barbara, Paula, Eustochium und Blesilla und die Mulier Amarior Morte. Die Frau als hochgeschätzte Partnerin und verachtetes Prinzip, in: E. Birnbaum/L. Schwienhorst-Schönberger (Hg.), Hieronymus als Exeget und Theologe (BETL 168), Leuven 2014, 191–211.

Grützmacher, Georg Konstans, Hieronymus. Eine biographische Studie zur alten Kirchengeschichte, Bd. II (SGTK 10), Berlin 1906.

Leanza, Sandro, Gerolamo e la tradizione ebraica, in: C. Moreschini/G. Menestrina, (Hg.), Motivi letterari ed esegetici in Gerolamo, Brescia 1997, 17–38.

Lössl, Josef, Die wahre Kirche und die Anderen. Antijüdische Substitutionstheologie und Häretikerpolemik im Koheletkommentar des Hieronymus, in: E. Birnbaum/L. Schwienhorst-Schönberger (Hg.), Hieronymus als Exeget und Theologe (BETL 168), Leuven 2014, 171–190.

Rebenich, Stefan, Jerome (The Early Church Fathers), London/New York, N. Y. 2002.

Schnabel, Norbert, Stendhal-Syndrom (Blog vom 27. Februar 2013), http://syndrome-de-stendhal.blogspot.com/2013/02/hieronymus-der-gelehrte-asket.html (10. April 2019).

Siquans, Agnethe, Art. Augustinus, in: wibilex: https://www.bibelwissenschaft.de/de/stichwort/16569/ (06.04.2019).

—, Frauenfeindlichkeit und Willkür? Patristische Auslegung frauenfeindlicher Aussagen in Kohelet, in: E. Birnbaum/L. Schwienhorst-Schönberger (Hg.), Hieronymus als Exeget und Theologe (BETL 168), Leuven 2014, 213–241.

Stemberger, Günter, Hieronymus und die Rabbinen, in: E. Birnbaum/L. Schwienhorst-Schönberger (Hg.), Hieronymus als Exeget und Theologe (BETL 168), Leuven 2014, 87–106.

Wriedt, Markus, Art. Ambrosius, in: wibilex: https://www.bibelwissenschaft.de/stichwort/49873/ (06.04.2019).

Anneliese Felber (Universität Graz)

Maria – Figuration des „Gottesvolkes"?

Überlegungen zur christlichen Identitätskonstruktion

1. Einführung und Fragestellung[1]

Differenzwahrnehmungen zwischen Gruppen stellen nach Martin Riesebrodt die Voraussetzung jeglicher „Identität" dar, wobei diese Wahrnehmungen stets unterschwellige Gemeinsamkeiten ausdrücken.

> Jede Religion bedarf einer solchen Differenzwahrnehmung, um sich selbst als Religion verstehen oder darstellen zu können. Alle sich neu konstituierenden oder expandierenden Religionen greifen deshalb auf Polemik zurück oder sind Gegenstand von Polemik. Polemik zielt jedoch nicht nur auf Abgrenzung nach außen, sondern dient oftmals primär der Erhöhung des Konformitätsdrucks nach innen.[2]

Diese Grenzziehung zu anderen Religionen ist deshalb notwendig, weil diese Grenzen in der Praxis oft von den Gläubigen ignoriert werden. Dass das Christentum in Abgrenzung zum Judentum wie auch der paganen Antike zu seiner Identität findet, ist völlig klar, wobei es als jüdische Sekte primär gegen das dominante Judentum seiner Zeit polemisiert.

Neue Religionen setzen sich von den Vorläufern ab oder reklamieren deren Erbe für sich. Es ist aber auch möglich, dass Religionen Elemente voneinander borgen und sich assimilieren. Das ist eine Strategie, andere Religionen in den eigenen Rahmen zu integrieren und ein- bzw. unterzuordnen. Als weitere Möglichkeit kommt Überlagerung in Frage, wobei der Anspruch besteht, den Vorgänger abzulösen und sich selbst an dessen Stelle zu setzen, ihn zu überbieten. Damit drückt sich gleichfalls eine grundsätzliche Anerkennung von Ähnlichkeit und Verwandtschaft beider Religionen aus.

Schüssler Fiorenza berichtet, dass sie in einer Vorlesung zu den Synoptikern an einer Katholischen Universität erklärte, dass Jesus Jude war, was heftige Diskussionen auslöste. Jesus sei Gottes Sohn, argumentierten die Studierenden. Als sie mehr Argumente für ihre Position anführte, sagte schließlich ein Student: Sie

1 Die Anregung habe ich durch das Buch von Lohfink/Weimer, Maria, erhalten.

2 Vgl. Riesebrodt, Cultus, bes. 43–57, Zitat 46.

können vielleicht Recht haben, dass Jesus Jude war, aber die Gottesmutter war's bestimmt nicht![3]

Die Fragestellung ist, ob Maria in der frühchristlichen Literatur für die bleibende Kontinuität der Kirche zu Israel steht oder den Bruch zwischen beiden markiert. Hat sie ähnlich wie Johannes der Täufer eine Scharnierfunktion zwischen beiden Testamenten?[4] Kann Maria als Figuration Israels gesehen werden oder ist sie Figuration des neutestamentlichen Gottesvolkes, der Kirche? Wenn Maria Urbild der Kirche ist, ist diese Aussage abgelöst vom alttestamentlichen Gottesvolk? Dabei sollen Riesebrodts Konzepte des Religionsbegriffs zur Anwendung kommen und anhand der Gestalt der Maria die christlichen Strategien der Abgrenzung und Polemik, aber auch der Assimilation und Identifikation aufgezeigt werden.

2. Maria als Figuration Israels im Neuen Testament

In neutestamentlichen Arbeiten ist schon verschiedentlich der alttestamentliche Hintergrund der lukanischen Kindheitsgeschichte herausgearbeitet worden. Thomas Hieke hat in einem jüngsten Sammelband das *Magnificat* als Brückentext zwischen zwei Geschichten Gottes mit seinem Volk bezeichnet und Vers für Vers die alttestamentlichen Prätexte, diese vor allem aus den Psalmen, angeführt. Wilfried Eisele zeigt in einem Artikel, dass die Begegnung Marias mit Elisabet nach dem Vorbild von Judit und Jael (Jdt 13,18; Ri 5,24) gezeichnet ist. Gerhard Lohfink bringt es auf den Punkt: „In der gesamten Vorgeschichte des Lukasevangeliums wird stets von Israel her gedacht."[5] Lk 1–2 sind voller Anspielungen und Zitate auf die Schriften Israels – zentrale Themen des Alten Testaments, zugespitzt auf die Option Gottes für die Armen, werden vergegenwärtigt, vor allem die Befreiung Israels aus Ägypten bis zu seiner Heimführung aus Babylon (Jes 41,8 f). In den vier Hymnen begegnet Israel in jeweils anderer Perspektive: Das *Magnificat* (Lk 1,46–55) preist Gottes Taten an seinem Volk, das *Nunc dimittis* (Lk 2,29–32) lenkt den Blick auf die Vollendung Israels (V 32 „Herrlichkeit für dein Volk Israel"), während das *Benedictus* (Lk 1,68–79) und das *Gloria* der Engel (Lk 2,14) das Gekommensein des Messias in Israel besingen.

Maria redet in ihrem Hymnus von Beginn an von Dingen, die schon geschehen sind, was Gott an Israel und an ihr selbst getan hat. Die von Gott gewirkte

3 Vgl. Schüssler Fiorenza, Christlicher Antijudaismus, 65. Italienische Version bei Lohfink/Weimer, Maria, 291.

4 Vgl. Felber, Johannes der Täufer, 29–39.

5 Vgl. Lohfink/Weimer, Maria, 218–298, Zitat 252. – Siehe grundsätzlich die Arbeit von Serra, Die Frau des Bundes.

Schwangerschaft stellt das Kind „ganz in den Raum des Handelns Gottes seit Abraham hinein".[6] Maria fasst im Loblied die gesamte Geschichte Israels zusammen und kommt zum Schluss nochmals auf sich selbst zu sprechen, dass Gott sich in ihr endgültig Israels angenommen und der Verheißungen gedacht hat, die er seit Abraham gegeben. Das *Magnificat* spannt einen Bogen von Abraham bis zu Maria und Maria repräsentiert wie Abraham das Gottesvolk.[7] Sie spricht das *Magnificat* stellvertretend für Israel, wie sie schon stellvertretend für Israel ihr Ja gesprochen hat. Damit steht Maria für Israel, ist Repräsentantin Israels. Der Hymnus beginnt mit Maria als niedriger Magd und endet mit dem Knecht Israel – Magd und Knecht bilden eine Klammer, beide sind Israel.

Ähnlich führt Lohfink zu Joh 2,1–12 (Kana-Wunder) aus, dass Maria auf der Schwelle zum Neuen steht, für Israel, das der messianischen Zeit entgegenhofft. In der Kreuzesszene (Joh 19,25–27) kommt Israel ans Ziel: Jesus konstituiert die endzeitliche Gemeinde Israel, die durch das Miteinander von Maria und dem Lieblingsjünger repräsentiert wird.[8]

Fazit: Maria ist bei Lukas und Johannes Inbild des alttestamentlichen Gottesvolkes, vor allem, soweit es geöffnet ist für die messianische Zukunft. Und wahrscheinlich schöpfen die frühchristlichen Theologen aus den Texten über Zion, wenn sie Maria als Tochter, Jungfrau, Braut und Mutter bezeichnen, auch das sind Figurationen für Israel.[9]

Wie haben nun die folgenden Jahrhunderte Maria gesehen?

3. Maria bei den Kirchenvätern

Wenn man an die dogmengeschichtliche Entwicklung denkt, wird klar, dass die Figur der Maria in christologische Kontroversen, z. B. um die Zweinaturenlehre Christi (vgl. Konzil von Ephesus 431), hineingenommen wird. Auf der anderen Seite zeigt sich, dass Maria auch in den antijüdischen Debatten eine Rolle spielen kann, mitunter selbst zum Gegenstand antijüdischer Argumentationsmuster wird. Wenn es der Argumentation dienlich ist, kann sich diese sogar gegen Maria richten. Andererseits wird jede Kritik an mariologischen Aussagen wie Gottesmutterschaft und (immerwährende) Jungfräulichkeit als jüdische oder judaisierende Tendenz wahrgenommen.[10]

---

6 Lohfink/Weimer, Maria, 257.

7 Bei Irenäus spricht Maria im Namen der Kirche das Magnificat: *Haer.* 3,10,2 (FC 8/3, 84f).

8 Vgl. Lohfink/Weimer, Maria, 260–267; weiters bes. Kästle, Mutter Jesu.

9 Vgl. Lohfink/Weimer, Maria, 237. Vgl. bes. Betz, Maria.

10 Vgl. Kampling, Jüdin, 16f.

Ich bringe im Folgenden vier Texte, die Jesu Begegnung mit seiner Familie thematisieren,[11] und drei Texte, chronologisch eingefügt, die Mirjam auf Maria deuten bzw. von den beiden Marien am Grab handeln, ziehe für eine Gesamtwertung die Arbeit von Heinz Schreckenberg heran und versuche, Riesebrodts Konzept anzuwenden.

3.1. Bekanntes Beispiel für die negative Erinnerung von Maria als Jüdin ist die Interpretation Tertullians von Mk 3,31–35 in *De carne Christi* (206 n.Chr.), wo Jesus in der missglückten Begegnung mit seiner Familie die wahre Familie Gottes konstituiert und kontrastiert:

> Aber es bedeutet noch mehr: In seiner Mutter, welche von ihm getrennt ist, liegt eine Figur der Synagoge und in seinen ungläubigen Brüdern eine Figur der Juden. In jenen befand sich Israel ‚draußen', die neuen Jünger aber, welche drinnen zuhörten und glaubten, sie, die Christus eng verbunden waren, skizzierten (bereits) das Bild der Kirche, welche er, nachdem er die Verwandtschaft dem Fleisch nach zurückgewiesen hatte, die ‚vortrefflichere Mutter' und die ‚würdigeren Brüder' nannte. In eben diesem Sinne antwortete er schließlich auch auf jenen bekannten Ausruf (vgl. Lk 11,27), wobei er nicht den Leib und die Brüste seiner Mutter verleugnete, sondern diejenigen als seliger bezeichnete, die das Wort Gottes hören (vgl. Lk 11,28) (FC 84, 197–199).[12]

Dass auf der Erzählebene Maria, die Brüder und die Zuhörer Juden sind, stört nicht Tertullians Argumentation. Entscheidend ist der Unglaube, der als jüdisches Verhalten gedeutet wird. Maria steht exemplarisch für Unglauben und wird typologisch auf die Synagoge bezogen. Tertullians Interpretation ist geprägt von Gegensätzen wie draußen/drinnen, Ferne/Nähe zu Jesus, Maria bzw. Brüder/Zuhörer (neue Schüler), die die Deutung auf Synagoge und Kirche zulassen. In welchem Kontext steht die Auslegung? Sie ist gegen Apelles, einen Schüler des Markion, gerichtet, der die Frage Jesu „Wer ist meine Mutter?" als Argument gegen Jesu Geborensein verwendete. Er leugnet zwar nicht, dass Christus einen wirklichen Leib aus himmlischer Materie analog zu den Engeln gehabt habe, wohl aber, dass er einen menschlichen Leib aufgrund einer Geburt hatte. „Aber vielleicht tat man

---

11 Es sind Texte, die sich schon bei Kampling, Jüdin, finden, und auf die ich mich beziehe. Kampling bringt noch zwei weitere Texte zu Euseb (zu Ps 68,9 LXX) mit einer gewundenen Exegese (S. 22–24) und zu Hieronymus (*Comm. Matt.* 2) mit Verschärfung auf Juden und die Völker (= Zuhörer, S. 26–28).

12 Tertullian, *Carn. Chr.* 7,13 (CCL 2, 889, 83–90): *Sed et alias: figura est synagogae in matre abiuncta et Iudaeorum in fratribus incredulis. Foris erat in illis Israel, discipuli autem novi, intus audientes et credentes cohaerentes Christo, ecclesiam deliniabant, quam potiorem matrem et digniorem fraternitatem recusato carnali genere nuncupavit. Eodem sensu denique et illi exclamationi *** respondit, non matris uterum et ubera negans, sed feliciores designans, qui verbum dei audiunt.*

das, dass man ihm Mutter und Brüder anmeldete, die er nicht hatte, um ihn zu versuchen?“ – so die Ansicht des Apelles. Tertullian muss Argumente gegen diese Interpretation finden und tut dies mit einer typologischen Deutung, indem er sich den antijüdischen Verstehenshorizont der LeserInnen zunutze macht.[13] Der Gegensatz Unglaube – Glaube des Textes begünstigt in heilsgeschichtlicher Perspektive die typologische Auslegung auf Synagoge und Kirche.

Heinz Schreckenberg[14] kommt in seiner Wertung zu Tertullian zu der Aussage, dass seine Einstellung zum Judentum unpolemisch und ohne verbale Feindseligkeiten sei, weil er auch kein Interesse an einer Judenmission erkennen lasse. Der Kampf gegen Heiden oder häretische Christen wie Gnostiker werde viel härter geführt. Wichtige christliche Positionen gilt es abzusichern, z. B. hier das Spezifikum der Inkarnation Jesu und damit der Auferstehung. Das trifft auch auf die Positionierung gegenüber dem Judentum zu, dessen politisch-rechtliche Situation vor der Zeit Konstantins eine wesentlich bessere war als die des Christentums. Tertullian hat auch nicht Judenchristen im Blick, sondern reduziert die neutestamentlichen Aussagen einer Kirche aus Juden und Heiden schon ganz auf eine reine Heidenkirche, aber die Kirche ist noch kein *Verus Israel* und nicht so ausschließlich Gottes Volk wie bei anderen frühchristlichen Autoren. Israel habe kein Heilsmonopol, auch den Heidenvölkern sei die Gnade Gottes zugedacht.

Tertullian geht es an dieser Stelle nicht um eine Debatte mit den Juden, sondern um Argumente gegen die Interpretation des Apelles mit allen theologischen Konsequenzen. Ob Antijudaismus schon ausgeprägt und Gemeingut war, wie Kampling[15] behauptet, möchte ich offenlassen. Auf jeden Fall geht es nicht um eine Auseinandersetzung mit einem realen jüdischen Gegenüber, sondern Antijudaismus wird für eine überzeugende Beweisführung innerhalb des Christentums eingesetzt. Es geht um ein innerchristliches Streitthema. Antijudaismus wird antihäretisch funktionalisiert. Fraglich ist, ob Apelles überzeugt werden sollte, da es von seiner Seite wahrscheinlich kein Legitimationsproblem gegenüber dem Judentum gab. Die Distanz zu der Vorläuferreligion scheint so weit fortgeschritten, dass ohne konkreten Bezug, völlig losgelöst, antijüdisch argumentiert werden konnte.

---

13 Vgl. Felber, Antijudaismus.

14 Vgl. Schreckenberg, Adversus-Judaeos-Texte, 216–225. Bei Tertullian zeigt sich schon die verbreitete Auslegungstradition, biblische Zweierpaare oppositionell zu deuten, und dadurch das Verhältnis von Kirche und Synagoge als eine Beziehung von Erben und Enterbten zu bestimmen, z. B. Jakob und Esau (Gen 25,23), der Ältere soll dem Jüngeren dienen; Kain und Abel (irdische und geistige Opfer der Christen) oder das Gleichnis vom verlorenen Sohn, wobei der ältere Sohn zumeist mit den Juden identifiziert wird wegen seiner Missgunst; weiters Sara und Hagar oder Rahel und Lea.

15 Vgl. Kampling, Jüdin, 33.

3.2. Auch Ambrosius, der in seinem Lukaskommentar (390 n.Chr.) die Formel Maria als Typos der Kirche[16] geprägt hat, deutet in seiner Auslegung zu Lk 8,19–21 die Draußenstehenden im geistigen Sinn, allerdings in stark abgeschwächter Form. Ambrosius betont, dass Jesus nicht pietätlos handle, sondern das Gesetz erfülle.[17] Er habe die geistigen Bande den familiären vorgezogen. Dass Jesus seine Mutter nicht verleugne, wie Häretiker meinen, zeige sich auch an Joh 19,26, wo er sie vom Kreuz herab anerkenne. Dann schließt sich der Satz an:

> Auch der Gedanke klingt nicht befremdlich, dass Christus den Juden, „von denen er dem Fleische nach abstammt" (Röm 9,5), sinnbildlich an seinen Verwandten zeigen will, dass der Kirche, welche den Glauben angenommen, der Vorrang gebührt.[18]

Es ist eine vorsichtige Formulierung – einerseits ist es keine völlige Gleichsetzung durch *per figuram*, andererseits spricht der Text von *parentes*,[19] das im weiteren Sinn Verwandte meint, die implizit dem Unglauben zugeordnet werden. Implizit kann auch Maria mitgemeint sein. Die Bevorzugung der Kirche aufgrund ihres Glaubens schließt eine Nachordnung der Juden ein. An den Verwandten Jesu – nicht an Maria – wird diese heilsgeschichtliche Sicht demonstriert.

3.2.1. Ambrosius setzt in seinen asketischen Schriften Mirjam/Maria, die Schwester des Mose, und die Mutter Jesu als Jungfrauen in Parallele, ohne biblische Grundlage bei Mirjam.[20] Wann immer auf Ex 15,20 angespielt ist, hat er die neutestamentliche Maria im Blick. Dabei wandelt sich Mirjam von der Anführerin eines Jungfrauenchores[21] über eine Heerführerin der Hebräer[22] zur Anführerin des ganzen Volkes der Hebräer.[23] Mirjam bekommt große heilsgeschichtliche Bedeutung, geht aber ganz in Maria auf. Es gibt eine einzige Stelle, wo Mirjam als Chorführerin Figuration der Kirche ist, *De virginibus* 1,3,12 (377/8 n.Chr.):

---

16 Ambrosius, *Exp. Luc.* 2,7 (CCL 14, 33).

17 Gemeint ist Gen 2,24 bzw. Eph 5,3 f, dass der Mensch Vater und Mutter verlassen müsse.

18 Ambrosius, *Exp. Luc.* 6,38, BKV^2 21, 288; CCL 14, 188, 404–407: *Illud quoque intellegere non abhorret, quia per figuram parentum demonstrat Iudaeis, ex quibus est Christus secundum carnem, ecclesiam quae credidit praeferendam.*

19 Kampling, Jüdin, 25 Fn. 35, übersetzt: „durch die Figur der Mutter" (!), und kommt daher zu einer klaren Entsprechung Marias mit dem Judentum.

20 Vgl. Neumann, Virgin Mary, 51–60. Vgl. ausführlich Siquans, Prophetinnen, 82–85.91–102, die Stellen aus Cyrill von Alexandrien und Johannes von Damaskus anführt mit Mirjam als Typos der Kirche; weiters Gregor von Nyssa, Chromatius, Petrus Chrysologus und den anonymen Dialog mit den Juden unter dem Aspekt der Jungfräulichkeit von Mirjam/Maria.

21 Z. B. Ambrosius, *Virg.* 1,3,12; 2,2,17.

22 Z. B. Ambrosius, *Epist. extra coll.* 15(42),7 (CSEL 82/3, 307); *Instit. virg.* 17,106 (PL 16, 331 bzw. Gori 186).

23 Z. B. Ambrosius, *Exh. virginit.* 5,28 (PL 16, 344; Gori 218–220): […] *virgo est ecclesia* (2 Kor 11,2).

> Auch Mirjam nahm die Pauke und führt die Chortänze in jungfräulicher Keuschheit an. Bedenkt aber, wessen Gestalt sie damals verkörperte. Nicht die der Kirche, die, als Jungfrau, unbefleckten Geistes, die frommen Volksscharen vereinigte, damit sie göttliche Lieder sängen? (FC 81, 118–121)[24]

Ob das auf die Einheit beider Testamente, auf die Präexistenz der Kirche oder eine Opposition gegenüber dem Judentum zielt, möchte ich offenlassen, auf jeden Fall ist es eine christliche Vereinnahmung der hebräischen Bibel. Man kann auch fragen, ob damit schon grundgelegt ist, was im Mittelalter zum Tragen kommt, dass Maria als Urbild der Kirche Mirjam als Urbild der Synagoge gegenübersteht.[25]

Schreckenberg[26] vermerkt zu Ambrosius, dass man bei ihm respektvolle Sätze zum Judentum finden kann, aber auch verbale Aggression insofern, weil Ambrosius Interesse an der Bekehrung von Juden hat, diese zumindest endzeitlich erhofft. Die scharfe Trennung Kirche – Israel setzt voraus, dass die Kirche sich inzwischen als wahres Israel versteht. Gemeinsamkeiten würden nicht mehr gesehen, ja vehement geleugnet. Da Ambrosius dem Gegenpapst Ursinus (zu Damasus 366/67) den Umgang mit Juden vorwirft, sei darauf zu schließen, dass er selber keinen persönlichen Umgang hatte. Das Beispiel der Zerstörung einer Synagoge im fernen Osten des Reichs und die Vereitelung des Wiederaufbaus durch Ambrosius zeige, dass einer relativ toleranten Einstellung des Kaisers in Bezug auf das Judentum die repressive Haltung eines Bischofs gegenüberstehe.

Die christliche Vereinnahmung des sog. Alten Testaments, hier in der Gestalt der Mirjam, deute ich als Strategie, das Judentum in den eigenen Rahmen zu integrieren, wodurch sich auch das Interesse des Ambrosius an der Bekehrung der Juden und seine Position gegen den Wiederaufbau der Synagoge erklären ließe. Mit typologischer Exegese wird die jüdische Bibel in Anspruch genommen, verchristlicht und die biblische Geschichte Israels zu einer Vorgeschichte des Christentums. Daher geht auch Mirjam vollständig in Maria auf.

---

24 *Et Maria tympanum sumens pudore virgineo choros duxit. Sed considerate cuius illa speciem tunc gerebat. Nonne ecclesiae, quae religiosos populi coetus, qui carmina divina concinerent, immaculato virgo copulavit?* (FC 81, 118–121; vgl. 2,2,17, ebd. 230). Heil, Seele, 40, erwähnt fälschlicherweise *De spiritu sancto* 3,4,20 (CSEL 32/2, 159) als Stelle, wo Mirjam anstelle der Maria als Führerin der Juden auftrete, es steht aber Mose im Text.

25 Vgl. Kloft, Jungfrau, 65. Maria als Urbild der Kirche ist im 14. Jh. Mirjam als Synagoge entgegengesetzt, Codex Paris, Bibl. Nat. lat. 9561 fol. 89. – Ambrosius hat eine Zweibrüdertheologie mit Vorzug des Jüngeren gegenüber dem Älteren: Der Jüngere (die Kirche) verdrängt diesen bzw. steht an dessen Stelle, vgl. Hahn, Gesetz, 476.

26 Vgl. Schreckenberg, Adversus-Judaeos-Texte, 303–310. Bei Ambrosius finden sich Elemente profaner Judenfeindschaft, die zum Teil mit theologischen Gesichtspunkten vermengt an das Mittelalter weitergegeben werden und über Luther bis in die Neuzeit wirken, wie Habgier, Unverstand, Zweifel an Sittlichkeit.

Wenn die neutestamentlichen Aussagen, wonach die Kirche eine „Kirche aus Juden und Heiden“ ist, verschärft formuliert werden, sodass die bleibende Erwählung Israels verloren geht, und die Kirche nur eine aus Heiden ist, ist das eine Kirche im Defekt, was damit überspielt wird, dass sie sich als das wahre Israel behauptet.[27] Man muss auch festhalten, dass die Kirche mit dem Bild vom wahren Israel und den damit verbundenen biblischen Inhalten wichtige Aspekte kirchlichen Selbstverständnisses entfaltet hat, die nicht ohne den jüdischen Wurzelgrund zu beschreiben gewesen wären.[28]

3.2.2. Zeno von Verona (2. Hälfte 4. Jh.) legt in einer Osterpredigt den Exodusbericht vom Durchschreiten des Roten Meeres durch das Gottesvolk (*dei populus*) mit dem Lied der Mirjam/Maria nach der Befreiung aus. In der anschließenden typologischen Erklärung ist Israel der *populus Christianus*, das Wasser Typos der Taufe, die Feuersäule Zeichen des Gerichts, Mirjam Typos der Kirche:

> Maria, die mit den Frauen die Pauke schlägt, ist das Vorbild der Kirche. Denn diese singt mit all den Kirchen, die sie geboren, das Loblied, schlägt die Brust, die wahre Pauke, und führt das Volk der Christen nicht in die Wüste, sondern in den Himmel (BKV² 10, 314).[29]

In die Exodus-Erzählungen werden christliche Deutungen hineingetragen, mit Überbietung: Maria führt in den Himmel! Ob Mirjam Vorbild der Kirche sei, stellt er nicht mehr als Frage. Er kämpft, zum Teil mit schwülstigem Pathos, gegen den jüdischen Hintergrund des Passafestes, vielleicht um judaisierenden Neigungen von Christen entgegenzuwirken in einer Zeit, wo nach Rainer Kampling das Judentum noch als Gefahr für die eigene Missionstätigkeit angesehen wurde.[30] Kampling bringt dafür Belege bis ins 9. Jh. Wir haben offensichtlich eine Konkurrenzsituation, wie sie auch Johannes Chrysostomus[31] bezeugt, und Zeno vermittelt in seinen Predigten die kirchliche Darstellung des Judentums.[32] Riesebrodt stellt fest, dass es tendenziell Funktionäre sind, denen es um die Reinheit der Praxis und Lehre

---

27 Vgl. Wengst, Identitätsbildung, 96 f.

28 Vgl. Dassmann, Kirche, 196.

29 Zeno von Verona, *Tract.* 2,26 (54),1 f (CCL 22, 200): *Maria cum mulieribus tympanum quatit; hymnus canitur; dei populus liberatur* […] *Maria, quae cum mulieribus tympanum quatit, typus ecclesiae fuit, quae cum omnibus ecclesiis, quas peperit, hymnum canens et pectoris verum tympanum quatiens populum Christianum ducit, non in eremum, sed ad caelum.*

30 Kampling, Darstellung der Juden, 25 Fn. 43, bringt Belege, dass den ChristInnen immer wieder die Teilnahme an jüdischen Festlichkeiten verboten wurde. Noch im 9. Jh. musste Papst Nikolaus I. gegen das Opfern eines Lammes in der Ostermesse als judaisierendes Element einschreiten.

31 Johannes Chrysostomus greift die Juden an, weil sie in Antiochia offensichtlich stark und attraktiv für Christen waren, vgl. dazu Nirenberg, Anti-Judaismus, 123; ausführlich Hahn, Gemeinde, 72–76.

32 Vgl. Schreckenberg, Adversus-Judaeos-Texte, 281–283.

geht, während sich die einfachen Religionsangehörigen weniger um diese Grenzen kümmern. Allerdings schaffe erst die Abgrenzung und die Systematisierung von Praktiken und Glaubensvorstellungen eine selbstbewusste Tradition.[33]

3.2.3. Petrus Chrysologus (gest. ca. 451) behandelt in seiner zweiten Auferstehungspredigt die Perikope, wo die beiden Marien (Mk 16,1; Mt 28,1) ans Grab kommen und die Auferstehung bezeugen. Die Doppelung des Namens soll die *ecclesia* aus zwei Völkern verdeutlichen. Die beiden Marien verschwimmen zu einer Figur, wie auch die Kirche aus Heiden und Juden besteht.[34] Bemerkenswert ist die Reihenfolge Heiden – Juden und das Zitat Mt 19,30. Die Stelle enthält nichts explizit Negatives, aber Maria wird durch die Namensgleichheit der Zeuginnen entjudaisiert.[35]

Diese Predigten des Petrus Chrysologus, die viel rhetorischen Prunk zeigen, werden im Mittelalter gerne gelesen, mit einer Bekehrung der Juden rechnet Petrus nicht mehr. Das zeigt sich in der Auslegung des verlorenen Sohnes, wo er andere Wege geht: Der zuhause gebliebene Sohn, der traditionell auf das Judentum ausgelegt wird, auch in seiner Missgunst, ist vom Festmahl ausgeschlossen. „Alles, was mein ist, ist auch dein" (Lk 15,31) hat keine Gültigkeit mehr.[36]

3.3. Ich bringe einen dritten Text zur missglückten Begegnung Jesu mit seiner Familie, aus dem *Opus imperfectum in Matthaeum*, verfasst von einem anonymen Autor im 5. Jh., vermutlich einem arianischen Presbyter:

> In geistlicher Betrachtung handelt der Text [...] von Maria, die nicht durch die Vereinigung des Fleisches, sondern aus Gnade des Glaubens durch Glauben Mutter Christi geworden ist. Daher verstehen wir Mutter und Brüder Christi, welche den Willen Gottes tun, nicht als die Synagoge, die nach dem Fleische Christus hervorbrachte (vgl. Röm 9,5), und die übrigen Juden. Nein, jene Synagoge erkennen wir in der Mutter, welche gerettet wurde als an Christus Glaubende und ihn nicht kreuzigte. Ähnlich muss man auch die Brüder verstehen, die nach dem Geiste Juden, nicht nach dem Fleische waren (Röm 2,28; 1 Kor 10,18; Gal 6,16), die Christus angehörten, den Willen tuend (Übers. Kampling, Jüdin, 30 Fn. 46).[37]

---

33 Vgl. Riesebrodt, Cultus, 47.

34 Petrus Chryologus, *Sermo* 75,3 (CCL 24A, 459 f): *Maria et Maria: sic altera ut ipsa, ipsa ut altera. Maria, maternum Christi unum nomen, duas geminatur in feminas, quia hic ecclesia ex duobus populis veniens, una figuratur ex duobus populis, id est ex gentibus et Iudaeis, quia* primi novissimi, et novissimi primi (Mt 19,30; Mk 10,31).

35 Vgl. Heil, Seele, 42.

36 Petrus Chryologus, *Sermo* 5,7 (CCL 24, 36–42, bes. 41 f): *nam venit Judaeus ad domum patris, id est, ad ecclesiam; stat foris per invidiam [...] Sed quia tu per invidiam perdere vis fratrem, paternas epulas, patris gaudia, dignus es non habere.*

37 *Opus imperfectum, Hom.* 30 (zu Mt 12,50) (PG 56, 791): *In qua cognatione spirituali nihilominus est haec Maria, quae non per coitum carnis, sed per gratiam fidei credendo facta est mater Christi. Deinde matrem et fratres Christi, facientes voluntatem Dei intelligimus non synagogam,*

Auch dieser Text verbindet die Typologie mit einer heilsgeschichtlichen Sicht, wobei allerdings das Jüdischsein der Maria nicht vollständig negativ akzentuiert wird. Das Motiv von Maria als Typos der Synagoge wird uminterpretiert zur *synagoga credens*. Der Autor unterscheidet zwischen Juden dem Fleische nach und die dies bleiben, die Christus gekreuzigt haben und nicht gerettet werden, und den Juden, die zum Glauben an Christus gekommen sind. Auch wenn Jesus fleischlich aus den Juden stammt (Röm 9,5), ist die fleischliche Abstammung aus dem Judentum nicht heilsrelevant. Der Autor scheint von paulinischen Texten geleitet zu sein, die Rechtfertigung aus Gnade und Glauben klingt an. Der Text erinnert positiv an die Anfänge, dass es Juden waren, die an Christus glaubten. Das mag banal erscheinen, ist aber eine einzigartige Aussage.

Kampling[38] spricht von einer positiven Uminterpretation des Motivs der Maria als Typos der ungläubigen Synagoge (deutlicher als bei Euseb) und von einem Gegenmodell und stellt die Vermutung an, ob sich diese positive Sicht auf das Judenchristentum mit der Situation des Autors als Arianer erklären lässt.

Nach Riesebrodt ordne ich das als Versuch einer Assimilation ein, wobei sogar das „Vokabular der Konkurrenz",[39] *synagoga credens*, übernommen und inkorporiert wird. Das mag durch Wettbewerb begründet sein, ist aber eine Strategie, eine andere Religion zu integrieren und unterzuordnen, und zeigt, dass sich Religionen wechselseitig wahrnehmen.

3.4. Gregor der Große führt zu Mt 12,46–50 (590/2 n.Chr.), zur Begegnung Jesu mit seiner Familie, aus:

> Was gibt er uns anderes durch diese Worte zu verstehen außer, dass er sich viele aus dem Heidentum sammelt, die seinen Geboten Folge leisten, und die Jüdin, aus deren Fleisch er geboren wurde, nicht kennen will? Und seiner Mutter nun, da sie gleichsam nicht erkannt wird, wird geheißen, draußen stehen zu bleiben. Offensichtlich wird dementsprechend die Synagoge von ihrem Urheber nicht wiedererkannt, da sie sich an die Gesetzesobservanz haltend, den geistigen Sinn verloren hat, und sich zur Wache des Buchstabens nach draußen stellte (Übers. Kampling, Jüdin, 31 Fn. 50).[40]

---

quae secundum corpus peperit Christum, caeterosque Iudaeos: sed illam synagogam intelligimus matrem quae salvata est credens in Christum, non crucifigens eum. Similiter est intelligendum et de fratribus, qui secundum spiritum erant Iudaei, non secundum corpus, qui Christi erant facientes voluntatem.

38 Vgl. Kampling, Jüdin, 29 f.

39 Riesebrodt, Cultus, 57.

40 Gregor der Große, *Hom. ev.* 3,1 (FC 28/1, 80 f): *Quibus nobis verbis quid aliud innuit, nisi quod obsequentes iussionibus suis multos ex gentilitate colligit, et Iudaeam, ex cuius carne est genitus, non agnoscit. Unde et mater eius cum quasi non agnoscitur, foris stare perhibetur: quia videlicet synagoga idcirco ab auctore suo non recognoscitur, quia legis observationem tenens, spiritalem intellectum perdidit, et sese ad custodiam literae foris fixit.* Fiedrowicz übersetzt FC 28/1, 81 f: „[…] das Judentum,

Den Text dominiert die Vorstellung von aufgegebenen Beziehungen. Maria wird als *Iudaea* bezeichnet und zum Demonstrationsobjekt des Schicksals der Synagoge. „In der Mutter vollzieht Jesus antizipierend, was das Judentum post Christi resurrectionem in seiner Gesamtheit trifft.“[41] Implizit wird auch auf den Juden Jesus verwiesen, der aber nach Interpretation Gregors nichts von seiner Herkunft wissen will. Die Lossagung Jesu vom Judesein verschärft sich durch die Betonung der *Iudaea*. Nicht ganz klar wird, wer mit Urheber der Synagoge gemeint ist. Man wird dabei wohl an die Erwählung Israels durch Gott denken müssen. Gregor weiß um die enge Bindung Jesu an das Judentum, aber er sieht darin nichts Bleibendes, bedingt durch die Gesetzesobservanz und den Literalsinn der Schrift. Die Zuhörer sind bei Gregor schon völlig als Christen aus den Völkern zu verstehen. Bemerkenswert ist allerdings, wie klar Gregor die Bindung Marias und Jesu an das Judentum bezeugt. Die Nähe wird benannt, um die Distanz zu unterstreichen. Bemerkenswert ist auch, dass Gregor einen Grund nennt; für Gregor ist das Schicksal des jüdischen Volkes von seiner Fähigkeit zur *spiritalis intelligentia* bestimmt. Diese fehlt den Juden bezüglich der Interpretation der Gestalt Jesu und der Exegese der Schrift, sodass sie nicht die wahre Gestalt Christi erkennen können und nicht zur Kirche gehören.[42]

Fiedrowicz kommt in seiner Dissertation zum Kirchenverständnis Gregors[43] zu dem Urteil, dass seine Haltung unpolemisch gegenüber dem Judentum sei, dass der Verlust des größten Teils des jüdischen Volkes für die Kirche einen großen Schmerz darstelle und dass es ursprünglich Verkündiger aus dem jüdischen Volk waren, die wie die ProphetInnen und Priester des Alten Bundes den kommenden Erlöser verkündigten. Nicht die heilsgeschichtliche Ablösung, sondern die Parallelität zwischen dem alten und neuen Volk Gottes interessiert ihn.

> Das alte Volk hatte Väter vor dem Gesetz, unter dem Gesetz und schließlich die Propheten. Im neuen Volk aber haben zunächst die Erstlinge der Hebräer geglaubt, dann ist die Fülle der Heiden im Glauben nachgefolgt, und schließlich wird am Ende der Welt der Rest der Hebräer gerettet werden.[44]

Seine Position ist von der Hoffnung auf endzeitliche Bekehrung bestimmt.[45]

---

von dem er leiblich abstammt, […]“. Warum er statt Jüdin Judentum übersetzt, ist nicht klar; vielleicht soll das der Versuch einer Glättung sein.

41 Kampling, Jüdin, 31.

42 Vgl. Fiedrowicz, Kirchenverständnis, 171.

43 Vgl. ebd., 163–179; auch 126–137.

44 Gregor der Große, *Hom. Ezech.* 2,4,5 (CCL 142, 261, 155–160).

45 Keine eschatologische Bekehrung Israels erwarten, weil die biblischen Verheißungen vom geretteten Israel auf die aus Juden und Heiden konstituierte Kirche gedeutet werden, z. B. Euseb, Athanasius und Cyrill von Jerusalem; die Auffassung einer Möglichkeit einer endzeitlichen Konversion vertreten Ambrosius, Hieronymus und Augustinus. Gregor schließt sich Tertullian, Cyprian und

Zu Joh 10,16[46] (*Hom. ev.* 14,4) führt Gregor aus, dass der Herr nicht allein das Judentum, sondern auch das Heidentum (andere Schafe) erlösen und aus zwei Herden eine einzige Hürde machen werde, weil er das jüdische und heidnische Volk im Glauben an sich vereinigt. Aus beiden Völkern erwählt er die Aufrichtigen zum ewigen Leben.[47] Zu Joh 20,4, wo Petrus als Kirche und Johannes als Synagoge zum Grab laufen, hält er fest, dass beide miteinander laufen, weil das Heidentum mit der Synagoge von der Zeit seines Anfangs bis ans Ende auf gleichem und gemeinsamem Weg, wenn auch nicht mit gleicher und gemeinsamer Gesinnung, gelaufen ist.[48]

Gregor[49] hat als politischer Repräsentant Interesse an der Rechtssicherheit der Juden und an Rechtskontinuität. In ca. dreißig seiner Briefe ist er mit der religionspolitischen Situation der Juden im Westen des Reichs befasst. Das sind das Recht freier Religionsausübung, Sicherung vor Zwangstaufen, er geht gegen antijüdische Übergriffe wie gegen jüdische Mission vor, meist geht es um den Besitz christlicher SklavInnen bei Juden. Das sind Bestimmungen, die in der päpstlichen Judenpolitik im Mittelalter weiterwirken. In einem Brief vom Juli 599 berichtet er, dass ein zum Christentum bekehrter Jude in die Synagoge in Cagliari eingedrungen sei mit einem Madonnenbild, dem Kreuz und seinem Taufgewand, um die Synagoge zur Kirche zu machen. Gregor ordnet die Entfernung der Gegenstände an und mahnt zu Respekt und störungsfreiem Besitz der Synagoge.[50] Im letzten Brief zum Judentum vom September 603[51] bestätigt er, was aus anderen Quellen bekannt ist, dass bei vielen Christen die Kultzeremonien des Judentums in Ansehen stehen, konkret geht es hier um die Einhaltung der Sabbatruhe. Das Judaisieren von Christen wird als ernste Gefährdung christlicher Identität empfunden.

In seinen exegetischen und homiletischen Werken wie den Ezechielhomilien und Moralia in Job aber finden sich die traditionellen theologischen Vorstellungen, allerdings mit Einschränkungen. So wird das Verhältnis von altem und neuem Bund als Fortschreiten verstanden.[52] Er hegt die Hoffnung auf Bekehrung der Juden,

---

Gregor von Nazianz an, die die Hoffnung auf endzeitliche Konversion bezeugen, und er gibt dieser Hoffnung breiten Raum (vgl. Fiedrowicz, Kirchenverständnis, 171 Fn. 49).

46 „Ich habe noch andere Schafe, die nicht aus diesem Stall sind; auch sie muss ich führen, und sie werden meine Stimme hören; dann wird es nur eine Herde geben und einen Hirten." (EÜ)

47 Gregor der Große, *Hom. ev.* 14,4 (FC 28/1, 230 f): [...] *Quasi enim ex duobus gregibus unum ovile efficit; quia iudaicum et gentilem populum in sua fide coniungit* [...] *Dum enim ad aeternam vitam ex utraque natione simplices eligit, ad ovile proprium oves deducit* (232).

48 Gregor der Große, *Hom. ev.* 22,2 (FC 28/1, 392 f): *Cucurrerunt ambo simul: quia ab ortus sui tempore usque ad occasum, pari et communi via, etsi non pari et communi sensu, gentilitas cum synagoga cucurrit* (394).

49 Vgl. Schreckenberg, Adversus-Judaeos-Texte, 424–435.

50 Vgl. ebd., 432.

51 Vgl. ebd., 433.

52 Vgl. in mittelalterlichen Kathedralplastiken die Apostel als Söhne der Propheten.

vor allem in der Endzeit. Gregor ist einer der wenigen, der in der Gottesmordfrage um die Mitschuld der Römer weiß bzw. um die Schuld aller bösen Menschen einschließlich der Christen.

Gregor nimmt die Differenz zwischen Juden- und Christentum wahr, ohne zu polemisieren. M. E. begründet er sie in sachlicher Weise.

4. Schlussfolgerungen

Ich versuche im Folgenden, ein paar Grundsätze zu formulieren, die, ohne den patristischen Antijudaismus relativieren zu wollen, dazu beitragen sollen, einen anderen Umgang mit diesen Texten zu pflegen. Es steht für mich außer Frage, dass die Rezeption dieser Texte den antijüdischen Ton entgegen der ursprünglichen Intention wesentlich verschärft hat.

- Wenn das Jüdischsein der Maria thematisiert wird, geschieht es zumeist negativ. Klar ist die Tendenz zu erkennen, sie zu entjudaisieren und auf die christliche Seite zu stellen.
- Die Betonung des Jüdischseins der Maria (und auch Jesu) lässt bei aller negativen Akzentuierung bzw. Negierung die Bindung des Christentums ans Judentum erkennen. Die Nähe des Christentums zum Judentum wird von christlicher Seite durch Abgrenzung zur Bestimmung der eigenen Identität kompensiert.
- Maria spielt eine zentrale Rolle bei der heilsgeschichtlichen Konfrontation zwischen JüdInnen und ChristInnen zur Bestimmung von Differenz und Distanz. Alle Überlegenheitsaussagen sind zu zähmen durch das Wissen, dass ohne Gottesvolk der Juden das neue Gottesvolk der Kirche nicht möglich ist.[53]
- Vor allem in der Predigtliteratur, die auf Wirkung bei der Zuhörerschaft abzielt, wird eine kirchliche Darstellung des Judentums vermittelt. Zwischen biblischem und zeitgenössischem Judentum wird nicht unterschieden. Antijudaismus kann zum Gradmesser für kirchliche Konformität werden.[54]
- Oft handelt es sich um Scheinpolemik, es ist nicht an Juden als Leser gedacht, sondern an Heiden, die zwischen Juden- und Christentum schwanken. Es sind „virtuelle" Juden[55] im Dienst immanent christlicher Verhältnisse.
- Das Judaisieren von ChristInnen, d. h. Kontakte und Beziehungen zwischen beiden Gruppen, wird als Gefährdung der eigenen christlichen Identität empfunden. Es bezeugt das „Ausmaß der christlich-jüdischen Koexistenz"[56].

---

53 Vgl. Dassmann, Kirche, 207.

54 Vgl. Kampling, Grenzgebiete, 342.

55 Vgl. Heil, Seele, 56.

56 Hahn, Gemeinde, 74.

- Aus den Texten kann nicht geschlossen werden, was ChristInnen allgemein über JüdInnen dachten. Es geht um eine Konstruktion von JüdInnen.
- Der Anspruch, wahres Israel zu sein, ist mehr als eine Metaphorik, weil die Kirche damit nicht eine Qualität in Anspruch nimmt, die von sonst niemandem beansprucht wird, sondern für sich reklamiert, was einem anderen abgesprochen wird. Land und Volk werden identitätsstiftend beansprucht bzw. verweigert.[57]
- Es gilt eine Ekklesiologie zu entwickeln, die der Ab- und Ausgrenzung nicht mehr bedarf.
- Es gilt eine Neudefinition des Gottesvolkes bzw. eine Veränderung der bisherigen Gottesvolk-Konzeption zu entwickeln, sodass jesusgläubige Nichtjuden in das Gottesvolk hineingenommen werden und dieses somit ausgeweitet wird – gegen die Substitutionstheorie, dass die christliche Gemeinde das wahre Israel sei und sich Teile des Judentums selbst aus dem Gottesvolk ausgeschlossen hätten.[58]
- Es gilt, was Günter Stemberger festgehalten hat, dass keine pauschalen und isolierten Aussagen über das Verhältnis der Kirchenväter zu den Juden möglich und sinnvoll sind.[59]

Literatur

Betz, Christina, Maria – „Tochter Zion"? Eine kritische Auseinandersetzung mit René Laurentins These zur lukanischen Kindheitsgeschichte, in: H.-U. Weidemann (Hg.), „Der Name der Jungfrau war Maria" (Lk 1,27). Neue exegetische Perspektiven auf die Mutter Jesu (SBS 238), Stuttgart 2018, 221–242.

Dassmann, Ernst, Die eine Kirche in vielen Bildern. Zur Ekklesiologie der Kirchenväter (Standorte in Antike und Christentum 1), Stuttgart 2010.

Eisele, Wilfried, Maria, Elisabet und die vielgepriesenen Frauen Israels (Lk 1,39–45), in: H.-U. Weidemann (Hg.), „Der Name der Jungfrau war Maria" (Lk 1,27). Neue exegetische Perspektiven auf die Mutter Jesu (SBS 238), Stuttgart 2018, 172–203.

Felber, Anneliese, Johannes der Täufer: Repräsentant Israels? Bemerkungen aus patristischer Sicht, PZB 4 (1995), 29–39.

—, Zum Problem des Antijudaismus in der Patristik, StPatr 40 (2006), 197–201 (= Anneliese Felber, Väterexegese: Brisanz und Vielfalt, Habilitationsschrift Graz 2011, 29–33).

Fiedrowicz, Michael, Das Kirchenverständnis Gregors des Großen. Eine Untersuchung seiner exegetischen und homiletischen Werke (RQ.S 50), Freiburg i.Br. 1995.

Hahn, Johannes, Die jüdische Gemeinde im spätantiken Antiochia. Leben im Spannungsfeld von sozialer Einbindung, religiösem Wettbewerb und gewaltsamem Konflikt, in:

57 Vgl. Dassmann, Kirche, 195.

58 Vgl. Neubrand, Volk aus Nichtjuden, 297.

59 Vgl. Stemberger, Kirchenväter, 46 f.

R. Jütte (Hg.), Jüdische Gemeinden und Organisationsformen von der Antike bis zur Gegenwart, Wien 1996, 57–89.

Hahn, Viktor, Das wahre Gesetz. Eine Untersuchung der Auffassung des Ambrosius von Mailand vom Verhältnis der beiden Testamente, Münster 1969.

Heil, Johannes, „... auch durch deine Seele wird ein Schwert dringen“. Zur Auslegung von Lk 2, 34–35 in der exegetischen und homiletischen Literatur von der Patristik zum Hochmittelalter, in: J. Heil/R. Kampling (Hg.), Maria – Tochter Sion? Mariologie, Marienfrömmigkeit und Judenfeindschaft, Paderborn 2001, 37–57.

Hieke, Thomas, Ein Psalm, der von der Zuverlässigkeit der Lehre überzeugt. Das Magnificat (Lk 1,46–55) als Brückentext zwischen zwei Geschichten Gottes mit einem Volk, in: ders., Studien zum Alten Testament im Neuen Testament (SBAB 67), Stuttgart 2018, 37–65.

Kästle, Philipp, Die Mutter Jesu im Johannesevangelium. Zeugin des irdischen Wirkens und Garantin der sarkischen Existenz Jesu, in: H.-U. Weidemann (Hg.), „Der Name der Jungfrau war Maria“ (Lk 1,27). Neue exegetische Perspektiven auf die Mutter Jesu (SBS 238), Stuttgart 2018, 301–334.

Kampling, Rainer, Die Darstellung der Juden und des Judentums in den Predigten des Zeno von Verona, Kairos 26 (1984), 16–27.

—, „... die Jüdin, aus deren Fleisch er geboren wurde ...“. Zu einem antijudaistischen und antimarianischen Modell der patristischen Auslegung, in: J. Heil/R. Kampling (Hg.), Maria – Tochter Sion? Mariologie, Marienfrömmigkeit und Judenfeindschaft, Paderborn 2001, 13–36.

—, Grenzgebiete – Zu Strukturelementen des spätantiken Antijudaismus, in: H. Frankemölle/J. Wohlmuth (Hg.), Das Heil der Anderen. Problemfeld: „Judenmission“ (QD 238), Freiburg i.Br. 2010, 337–357.

Kloft, Matthias Theodor, „Die heilige Jungfrau ist gleichsam die Vollendung der Synagoge“. Maria und die Juden in der Theologie des Hochmittelalters, in: J. Heil/R. Kampling (Hg.), Maria – Tochter Sion? Mariologie, Marienfrömmigkeit und Judenfeindschaft, Paderborn 2001, 59–68.

Lohfink, Gerhard/Weimer, Ludwig, Maria – nicht ohne Israel. Eine neue Sicht der Lehre von der Unbefleckten Empfängnis, Freiburg i.Br. 2008.

Neubrand, Maria, „Ein Volk aus Nichtjuden“ (Apg 15,14). Die bleibende Erwählung Israels und die Erwähnung aus den Völkern im lukanischen Doppelwerk, in: H. Frankemölle/J. Wohlmuth (Hg.), Das Heil der Anderen. Problemfeld: „Judenmission“ (QD 238), Freiburg i.Br. 2010, 289–310.

Neumann, Charles W., The Virgin Mary in the Works of Saint Ambrose, Fribourg 1962.

Nirenberg, David, Anti-Judaismus. Eine andere Geschichte des westlichen Denkens, München 2015.

Riesebrodt, Martin, Cultus und Heilsversprechen. Eine Theorie der Religionen, München 2007.

Serra, Aristide, Die Frau des Bundes. Präfigurationen Marias im Alten Testament (MSt 23), Regensburg 2015.

Schreckenberg, Heinz, Die christlichen Adversus-Judaeos-Texte und ihr literarisches und historisches Umfeld (1.–11. Jh.), Frankfurt a. M. 1982.

Schüssler Fiorenza, Elisabeth, Christlicher Antijudaismus aus feministischer Perspektive, in: C. Kurth/P. Schmid (Hg.), Das christlich-jüdische Gespräch. Standortbestimmungen, Stuttgart 2000, 56–75.

Siquans, Agnethe, Die alttestamentlichen Prophetinnen in der patristischen Rezeption. Texte – Kontexte – Hermeneutik (HBS 65), Freiburg i.Br. 2011.

Stemberger, Günter, Antike Kirchenväter und ihr Judenbild, in: C. Müller/G. Förster (Hg.), Augustinus – Christentum – Judentum. Ausgewählte Stationen einer Problemgeschichte. Beiträge des 13. Würzburger Augustinus-Studientages vom 12./13. November 2015, Würzburg 2018, 33–48.

Wengst, Klaus, Christliche Identitätsbildung im Gegenüber und im Gegensatz zum Judentum zwischen 70–135 d. Zt., in: C. Kurth/P. Schmid (Hg.), Das christlich-jüdische Gespräch. Standortbestimmungen, Stuttgart 2000, 91–99.

Gerhard Langer (Universität Wien)

Mirjam in rabbinischen Midrasch-Texten

Eine Gegenfigur zu Maria?

Mirjam ist Gegenstand zahlreicher rabbinischer Betrachtungen über die Jahrhunderte. Spätere Texte[1] scheinen allerdings die Traditionen noch besonders zuzuspitzen und anzureichern und sie sind zweifellos interessant für einen direkten Vergleich mit christlichen Auslegungen.

Der folgende Beitrag konzentriert sich auf wenige Beispiele und versucht einen thematischen Zugang, der sich auf die Bedeutung Mirjams im Hinblick auf Sexualität, Geburt und den Erhalt des Volkes konzentriert. Damit ist auch ihre vorbereitende Rolle im Hinblick auf den „Erlöser" verbunden.[2]

Mirjams Name leitet sich der Tradition nach von *mar* ab, was „bitter" bedeutet. So verbindet man – z. B. in *Pesiqta Rabbati* 15:11 – den Namen mit Bezug zu Ex 1,14 auf die Bitternis der harten Arbeit der Israeliten.

Prägnant drückt es auch der mittelalterliche Midrasch *Wa-joscha* aus, wenn dort der Völkerengel Uzza mit Gott spricht und das Schicksal des Volkes Israel mit dem Schicksal der Mirjam in eins zu setzen scheint:

> Sofort begann Uzza und sprach vor Ihm: „Herr der Welten! Du hast diesem Volk verordnet, dass es unter meinem Volk vierhundert Jahre lang in Knechtschaft dienen soll, und bisher haben sie bei ihnen erst 86 Jahre gedient seit dem Tage, an dem Miriam geboren wurde. Denn deshalb ist ihr Name Miriam, weil die Ägypter ihr Leben verbitterten. Und so wie du ein Beständiger bist, so wird auch deine Verordnung beständig sein.[3]

Mar kann sich zudem, wie Jes 40,15 zeigt, auf Wasser beziehen. Wasser ist ein in ganz besonderer Weise mit Mirjam verbundenes Element. Seine Bedeutung in der biblischen und rabbinischen Tradition ist intensiv mit dem Erhalt, aber auch dem Verlust von Leben verbunden. Im metaphorischen Sinn wird Wasser dann gern auf die Tora und die Lehre gedeutet. Ein Lehrer wie R. Eliezer wird gern als Zisterne, Elazar ben Arakh als Quelle bezeichnet (*Avot* 2:8).

---

1 Der Ausdruck „späterer Midrasch" ist freilich recht unspezifisch, meint hier aber Texte, die vom Ende der Talmudwerdung bzw. ins Mittelalter hineinreichen. Früheres Material wird dabei integriert und transformiert.

2 Einen guten Überblick über die Mirjam-Tradition in der rabbinischen Literatur bietet bereits Steinmetz, A Portrait of Miriam.

3 Übersetzung Wies-Campagner, Midrasch Wajoscha, 263.

Die wohl bekannteste mit Mirjam verbundene Episode bezieht sich auf den Brunnen, der die Israeliten in der Wüste begleitete. In der Tosefta *Sota* 11:8 heißt es dazu:

> Als Israel aus Ägypten auszog, wurden ihnen drei gute Führer (*parnassim*) bestellt, und zwar Mose, Aaron und Mirjam. Durch ihr Verdienst wurden ihnen drei Gaben zuteil: Die Wolkensäule, das Manna und der Brunnen. Der Brunnen durch das Verdienst Mirjams, die Wolkensäule durch das Verdienst Aarons und das Manna durch das Verdienst Moses. Als Mirjam starb, hörte der Brunnen auf, kam aber wieder durch das Verdienst Moses und Aarons.[4]

Damit unterscheiden sich die Rabbinen von der Tradition im *Liber Antiquitatum Biblicarum*, einer Schrift, deren zeitliche Einordnung zwischen dem 1. Jh. v. und dem 2. Jh. n.Chr. schwankt. Dort wird der Brunnen auf das Verdienst des Mose zurückgeführt.[5]

Grundlage ist die Bemerkung in Num 20,1–2, wonach das Volk nach dem Tod der Mirjam kein Wasser mehr hatte. Die Rabbinen füllen demnach logische Lücken im Text, ein zentrales Verfahren rabbinischer Auslegung. Das Murren des Volkes wegen des fehlenden Wassers findet sich bereits in der Episode in Ex 15,22–24, direkt nach der Erzählung über Mirjams Gesang am Schilfmeer:

> Mose ließ Israel vom Roten Meer aufbrechen und sie zogen zur Wüste Schur weiter. Drei Tage waren sie in der Wüste unterwegs und fanden kein Wasser. Als sie nach Mara kamen, konnten sie das Wasser von Mara nicht trinken, weil es bitter war. Deshalb nannte man es Mara. Da murrte das Volk gegen Mose und sagte: Was sollen wir trinken?

Besonders deutlich wird es in Num 20,10–13.24; 27,14 zum Ausdruck gebracht:

> 20,10 Mose und Aaron riefen die Versammlung vor dem Felsen zusammen und Mose sagte zu ihnen: Hört, ihr Meuterer, können wir euch wohl aus diesem Felsen Wasser fließen lassen? 11 Dann hob er seine Hand hoch und schlug mit seinem Stab zweimal auf den Felsen. Da kam Wasser heraus, viel Wasser, und die Gemeinde und ihr Vieh konnten trinken […] 13 Das ist das Wasser von Meriba, Streit, weil die Israeliten mit dem HERRN gestritten haben und er sich als der Heilige erwiesen hat […] 24Aaron wird jetzt mit seinen Vorfahren vereint; er wird nicht in das Land kommen, das ich für die Israeliten bestimmt habe; denn ihr habt euch am Wasser von Meriba gegen meinen Befehl aufgelehnt.

---

4 Übersetzung Stemberger, Mose, 145. Parallelen finden sich auch in *Seder Olam Rabba* 10, in der *Mekhilta Wajassa* 6 und *bTaanit* 9a.

5 Nach *Avot* 5:6 gehört der Brunnen (oder genauer die Öffnung des Brunnens – *pi ha-be'er*) zu den (zehn) Dingen, die bereits im Zwielicht des Schabbat bei der Weltschöpfung erschaffen wurden. Von Mirjam ist dort nicht die Rede. Nach *bSchabbat* 35a kann man den Brunnen immer noch vom Karmel aus sehen. Nach Rav ist er eine rituell reine Quelle, die sich von Ort zu Ort bewegt. Weitere Traditionen haben ihn auch im See Genezaret verortet (*Lev. Rab.* 22:4; *Qoh. Rab.* 5:8), wo er noch wundersame Heilungen bewirkt.

> 27,14 denn ihr habt euch in der Wüste Zin meinem Befehl widersetzt, als die Gemeinde haderte und ihr durch das Wasser vor ihren Augen hättet bezeugen sollen, dass ich der Heilige bin. Das ist das Haderwasser von Kadesch in der Wüste Zin.

Murren, Streiten und Hadern sind eng verzahnt mit dem bitteren Wasser und klingen sprachlich zusammen. In der rabbinischen Kombination entsteht daraus die Assoziation mit Mirjam. Im Prinzip ist es also Mirjam als Spenderin des Wassers, deren Verlust beklagt wird.

Mirjams eigentliches Murren betraf ihren Bruder Mose und findet sich in Num 12,1–3:

> Als sie in Hazerot waren, redeten Mirjam und Aaron gegen Mose wegen der kuschitischen Frau, die er sich genommen hatte. Er hatte sich nämlich eine Kuschiterin zur Frau genommen. Sie sagten: Hat der HERR etwa nur durch Mose gesprochen? Hat er nicht auch durch uns gesprochen? Das hörte der HERR. Mose aber war ein sehr demütiger Mann, demütiger als alle Menschen auf der Erde.[6]

Der Gegenstand des Unmuts ist einerseits die „neue" kuschitische Frau des Mose, andererseits der exklusive Autoritätsanspruch des Mose,[7] dem sich Mirjam, aber auch Aaron widersetzen. Die Rabbinen identifizieren die kuschitische Frau mit Zippora, da sie vermeiden wollen, eine zusätzliche namenlose Gemahlin für Mose anzunehmen. Es gibt schließlich einen ganz besonderen Grund für den Aufruhr:

---

6 Der folgende Text Num 12,4–16 schildert die Reaktion Gottes und die Bestrafung der Mirjam: „Da sprach der HERR plötzlich zu Mose, Aaron und Mirjam: Geht ihr drei hinaus zum Offenbarungszelt! Da gingen die drei hinaus. Der HERR kam in der Wolkensäule herab, blieb am Zelteingang stehen und rief Aaron und Mirjam. Beide traten vor und der HERR sprach: Hört meine Worte! Wenn es bei euch einen Propheten gibt, so gebe ich mich ihm in einer Vision als der HERR zu erkennen, im Traum rede ich mit ihm. Anders bei meinem Knecht Mose. Mein ganzes Haus ist ihm anvertraut. Von Mund zu Mund rede ich mit ihm, in einer Vision, nicht in Rätseln. Die Gestalt des HERRN darf er sehen. Warum habt ihr euch nicht gefürchtet, gegen meinen Knecht, gegen Mose, zu reden? Da entbrannte der Zorn des HERRN gegen sie und er ging weg. Als die Wolke vom Zelt gewichen war, siehe, da war Mirjam weiß wie Schnee vor Aussatz. Aaron wandte sich Mirjam zu und siehe, sie war aussätzig. Da sagte Aaron zu Mose: Mein Herr, ich bitte dich, lege uns die Sünde nicht zur Last, mit der wir töricht gehandelt haben und mit der wir uns versündigt haben! Mirjam soll nicht wie eine Totgeburt sein, halb verwest, wenn sie den Schoß der Mutter verlässt. Da schrie Mose zum HERRN: O Gott, heile sie doch! Der HERR antwortete Mose: Wenn ihr Vater ihr ins Gesicht gespuckt hätte, müsste sie sich dann nicht sieben Tage lang schämen? Sie soll sieben Tage lang aus dem Lager ausgesperrt sein; erst dann soll man sie wieder hereinlassen. So wurde Mirjam sieben Tage aus dem Lager ausgesperrt. Das Volk brach nicht auf, bis man Mirjam wieder hereinließ. Danach brach das Volk von Hazerot auf und schlug sein Lager in der Wüste Paran auf."

7 Eine kritisch-feministische Lektüre zu dem Text bietet Fischer, Die Autorität Mirjams. In dem Sammelband von Brenner, A Feminist Companion to Exodus to Deuteronomy, sind verschiedene Beiträge zu Mirjam einschlägig.

„Wegen der Frau", nämlich über die Sache von der Trennung (Moses) von der Frau. Sie sagten: Ein stolzer Mensch ist Mose. Hat denn der Heilige, gepriesen sei er, mit ihm allein gesprochen? Er hat doch mit vielen Propheten und mit uns gesprochen, und wir haben uns nicht von unseren Frauen getrennt, wie er sich getrennt hat; denn es heißt: „Hat etwa der Herr nur mit Mose gesprochen?" [...] Er hat doch mit uns gesprochen, auch mit unseren Vätern. Nur haben wir uns nicht so verhalten und waren auch nicht verpflichtet, uns so zu verhalten [...] „Das hörte" – ist es denkbar; dass es nur Gott gehört hat? Woher (weiß ich), dass es auch Mose gehört hat? Die Schrift lehrt: das hörte der Herr und der Mann Mose" (*Sifre Zuta Num* 12,1–3).[8]

Stemberger hat völlig recht mit der Ansicht, dass hier kunstvoll Lücken im Bibeltext geschlossen werden und gleichzeitig die Frage beantwortet wird, warum Mose sich vom Geschlechtsverkehr mit seiner Frau enthielt, nämlich nicht aus Stolz, wie man annehmen könnte, sondern aus der besonderen Bereitschaft, jederzeit für die Offenbarung Gottes bereit zu sein, wie sie den Israeliten am Sinai zuteilwurde, die sich dort drei Tage von ihren Frauen fernhielten (Ex 19,15; vgl. dazu *Sifre Num* 103; *Sifre Zuta Num* 12,8).

Eine ganz ähnliche Argumentation vertritt auf christlicher Seite Aphrahat (4. Jh.), der allerdings neben Mose dann auch Josua, Jeremia, Elija und Elischa nennt: Auch sie hatten wegen ihrer Aufgabe keine sexuellen Beziehungen.[9]

Diese relativ frühen Belege zeigen Mirjams Ärger über die sexuelle Abstinenz des Mose. Im babylonischen Midrasch des Talmud *Sota* wird dieser Aspekt aufgegriffen und mit einer Episode verbunden, die vor der Geburt des Mose liegt. Der Text von *Sota* 12a–13a ist von besonderem Interesse, da er mit großer Wahrscheinlichkeit bereits auf die Evangelien von Matthäus und Lukas zur Geburt Jesu reagiert. Doch bleiben wir vorerst am Text, der sich direkt auf Mirjam (und Jochebed) bezieht. Er ist im entscheidenden Teil chiastisch gegliedert:

„*Ein Mann aus einer levitischen Familie ging hin*" (Ex 2,1).

Wohin ging er? Es sagte R. Jehuda bar Zevina: Er ging nach dem Rat seiner Tochter.

A

Es wird gelehrt: Amram war der Größte seiner Generation. Als er sah, dass der Pharao dieses Dekret erlassen hatte [d.h. Ex 1,22: „*Alle Knaben, die geboren werden, werft in den Nil*"] sagte er: Umsonst mühen wir uns. Er stand auf und schied sich von seiner Frau. Und alle standen auf und schieden sich von ihren Frauen.

8 Übersetzung Stemberger, Mose, 147.

9 Vgl. ebd., 148.

B

Da sagte ihm seine Tochter: Vater, dein Erlass ist härter als der Erlass des Pharao. Der Pharao hat nur gegen die Knaben einen Erlass verhängt, du aber gegen Mädchen und Knaben; der Pharao nur für diese Welt, du aber für dieseWelt und für die kommende Welt! Der Pharao ist böse und es ist zweifelhaft, ob sein Erlass eingehalten wird oder nicht. Du aber bist gerecht und dein Erlass wird wirklich eingehalten; denn vom Gerechten steht geschrieben: *„Beschließt du etwas, dann trifft es ein*" (Hiob 22,28).

A′

In derselben Stunde stand er auf und nahm seine Frau zurück. Alle standen auf und nahmen ihre Frauen zurück.

„Und nahm [zur Frau]" (2,1).

„Nahm zurück", müsste es heißen! Es sagte R. Jehuda bar Zevina: Er behandelte sie wie bei der Heirat. Er setzte sie in eine Sänfte: Aaron und Mirjam tanzten vor ihr und die Dienstengel sagten: *„Die Mutter freut sich an ihren Kindern*" (Ps 113,9).

„Die Tochter Levis" (2,1).

Ist das möglich? Sie war doch 130 Jahre alt, und da nennt er sie eine Tochter?! Es sagte ja R. Chama bar Chanina: Das ist Jochebed, deren Empfängnis auf dem Weg [der Familie Jakobs nach Ägypten] und deren Geburt in den Mauern [Ägyptens] stattfand. Denn es heißt: *„(Die Frau Amrams hieß Jochebed, die Tochter Levis). Sie war dem Levi in Ägypten geboren worden*" (Num 26,59). Ihre Geburt war in Ägypten, nicht aber ihre Empfängnis in Ägypten. Und er nennt sie Tochter?! Es sagte R. Jehuda bar Bizna: Es entstanden ihr wieder Zeichen der Jugend.[10]

Wieder richtet sich Mirjams Aufruhr gegen die Verweigerung von Sexualität. Sie ist das Ergebnis allgemeiner Frustration angesichts der harten Fronarbeit in Ägypten. Diese ist bereits bei Flavius Josephus *A. J.* 2,210–215 und im Liber *Antiquitatum Biblicarum* 9,9 bezeugt. Dort wird berichtet, dass Mirjam von einem göttlichen Geist im Traum die Botschaft vom rettenden Kind erhält. Die Eltern, so heißt es, hätten ihr nicht geglaubt. Ihr persönlicher Einsatz gegen den Vater und den Sanhedrin wird jedoch nicht erzählt. In *Sota* 12a wird äußerst konzentriert und knapp berichtet. Vor allem das in den Elementen A und A′ parallel geschilderte Handeln der Männer ist geradezu holzschnittartig verknappt:

עמד וגירש את אשתו עמדו כולן וגירשו את נשותיהן
עמד והחזיר את אשתו עמדו כולן והחזירו את נשותיהן

10 Übersetzung ebd., 18 f.

Mirjam erscheint in ihrer zentralen Rede selbstbewusst und klar. Eine erweiterte Fassung bietet *Pesiqta Rabbati* 43:14–16. Hier ist der Kontext von Bedeutung, der auf biblische Frauen eingeht, die kinderlos waren und schließlich mit Kindern gesegnet wurden, allen voran Sara. Dabei wird Mirjams und Moses Mutter Jochebed thematisiert und Ps 113,9 auf sie ausgelegt. Die unfruchtbare (*aqara*) wurde nach dem Dekret Amrams und seines Sanhedrin von ihrem Haus „entwurzelt" (*nitaqra*). Der Appell der als erst sechsjährige geschilderten Mirjam gegen den Erlass wird geradezu wörtlich übernommen. Amram nimmt Mirjam zum Sanhedrin mit, der das Dekret offiziell auflöst. Wie im Talmud wird Jochebed mit einer Sänfte heimgeleitet.

Jochebed, so der Text, wird – obwohl bereits 130 Jahre alt – auf wundersame Weise wieder zu einer jungen Frau und feiert erneut Hochzeit. Sie wird ohne Schmerzen – wie alle gerechten Frauen – schwanger und gebiert ohne Schmerzen den Mose. Das Wunder der Verjüngung wird im Talmud *Bava Batra* 119b–120a auf Hautstraffung und Faltenglättung ausgedeutet, was wie in einer Werbebroschüre einer modernen Beauty-Klinik klingt.

Die erwähnte Schmerzlosigkeit der Geburt wird, wie Stemberger festhält, sehr wahrscheinlich auch eine Reaktion auf eine frühe Mariologie sein.[11] Bereits die Mutter des Mose hat diesen ohne Schmerzen empfangen. Allerdings gehen die Rabbinen noch einen Schritt weiter. Alle gerechten Frauen sind vom Dekret gegenüber Eva ausgeschlossen. Dies greifen auch spätere Varianten der Erzählung von der Geburt der Kinder in Ägypten auf, u. a. der schon erwähnte Midrasch Wa-*joscha*, wo es heißt:

> Du bist Der (der Ewige), der uns aus der Hand Ägyptens errettet hat, zur Stunde, als man (uns der Pharao) verordnete, *jeden neugeborenen Sohn sollt ihr in den Fluss werfen (jede Tochter aber lasst am Leben)* [Ex 1,22]. Und unsere Mütter gingen aufs Feld, und du in deiner großen Barmherzigkeit hast über sie einen Schlaf gesenkt. Und im Schlaf haben sie geboren, ohne Schmerz und ohne Not.[12]

Die Tat der Mirjam wird in gewisser Weise zum Rollenmodell der israelitischen Frau, das bereits knapp vor dem besprochenen Text in *Sota* herangezogen wird. So heißt es in *Sota* 11b[13] (siehe auch die Variante in *Exod. Rab.* 1:12):

> Durch das Verdienst der gerechten Frauen, welche in dieser Generation waren, wurde Israel aus Ägypten befreit. In der Stunde, in der sie hinausgingen, um Wasser zu schöpfen, füllte ihnen der Heilige, gepriesen sei er, kleine Fische in ihre Krüge, und sie schöpften zur Hälfte Wasser und zur Hälfte Fische; und sie setzten dann zwei Töpfe auf, einen mit warmem [Wasser] und einen mit Fischen; und sie brachten sie zu ihren

11 Vgl. ebd., 29 f.

12 Übersetzung Wies-Campagner, Midrasch Wajoscha, 215.

13 Zu Übersetzung, Motiv und Kontext vgl. Langer, Das Drama des Bundes.

Männern aufs Feld; und sie wuschen sie und salbten sie und gaben ihnen zu essen und zu trinken und wohnten ihnen bei zwischen den Hürden, wie es heißt: „Was treibt ihr Beischlaf zwischen den Hürden?" (Ps 68,14).

Die Frauen argumentieren hier weniger verbal mit ihren Männern, als dass sie sie auf wenig subtile Weise „überzeugen", doch Nachkommen zu zeugen. Ihre Gerechtigkeit besteht im Handeln, bei Mirjam ist es die prophetische Rede, die den Umschwung bewirkt.

Diese prophetische Rede wird in *Sota* 12a durch ein Zitat aus Ex 15,20 bekräftigt und es heißt:

„Da nahm Mirjam, die Prophetin, die Schwester Aarons (die Pauke in ihre Hand und alle Frauen zogen mit Pauken und Tanz hinter ihr her)" (15,20). Die Schwester Aarons und nicht auch die Schwester Moses?! Es sagte R. Amram, es sagte Rav, und andere sagen: es sagte R. Nachman, es sagte Rav: Das lehrt, dass sie die Schwester Aarons war, als sie prophezeite: Mutter wird einen Sohn gebären, der Israel erlösen wird. Als Mose geboren wurde, füllte sich das ganze Haus mit Licht. Da stand ihr Vater auf und küsste sie auf den Kopf und sagte zu ihr: Meine Tochter, deine Prophezeiung hat sich erfüllt. Doch als sie ihn in den Nil warfen, stand ihre Mutter auf, schlug ihr auf den Kopf und sagte zu ihr: Meine Tochter, was ist aus deiner Prophezeiung geworden? Das bedeutet es, wenn geschrieben steht: *„Und seine Schwester stellt sich von ferne hin (um zu erfahren, was mit ihm geschehe)"* (2,4) – um zu erfahren, was aus ihrer Prophezeiung würde.[14]

Diese Episode ist durchaus interessant, nicht nur, weil sie die Frage klärt, warum im Bibeltext in Ex 15 Mirjam nur als Schwester des Aaron bezeichnet wird, weil eben die Prophetie auf die vorgeburtliche Verkündigung des Mose zu beziehen ist, sondern auch im Hinblick auf die Rolle der Eltern. Es wird nicht genügen, die Aktion der Jochebed als Folge der Sorge um ihren Sohn abzutun, man wird darin wohl auch ein Indiz dafür finden, dass die Rabbinen eine gewisse Konkurrenz zwischen Mutter und Tochter sehen. Auch wenn, was wir noch öfter bemerken werden, die Geschichte Mirjams viele Parallelen zu jener Jochebeds hat, so scheint mir Mirjam ihr gegenüber doch noch ein Stück bedeutsamer geschildert, aktiver und – wie hier – letztlich ein wenig näher bei Gott und seinem dauerhaften Plan. In Bezug auf ihre prophetische Rolle ist kurz auch ein Blick auf die *Mekhilta de-Rabbi Jischmael Schira* 10 zu werfen, der wohl älter als der Talmudtraktat *Sota* ist. Dort heißt es:

Und es nahm die Prophetin Mirjam (Ex 15,20): Wo finden wir denn, daß Mirjam prophezeit hat? Sie hatte zu ihrem Vater gesagt: Du wirst noch einen Sohn zeugen, der aufstehen und Israel erlösen wird. Es heißt ja: „Ein Mann aus einer levitischen Familie ging (und nahm eine Frau aus dem gleichen Stamm). Die Frau wurde schwanger

14 Übersetzung Stemberger, Mose, 23.

(und gebar einen Sohn) … Als sie ihn nicht mehr verborgen halten konnte …" (Ex 2,1–3). Da schalt sie ihre Mutter und sagte zu ihr: Mirjam, wo ist jetzt deine Prophezeiung? Sie aber hielt an ihrer Prophetie fest. Es heißt ja: „Seine Schwester aber stand von ferne, (um zu wissen, was ihm getan wurde)" (Ex 2,4). „Stehen" bedeutet überall den heiligen Geist […] „Von ferne": „Von ferne" bedeutet immer den heiligen Geist […] „Um zu wissen." „Wissen" bedeutet immer den heiligen Geist […] „Was ihm getan wurde": „Tun" bedeutet immer den heiligen Geist […] *Die Schwester Aarons*: War sie denn nicht die Schwester von beiden? Was lehrt dann die Schrift mit *die Schwester Aarons*? Doch nur: Weil er sein Leben für seine Schwester einsetzte, wird seine Schwester nach ihm genannt. Ebenso heißt es: „Da griffen zwei Söhne Jakobs, Simeon und Levi, die Brüder Dinas, zum Schwert" (Gen 34,25). War sie denn nicht die Schwester aller Stämme? Was lehrt dann die Schrift mit „die Brüder Dinas"? Doch nur: Weil sie ihr Leben für ihre Schwester einsetzten, wird ihre Schwester nach ihnen genannt. Ebenso heißt es: „in der Sache Kosbis, der Tochter eines Fürsten Midians, ihrer Schwester" (Num 25,18). War sie denn ihre Schwester? War sie nicht vielmehr eine Anführerin in ihrem Volk? Es heißt doch: „Der Priester von Midian hatte sieben Töchter" (Ex 2,16). Was lehrt dann die Schrift mit „ihre Schwester"? Doch nur: Weil sie ihr Leben für ihr Volk einsetzte, wird ihr Volk nach ihr genannt. *Die Pauke in die Hand*: Woher hatten denn die Israeliten Pauken und Flöten in der Wüste? Doch die Gerechten waren voll Vertrauen und wußten, daß Gott ihnen Wunder und Machttaten bei ihrem Auszug aus Ägypten tun werde, und sie bereiteten sich Pauken und Flöten vor. *Mirjam sang ihnen vor.* Der Schriftvers besagt: So wie Mose den Männern das Lied vortrug, so trug es Mirjam den Frauen vor: *Singt dem Herrn ein Lied, denn er ist hoch und erhaben* usw.[15]

Neben der alternativen Erklärung, warum Mose nicht erwähnt wird, betont die Mekhilta die Gabe des Heiligen Geistes auf Mirjam mit einer Reihe von Bibelbelegen. Die Geschlechterteilung am Ende des Abschnittes ist zwar ein wenig ernüchternd, aber bemerkenswert ist die enge Verbindung zwischen dem Lied der Mirjam und der Prophetie von der Geburt des Mose allemal. Agnethe Siquans hat in einem Beitrag in den Protokollen zur Bibel die patristische Tradition der Mirjam analysiert. Darin heißt es:

[…] der Großteil der christlichen Autoren [ist] der Ansicht, dass Mirjam eine Jungfrau gewesen sei. Dazu kommt, dass Mirjams griechischer Name Maria dem Namen der Mutter Jesu gleicht, was sie zu einem idealen Typus dieser Jungfrau schlechthin werden lässt. Mirjams Pauke verstärkt die asketische Interpretation: Die Bespannung besteht aus trockener Haut. Trockenheit wird jedoch als ein Zeichen für Unfruchtbarkeit verstanden, während Feuchtigkeit Fruchtbarkeit signalisiert – ein Bild, das leicht nachzuvollziehen ist. Daher steht das Tamburin symbolisch für das asketische Leben. Ein Ausschnitt aus Gregor von Nyssas Traktat *De virginitate* soll exemplarisch diese Interpretation veranschaulichen. Der Abschnitt enthält alle angesprochenen Aspekte und verdeutlicht gut die Zusammenhänge: „Vielleicht deutet das Wort durch die Pauke,

15 Übersetzung ders., Mekhilta, 190–191.

wie es scheint, die Jungfräulichkeit an, die Mirjam als erste erfolgreich praktiziert hat, durch die, meine ich, auch die Gottesgebärerin Maria im Voraus abgebildet ist. Denn so wie die Pauke ein widerhallendes Geräusch von sich gibt, fern von jeglicher Feuchtigkeit und extrem trocken, so wird auch die Jungfräulichkeit leuchtend und berühmt, weil sie von der zum Leben gehörigen Feuchtigkeit dieses (irdischen) Lebens nichts in sich aufnimmt. Wenn also die Pauke, die Mirjam in die Hand nahm, ein toter Körper ist, die Abtötung des Körpers aber die Jungfräulichkeit ist, ist vielleicht die Wahrscheinlichkeit nicht weit entfernt, dass die Prophetin eine Jungfrau war. Aber das ist (eine Sache) von Mutmaßungen und Annahmen, nicht von klarer Beweisführung, so wie wir an der Annahme festhielten, dass die Prophetin Mirjam den Chor der Jungfrauen anführte, wenn auch viele von denen, die sich damit beschäftigten, deutlich aufzeigten, dass sie unverheiratet war, weil nirgends in der Geschichte Heirat und Geburt von Kindern von ihr erwähnt werden. Sicherlich wäre sie nicht nach ihrem Bruder Aaron, sondern nach ihrem Mann benannt und bekannt, wenn sie einen hätte, denn als Haupt der Frau wird nicht der Bruder, sondern der Mann bezeichnet (vgl. 1 Kor 11,3; Eph 5,23).«[16]

Diese Auslegung steht in einer faszinierenden Spannung zu den rabbinischen Traditionen. Mirjam und Maria werden in beiden Auslegungen m. E. deutlich in Verbindung gesetzt. Während Gregor die Jungfräulichkeit und Ehelosigkeit der Mirjam betont und dabei auch die Beschaffenheit der Pauke bemüht, argumentieren die Rabbinen zuerst ebenfalls mit einer Art der Unfruchtbarkeit, der symbolischen „Austrocknung" zuerst bei Jochebed, später aber auch bei Mirjam, ein Zustand, der sich jedoch wundersam wandelt. Ein zentraler Text dazu findet sich in *Sifre Num* 78, das zur Vorlage weiterer Auslegung in *Sota* 11b, *Pesiqta Rabbati* 45 und *Exod. Rab.* 1 wird:

> *Da befahl der König Ägyptens den Hebammen der Hebräerinnen [, von denen die eine Schifra, die andere Pua hieß]. (Ex 1,15) Schifra,* das ist Jochebed. *Pua,* das ist Mirjam. *Schifra,* weil sie fruchtbar war (*sche-para*) und sich vermehrte. *Schifra,* weil sie die Neugeborenen reinigte (*meschaperet*). *Schifra,* weil Israel in ihren Tagen fruchtbar war und sich mehrte. *Pua,* weil sie ihres Bruders wegen schrie (*poa*) und weinte. Denn es heißt: *Seine Schwester aber stellte sich von ferne hin, um zu erfahren, was mit ihm geschehen würde.* (Ex 2,4) *Und [Pharao] sprach: Wenn ihr die Hebräerinnen entbindet … Aber die Hebammen fürchteten Gott (Ex 1,16–17). [Und weil die Hebammen Gott fürchteten, machte er ihnen Häuser. (Ex 1,21)]* Ich weiß nicht, was jene Häuser sein sollen. Wie [in dem Fall] wenn es heißt: *Nach dem Verlauf von 20 Jahren, in denen Salomo die beiden Häuser gebaut hatte. (1.Kö 9,10) Das Haus des HErrn* – Das ist das Priestertum. *Und das Haus des Königs* – Das ist das Königtum. Jochebed erwarb sich das Verdienst des Priestertums und Mirjam das des Königtums, denn es heißt: *Qots aber zeugte Anub und Hatsobeba und die Familien des Acharchel, des Sohnes Harums. (1.Chron 4,8) Acharchel* – das ist Mirjam, denn es heißt: *Und alle Frauen zogen hinter*

16 Siquans, Kontextuelle Bibelauslegung, 118–119. Der Ausschnitt aus Gregor von Nyssa stammt aus *De virginitate* 19,1–20 (SC 119, 486–488).

> *ihr her (achareha). (Ex 15,20)* Des Sohnes Harums, das ist Jochebed, denn es heißt: *Alles Banngut (cherem) in Israel soll dir gehören. (Nu 18,14)* Mirjam wurde [mit] Kaleb verheiratet, denn es heißt: *Und als Asuba gestorben war, nahm sich Kaleb Efrat [zur Frau] und sie gebar ihm Chur. (1.Chron 2,19) Und diese waren die Söhne Kalebs, des Sohnes Churs [, des Erstgeborenen der Efrata]. (1.Chron 2,50)* Und es heißt: *David aber war der Sohn jenes Efratiten aus Bethlehem in Juda. (1.Sa 17,12)* Es ergibt sich [daraus], daß David zu den Nachkommen Mirjams gehörte. Also, jeden, der sich selbst [Gott] nähert, den nähert man sich vom Himmel her.[17]

Hier werden viele Informationen gebündelt. Zentral ist die Identifikation von verhältnismäßig unbekannten Personen aus dem Bibeltext – vor allem der Chronikbücher – mit sehr wichtigen Figuren der jüdischen Tradition. Jochebed und Mirjam stehen im Mittelpunkt. Mirjam wird hier zur Ehefrau Kalebs gemacht, was man aus dem Bibeltext in 1 Chr ableitet. Mirjams Lebenslauf ist in gewisser Weise eine Kopie des Lebenswegs ihrer Mutter. Wie jene *aqara*/unfruchtbar genannt wurde, so hieß sie *Asuba*/*azuva*, Verlassene, eine Frau, die „gestorben" war und „wiedererweckt" wurde als Efrat, als Blühende, Fruchtbare. Im Hintergrund steht dabei die Episode, in der sie wegen ihrer Aufmüpfigkeit gegen Mose mit Lepra geschlagen wurde (Num 12).[18] In der Folge war sie offensichtlich für die Männer tabu. Aber wie aus der verlassenen Jochebed Mose entsteht, so aus der „wiederbelebten" Mirjam David. Beide messianisch aufgeladenen Figuren haben demnach Erzmütter, die ein besonderes Schicksal teilen. In ihrer Kindheit wird Mirjam mit Pua, einer der Hebammen des Mose, identifiziert. Ihre Sorge um Mose wird ihr als Verdienst angerechnet.

In der Variante *Exod. Rab.* 1:13 wird die Episode des Aufstehens der Mirjam gegen Amram direkt mit ihrem Namen Pua verbunden, der hier als *hofia panim*, als „jemandem ins Antlitz widerstehen", ausgedeutet wird. Erstaunlicherweise findet sich dieser Begriff ein zweites Mal knapp vor der Auseinandersetzung mit dem Vater, und es heißt, dass Mirjam sich dem Pharao mit den prophetischen Worten „Wehe diesem Mann, dass Gott kommt, um ihn unseretwillen zu bestrafen (*lippara mimmenu*)[19]" widersetzt habe und nur mit viel Glück durch

17 Text nach Börner-Klein, Sifre zu Numeri, 129–130.

18 Interessant ist hier die biblische und rabbinische Tradition, die dem Volk große Sympathien für Mirjam nachsagt, aber mehr noch: „Das soll dich lehren, daß ‚mit dem Maß, mit dem ein Mensch mißt, auch ihm gemessen wird'. Mirjam wartete auf Mose eine Stunde lang. Es heißt ja: ‚Seine Schwester blieb von ferne stehen' (Ex 2,4) usw., und Gott hielt ihretwegen in der Wüste die Lade und die Schechina, die Priester, die Leviten und die sieben Wolken der Herrlichkeit auf. Es heißt ja: ‚Das Volk brach nicht auf, bis man Mirjam wieder hereinließ.'" (*Mekhilta Beschallach* 1; *mSota* 1:7) (Übersetzung Stemberger, Mekhilta, 104). Mirjam wird also die Sorge um das Wohl des Mose in seiner Kindheit angerechnet.

19 Die Verwendung des Begriffes *para* ist hier ein Wortspiel mit Pharao. Es bedeutet eigentlich „etwas lösen", „aufmachen", aber auch „zerstören". Die hier verwendete Form *niphra min* wird üblicherweise mit „bestrafen" oder „eine Schuld einfordern" übersetzt.

die Fürsprache ihrer Mutter seinem Zorn entkam. Das Argument der Schifra/Jochebed, das den Pharao besänftigte, war hier: „Sie ist ein Kind (*tinoqet*) und weiß nichts." Diese Schutzbemerkung gegenüber dem Pharao, in der jegliche prophetische Gabe der Mirjam geleugnet und auf ihren kindlichen Unverstand rekurriert wird, passt natürlich auch ganz gut zur Skepsis der Jochebed, die schon an anderer Stelle erwähnt wurde.

Doch gehen wir einen Schritt zurück zum Talmud *Sota* 11b und zur dort erwähnten Ehe mit Kaleb, über dessen Herkunft und Namen ausführlich diskutiert wird. Es heißt schließlich weiter in Auslegung von 1 Chr 2,24 („Nach dem Tod Hezrons kam Kaleb zu Efrata. Eine Frau Hezrons war Abija; sie gebar ihm Aschhur, den Vater Tekoas."):

> Aschhur ist Kaleb. Und warum heißt er Aschhur? Weil sein Antlitz sich vom vielen Fasten verfinsterte (von *schachar* – dunkel, schwarz).
> „Der Vater" – weil er für sie zum Vater wurde.
> „Tekoas" – weil er sein Herz an seinem Vater im Himmel festmachte (*taqa*).

Kaleb ist der Gerechte, der nicht dem Rat der Kundschafter folgt, die das verheißene Land schlechtmachen. Kaleb fastet und widmet sich gänzlich Gott. Im Zentrum dieser kleinen chiastischen Einheit steht jedoch seine „Vaterschaft". Sie meint wohl nicht, dass er tatsächlich Mirjam wie ein Vater behandelte, sondern eher, dass er ihr gegenüber die Bereitschaft zur Vaterschaft erkennen ließ und mit ihr Kinder zeugte. So gelesen imitiert Kaleb Amram, und sein Fasten und seine strikte Gottesnähe können als Enthaltsamkeit gedeutet werden, die erst Mirjam ändert. Die „Vaterschaft" des Kaleb ist natürlich auch ein Pendant zur in *Sota* 12a Amram zugeschriebenen Benennung Jochebeds als „Tochter". Beide Male steht im Hintergrund nicht eine in rabbinischen Texten oft vorkommende – und uns inzwischen fremd gewordene – Bezeichnung für ein Näheverhältnis zwischen Liebenden,[20] sondern ein Hinweis auf eine wundersame und erotisch aufgeladene Verjüngung. Im Midrasch Levitikus Rabba wird eine weitere Erklärung zu Kalebs und Mirjams Verbindung gebracht, in der der Begriff der Tochter ebenfalls eine Rolle spielt. Dort heißt es als Erklärung für den Namen Bitja im Chronikbuch:

20 Bemerkenswert ist beispielsweise das Gleichnis in *Hohelied Rabba* 3:11:2, das eine Abfolge von Bezeichnungen nahelegt, die Beziehungen prägen: „Ihr Töchter Jerusalems, kommt heraus und schaut, ihr Töchter Zions, König Salomo mit der Krone! Damit hat ihn seine Mutter gekrönt am Tage seiner Hochzeit, an dem Tag seiner Herzensfreude" (Hld 3,11). (*Maschal*) von einem König, der eine einzige Tochter hatte, die er über die Maßen liebte und sie *meine Tochter* nannte. Er hörte nicht auf, sie zu lieben, bis er sie *meine Schwester* nannte. Er hörte nicht auf, sie zu lieben, bis er sie *meine Mutter* nannte.

> „Das waren die Söhne der Bitja [, der Tochter des Pharao, die Mered geheiratet hatte]" (1 Chr 4,18) – (das ist) die Tochter des Herrn (*bat ja*), „die Mered geheiratet hatte" – das ist Kaleb: R. Abba bar Kahana und R. Jehuda bar Simon (diskutieren): einer sagte: jener ist der Rebell gegen den Rat der Kundschafter und jene ist die Rebellin gegen den Rat ihres Vaters. Der Rebell kam und heiratete die Rebellin.

Auf diese Weise wird Mirjam zum einen als Bat Ja mit der Bitja identifiziert, zum anderen eine Erklärung für die Ehe gegeben, die recht sympathisch klingt. Zwei Rebellen vereinigen sich.

Noch einmal zurück zu *Sota* 11b. Hier wird nun 2 Chr 4,5 („Aschhur, der Vater Tekoas, hatte zwei Frauen, Hela und Naara") ausgelegt:

> „Hatte zwei Frauen" – Mirjam war wie zwei Frauen. „Hela und Naara" – nicht Hela und Naara, sondern: am Anfang war sie kränklich (*chal'a*) und am Ende eine junge Frau (*na'ara*).

Wieder steht Mirjam in der Nachfolge der Jochebed. Auch sie wird zu einer jungen Frau durch die Heirat mit Kaleb. Doch noch nicht genug. Es heißt weiter:

> „Die Söhne der Hela waren: Zeret, Zohar und Etnan" (1 Chr 4,7). Zeret, weil sie (Mirjam) ihren Nachbarinnen eine Rivalin wurde; Zohar, weil ihr Gesicht der Mittagssonne (*zohorajim*) glich; Etnan, weil jeder, der sie sah, seiner (eigenen) Frau ein Geschenk (*etnan*) machte.

Die unverhohlenen Anspielungen auf die Schönheit der Mirjam als Folge des Transformationsprozesses nach der Ehe mit Kaleb wirken geradezu provokativ. Mirjam ist begehrenswert schön, dass sie Eifersucht erzeugt und andere Männer stimuliert.

All dies wird bereits vor der Episode mit ihrem Vater Amram erzählt, sodass bei den Lesenden oder Hörenden des Abschnitts die paradoxe Situation eintritt, dass sie noch vor der Geburt des Mose die weitere Heilsgeschichte als Genealogie nach Mirjam erzählt bekommen. Dies ist vielleicht nicht überzubewerten, aber es bleibt doch zu überlegen, in welchem Verhältnis Mirjam hier auch gegenüber ihrer Mutter und ihrem Bruder Mose steht. Während nämlich Jochebed vergleichsweise passiv bleibt, stellt sich Mirjam in den Vordergrund und scheut auch nicht die Konfrontation mit den starken und mächtigen Männern. Günter Stemberger, der mit gutem Grund die Kindheitsgeschichten Jesu mit der Episode aus dem babylonischen Talmud *Sota* vergleicht, schreibt:

> Die Rolle des Engels in Mt 2,20 erfüllt im Talmud das Mädchen, noch ein Kind (laut *PesR* 43:15 sechs Jahre alt), dessen Aussage durchaus nicht altersgemäß ist, damit als gottgelenkt betrachtet werden kann. Die Vorhersage des Engels: „Sie wird einen Sohn gebären, ihm sollst du den Namen Jesus geben; denn er wird sein Volk von seinen

Sünden erlösen" (2,21) hat ihr Gegenstück in Mirjams Weissagung [...]: „Mutter wird einen Sohn gebären, der Israel erlösen wird."[21]

Dies ist einerseits völlig richtig, aber gleichzeitig eine Verkürzung der Rolle der Mirjam im Vergleich mit dem Evangelium. Während der himmlische Bote die Jungfräulichkeit Marias betont und auch Josef sich Maria nicht nähert, bekräftigt Mirjam die positive und heilsgeschichtlich notwendige Funktion von Sexualität. Sie ist zudem nicht einfach nur Botin, sondern in Weiterführung zu Jochebed viel mehr noch eigenständige und entscheidende Mittlerin der zukünftigen Erlösung. Versteht man ihr Murren gegen Mose als Aufruhr gegen seine Verweigerung von Sexualität, der die Bestrafung durch Aussatz, mehr aber noch die erzwungene Enthaltsamkeit durch die daraus sich ergebende offensichtliche Weigerung der Männer Israels folgt, sich mit Mirjam einzulassen, so bricht der Gerechte Kaleb – ein Gegenstück zum eher vorsichtigen Josef der Evangelien – den Bann, indem er sich auf Sexualität mit Mirjam einlässt und dadurch die Geburt Davids und – in weiterer Folge – des zukünftigen Messias ermöglicht.

Eines wird in jedem Fall in *Sota* bereits klargestellt. In der Geburtsgeschichte des Mose ist kein Platz für „Fremde":

„*Die Tochter des Pharao kam herab, um im Nil zu baden*" (2,5).

Es sagte R. Jochanan im Namen des R. Simeon bar Jochai. Das lehrt, dass sie herabkam, um sich (im Nil) von den Götzen ihres Vaterhauses abzuwaschen; so sagt (die Schrift): „*Wenn der Herr ... von den Töchtern Zions den Kot abgewaschen*" (Jes 4,4). [„Im Nil" – wegen der Sache mit dem Nil]. „*Und ihre Dienerinnen gingen*" (2,5). Es sagte R. Eleazar [...] „Gehen" ist nur ein Ausdruck für Sterben; und so sagt (die Schrift): „*Siehe, ich gehe sterben*" (Gen 25,32).
„*Da sah sie im Schilf das Kästchen*" (2,5). (Die Dienerinnen) sagten zu ihr: Unsere Herrin! Es ist der Brauch der Welt – ein König aus Fleisch und Blut verhängt einen Erlass; wenn auch die ganze Welt ihn nicht einhält, seine Kinder und die Angehörigen seines Hauses halten ihn ein. Und du übertrittst den Erlass deines Vaters?! Da kam Gabriel und schlug sie zu Boden.[22]

In der prophetischen Rede Mirjams mit ihrem eigenen Vater war davon die Rede gewesen, dass der Pharao als Böser vielleicht sein eigenes Dekret nicht ernst nimmt. Zumindest im engsten Kreis der Familie, so wird hier suggeriert, sollte dies jedoch sehr wohl der Fall sein, weshalb die Dienerinnen der Tochter des Pharao insistieren, das Bastkörbchen nicht an Land zu holen. Dafür straft sie niemand geringerer als der Erzengel Gabriel mit dem Tod. Die Tochter des Pharao hingegen konvertiert zum Judentum, noch ehe sie den kleinen Mose berührt. So wächst dieser

21 Stemberger, Mose, 63.
22 Übersetzung ebd., 20.

ausschließlich unter jüdischer Fürsorge auf, da ja auch die Hebammen jüdisch sind. Der Erzengel Gabriel fungiert oft als „Nothelfer“ für Israel. Aber er ist natürlich hier auch eine kritische Anspielung auf den Verkündungsengel der Maria. Für *Sota* ist klar: Wer den „Erlöser“ Israels gefährdet, wird nicht überleben. Wie schon zu Beginn meiner Ausführungen zum Brunnen der Mirjam geschieht das Entscheidende am und mit Wasser. Die ein Konversionsbad nehmende Tochter des Pharao rettet das im Wasser schwimmende Baby.

Mirjam als beherzte, vom Heiligen Geist getriebene rebellische Prophetin stirbt schließlich, wie es etwa *Bava Batra* 17a klarlegt, durch den Kuss Gottes und ist damit neben Abraham, Isaak, Jakob, Mose und Aaron die einzige Frau, der dieses Privileg zuteilwurde.

Zusammenfassung

Mirjams Bedeutung für die Geschichte Israels, ihre prophetische Stimme, ihre Aufmüpfigkeit gegenüber männlichen Autoritäten wurde vielfach gesehen und auf unterschiedliche Weise gewürdigt. Die Frage, inwieweit Mirjam ein Gegengewicht zur neutestamentlichen Maria darstellt, ist differenziert zu betrachten. In den behandelten Texten (allen voran aus *bSota*) steht Mirjam deutlich in Parallele zu Jochebed, ihrer Mutter. Die Darstellung ihrer schwierigen Situation vor der Geburt und der weiteren Stationen hat zweifellos Parallelen im Evangelium und wahrscheinlich ist Stemberger recht zu geben, dass der in byzantinischer Zeit entstandene Text von *Sota* sich auf die Evangelien zurückbezog und dabei Mirjam die Funktion erhält, die der Engel gegenüber Maria hat. Mirjams Bedeutung geht jedoch deutlich über die einer prophetischen Verkündigerin hinaus. Gerade dort, wo sie augenscheinlich mit Jochebed verglichen wird, überragt sie diese letztlich sogar. Während Jochebed noch zweifelt, hat Mirjam völlige Zuversicht in Gott. Aus ihr wird David erstehen, der kommende Messias.

Mirjam ist die Verkünderin von Leben und Lebensspenderin. Dies wird durch den Brunnen bzw. die nie versiegende Quelle deutlich, die sich eng an ihre Existenz bindet und gewissermaßen zum Symbol des Lebens für das Volk im Exil schlechthin wird. Mirjam verkörpert die Überlebens- und Lebenshoffnung. Sie tut dies nicht zuletzt, indem sie den sexuellen Kontakt zwischen Eheleuten auch in schwierigen Zeiten einmahnt. Sie ist gerade kein Vorbild sexuell abstinenter Lebensweise und stellt insofern ein Gegengewicht zu christlicher Marienverehrung, aber auch Tendenzen der Askese dar. Ihr Murren, so finden es die Rabbinen, ist ein Aufschrei für Sexualität, ohne die es keine Zukunft geben kann. Mehr noch als Jochebed, deren wundersame Verjüngung vor allem im Zusammenhang mit der Möglichkeit der Fortpflanzung steht, wird Mirjam als sexuell anziehend beschrieben. Sie macht die Frauen in ihrer Umgebung eifersüchtig und ermutigt gleichzeitig die Männer dazu, durch Geschenke ihre Frauen wieder ihnen (wohl auch sexuell) zugeneigt zu machen. Freilich dient auch hier Sexualität letztlich der Weitergabe von Leben und im Endeffekt der Geburt des messianischen Königs.

Literatur

Börner-Klein, Dagmar, Der Midrasch Sifre zu Numeri (Rabbinische Texte Reihe 2, Tannaitische Midraschim 3), Stuttgart 1997.

Brenner, Athalya (Hg.), A Feminist Companion to Exodus to Deuteronomy. (The Feminist Companion to the Bible, Second Series 5), Sheffield 2000.

Fischer, Irmtraud, Die Autorität Mirjams. Eine feministische Relektüre von Num 12 – angeregt durch das jüdische Lehrhaus, in: M. Halmer u. a. (Hg.), Anspruch und Widerspruch (FS E. Krobath), Klagenfurt 2000, 23–38 (= engl. Übersetzung: The Authority of Miriam. A Feminist Rereading of Numbers 12 Prompted by Jewish Interpretation, in: A. Brenner [Hg.], A Feminist Companion to Exodus to Deuteronomy. [The Feminist Companion to the Bible, Second Series 5], Sheffield 2000, 159–173).

Langer, Gerhard, Das Drama des Bundes. Ezechiel 16 in rabbinischer Perspektive (HBS 11), Freiburg i.Br. 1997.

Siquans, Agnethe, Kontextuelle Bibelauslegung. Die Kirchenväter und die Prophetinnen, in: PZB 20 (2011), 111–124.

Steinmetz, Devorah, A Portrait of Miriam in Rabbinic Midrash, Prooftexts 8 (1988), 35–65.

Stemberger, Günter, Die Mekhilta de-Rabbi Jishma'el. Ein früher Midrasch zum Buch Exodus, Berlin 2010.

—, Mose in der rabbinischen Tradition, Freiburg i.Br. 2016.

Wies-Campagner, Elisabeth, Midrasch Wajoscha. Edition – Tradition – Interpretation, Berlin/Boston, Mass. 2009.

Stellenregister

Bibelstellenregister

Old Testament/Altes Testament

Antike Autoren

Rabbinische Schriften

Autorenregister